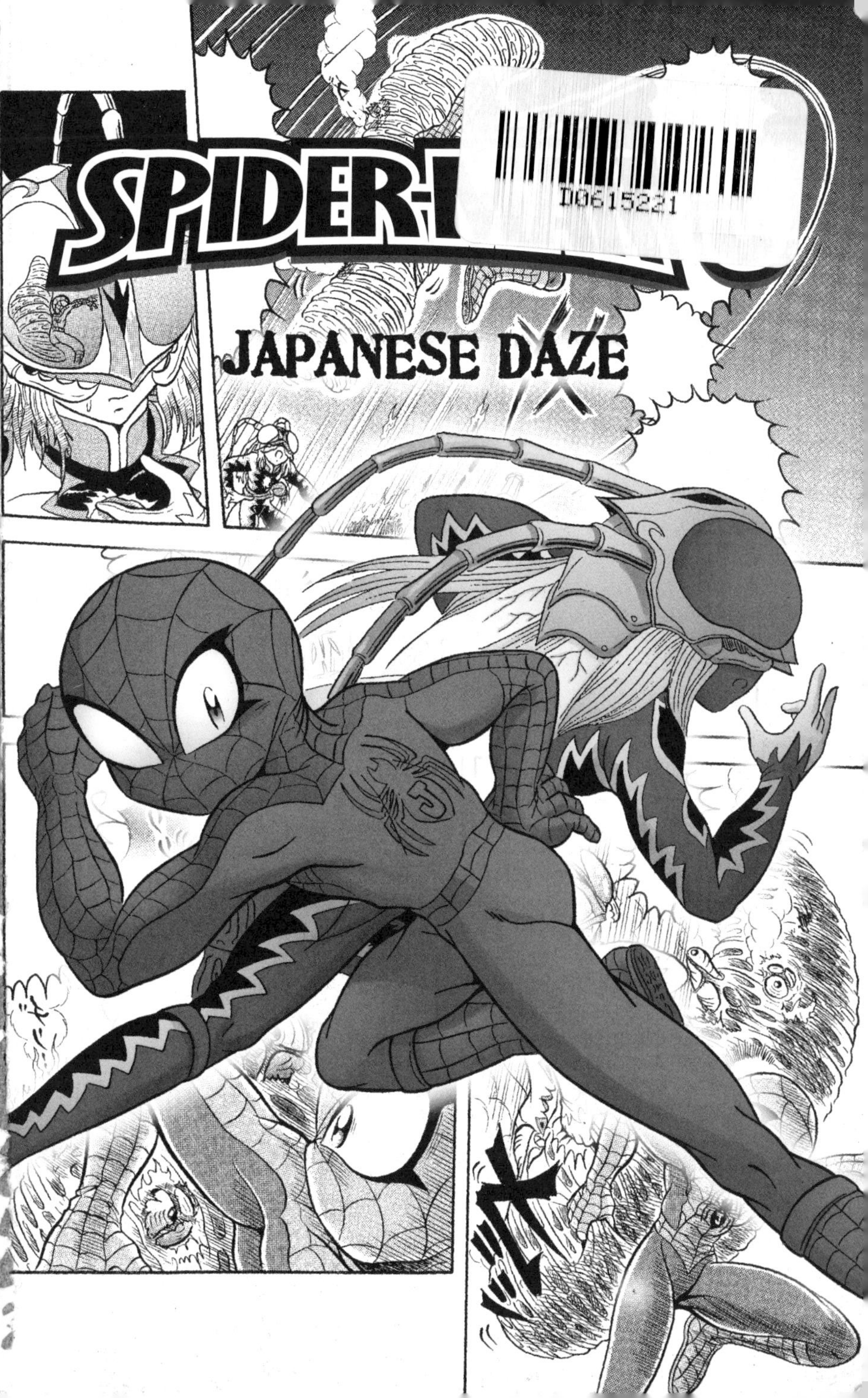
SPIDER-
JAPANESE DAZE

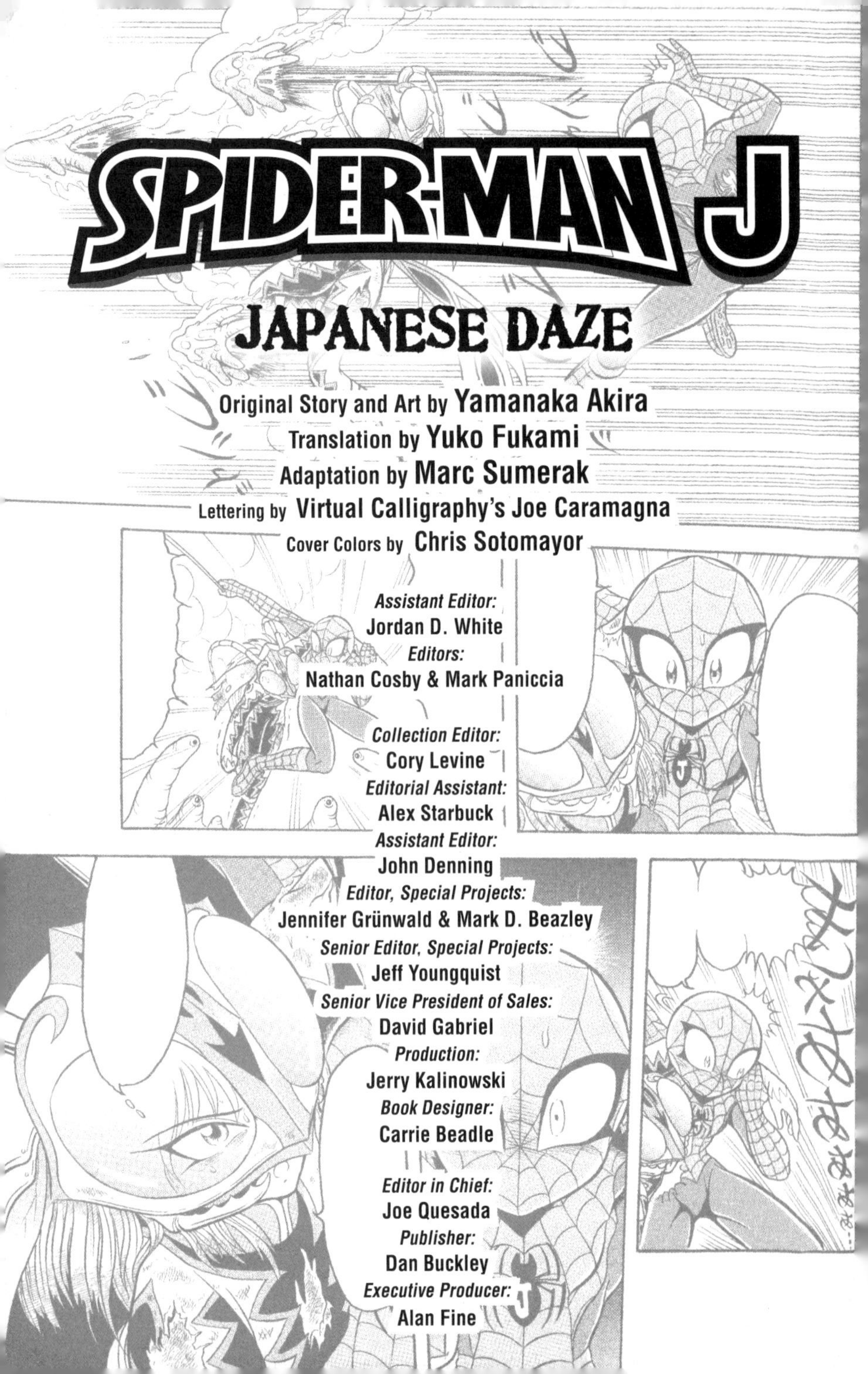

SPIDER-MAN J

JAPANESE DAZE

Original Story and Art by **Yamanaka Akira**

Translation by **Yuko Fukami**

Adaptation by **Marc Sumerak**

Lettering by **Virtual Calligraphy's Joe Caramagna**

Cover Colors by **Chris Sotomayor**

Assistant Editor:
Jordan D. White
Editors:
Nathan Cosby & Mark Paniccia

Collection Editor:
Cory Levine
Editorial Assistant:
Alex Starbuck
Assistant Editor:
John Denning
Editor, Special Projects:
Jennifer Grünwald & Mark D. Beazley
Senior Editor, Special Projects:
Jeff Youngquist
Senior Vice President of Sales:
David Gabriel
Production:
Jerry Kalinowski
Book Designer:
Carrie Beadle

Editor in Chief:
Joe Quesada
Publisher:
Dan Buckley
Executive Producer:
Alan Fine

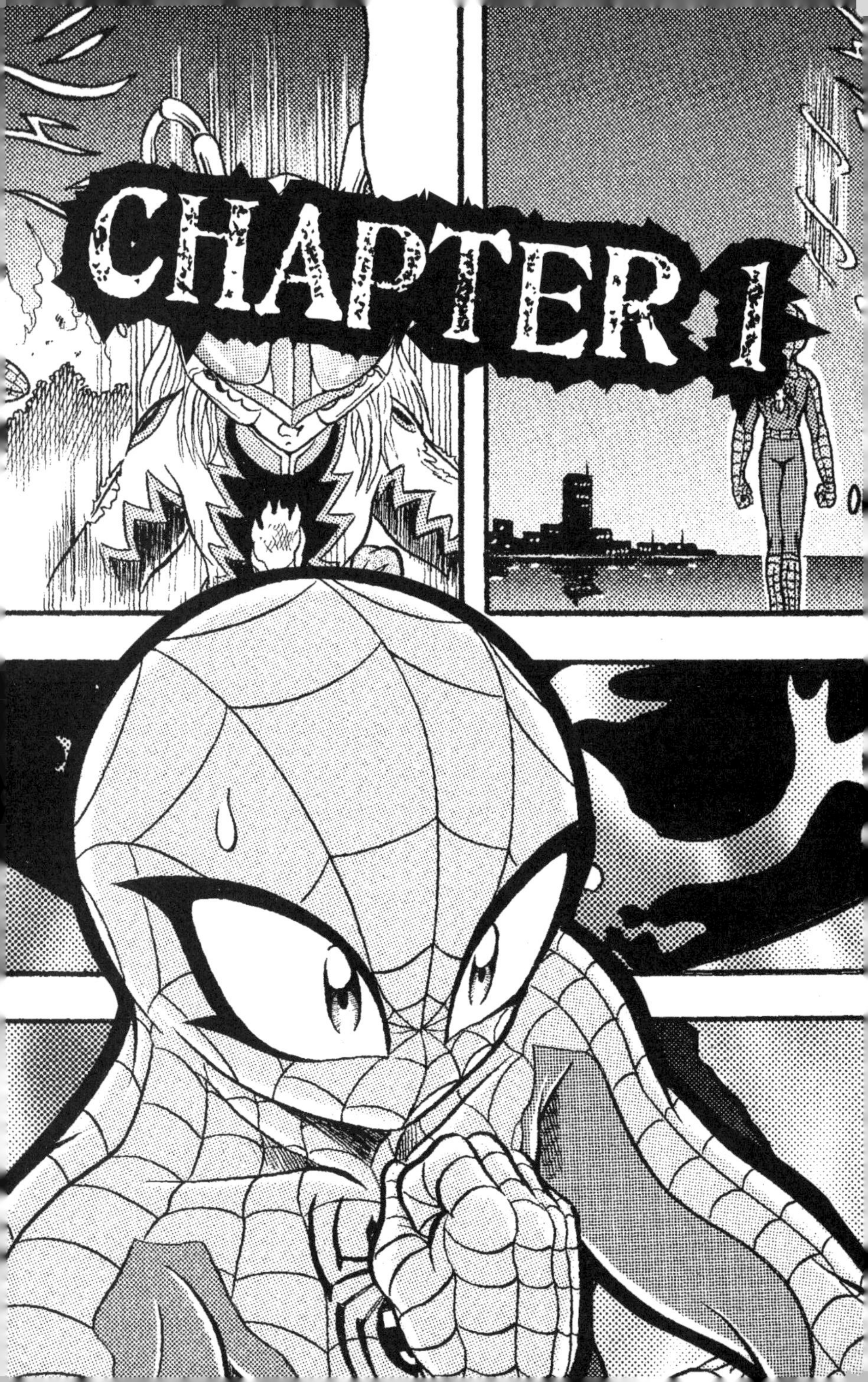
CHAPTER 1

Each corner of the globe has its own unique take on the AMAZING SPIDER-MAN! Direct from Japan, Marvel is proud to present...

SPIDER-MAN J "The Moth & The Flame"

ORIGINAL STORY AND ART BY YAMANAKA AKIRA

YUKO FUKAMI TRANSLATION | MARC SUMERAK ENGLISH ADAPTATION | VC'SJOE CARAMAGNA LETTERING | JORDAN D. WHITE ASST. EDITOR | NATHAN COSBY & MARK PANICCIA EDITORS | JOE QUESADA EDITOR IN CHIEF | DAN BUCKLEY PUBLISHER

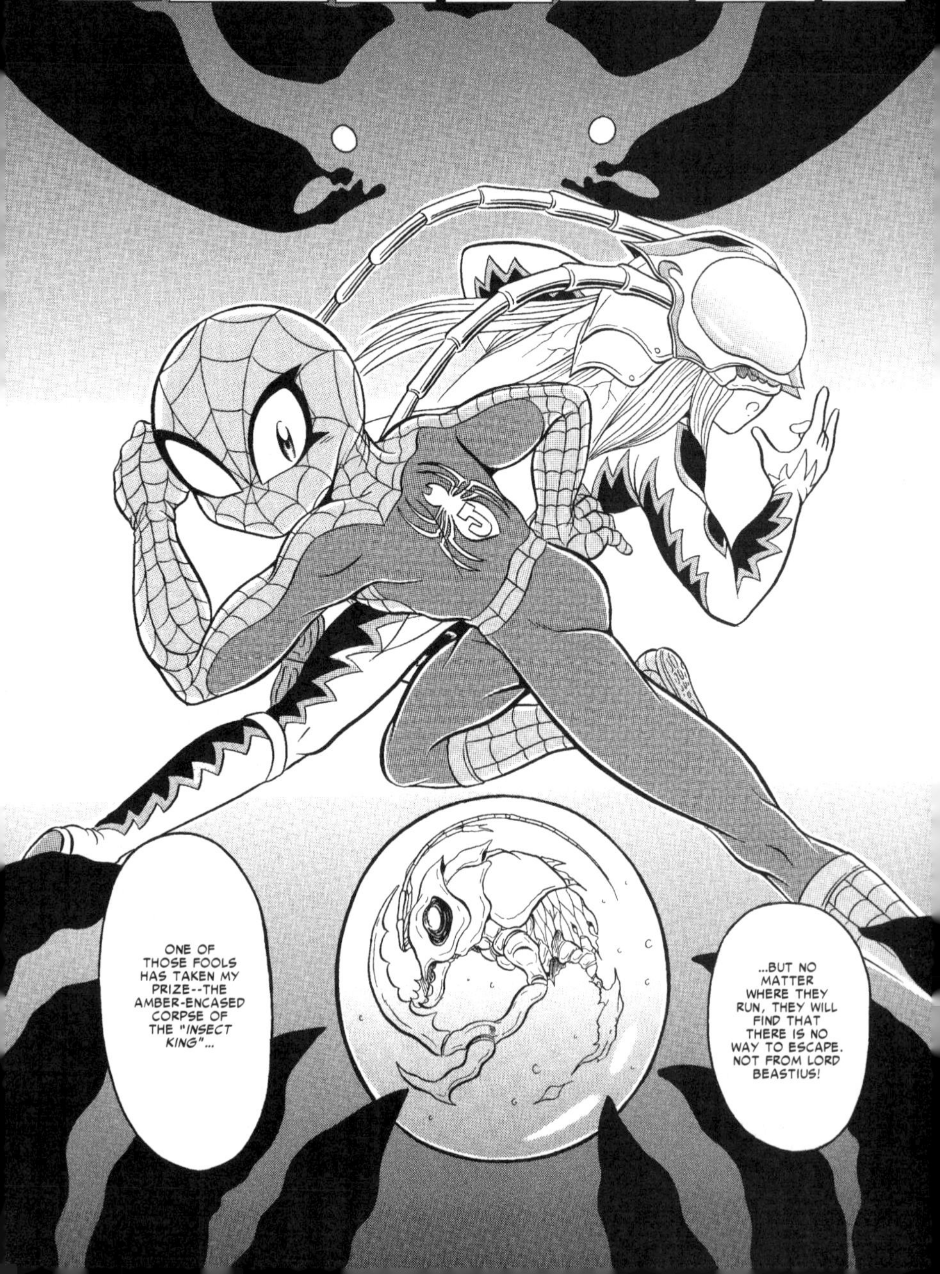

ONE OF THOSE FOOLS HAS TAKEN MY PRIZE--THE AMBER-ENCASED CORPSE OF THE "INSECT KING"...
...BUT NO MATTER WHERE THEY RUN, THEY WILL FIND THAT THERE IS NO WAY TO ESCAPE. NOT FROM LORD BEASTIUS!

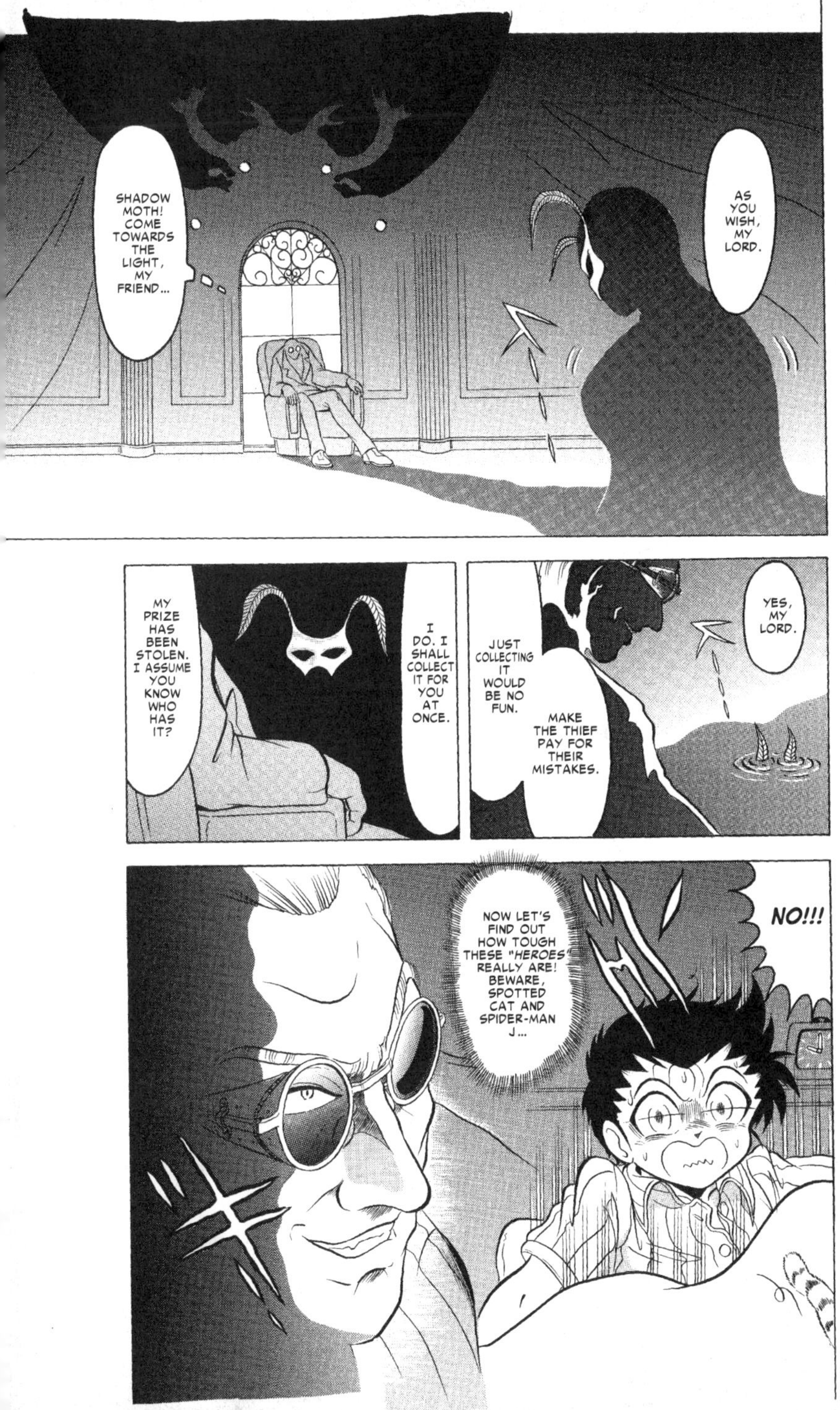
SHADOW MOTH! COME TOWARDS THE LIGHT, MY FRIEND...
AS YOU WISH, MY LORD.
MY PRIZE HAS BEEN STOLEN. I ASSUME YOU KNOW WHO HAS IT?
I DO. I SHALL COLLECT IT FOR YOU AT ONCE.
JUST COLLECTING IT WOULD BE NO FUN.
MAKE THE THIEF PAY FOR THEIR MISTAKES.
YES, MY LORD.
NOW LET'S FIND OUT HOW TOUGH THESE "HEROES" REALLY ARE! BEWARE, SPOTTED CAT AND SPIDER-MAN J...
NO!!!

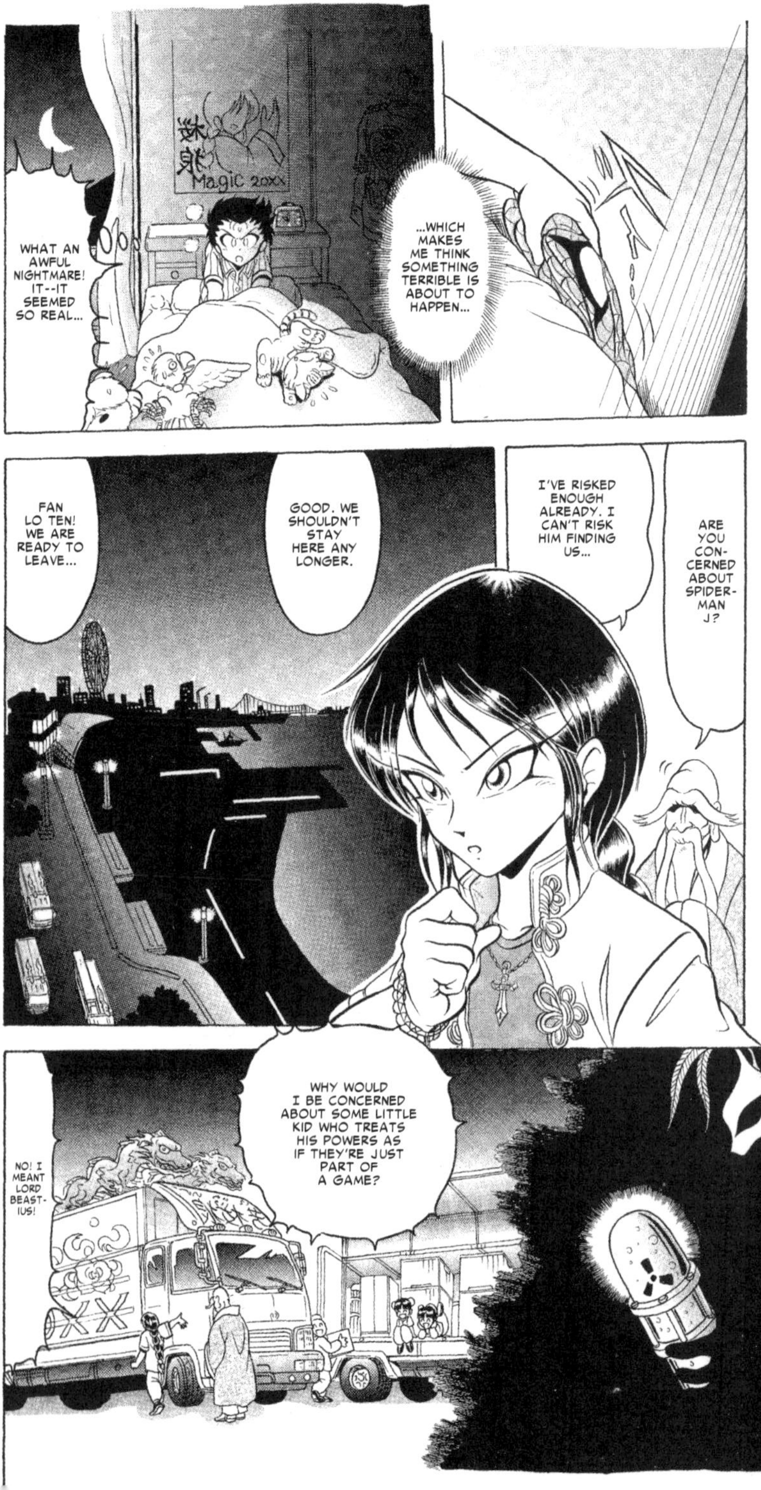

Magic 20XX
WHAT AN AWFUL NIGHTMARE! IT--IT SEEMED SO REAL...
...WHICH MAKES ME THINK SOMETHING TERRIBLE IS ABOUT TO HAPPEN...
FAN LO TEN! WE ARE READY TO LEAVE...
GOOD. WE SHOULDN'T STAY HERE ANY LONGER.
ARE YOU CONCERNED ABOUT SPIDER-MAN J?
WHY WOULD I BE CONCERNED ABOUT SOME LITTLE KID WHO TREATS HIS POWERS AS IF THEY'RE JUST PART OF A GAME?
NO! I MEANT LORD BEASTIUS!
I'VE RISKED ENOUGH ALREADY. I CAN'T RISK HIM FINDING US...

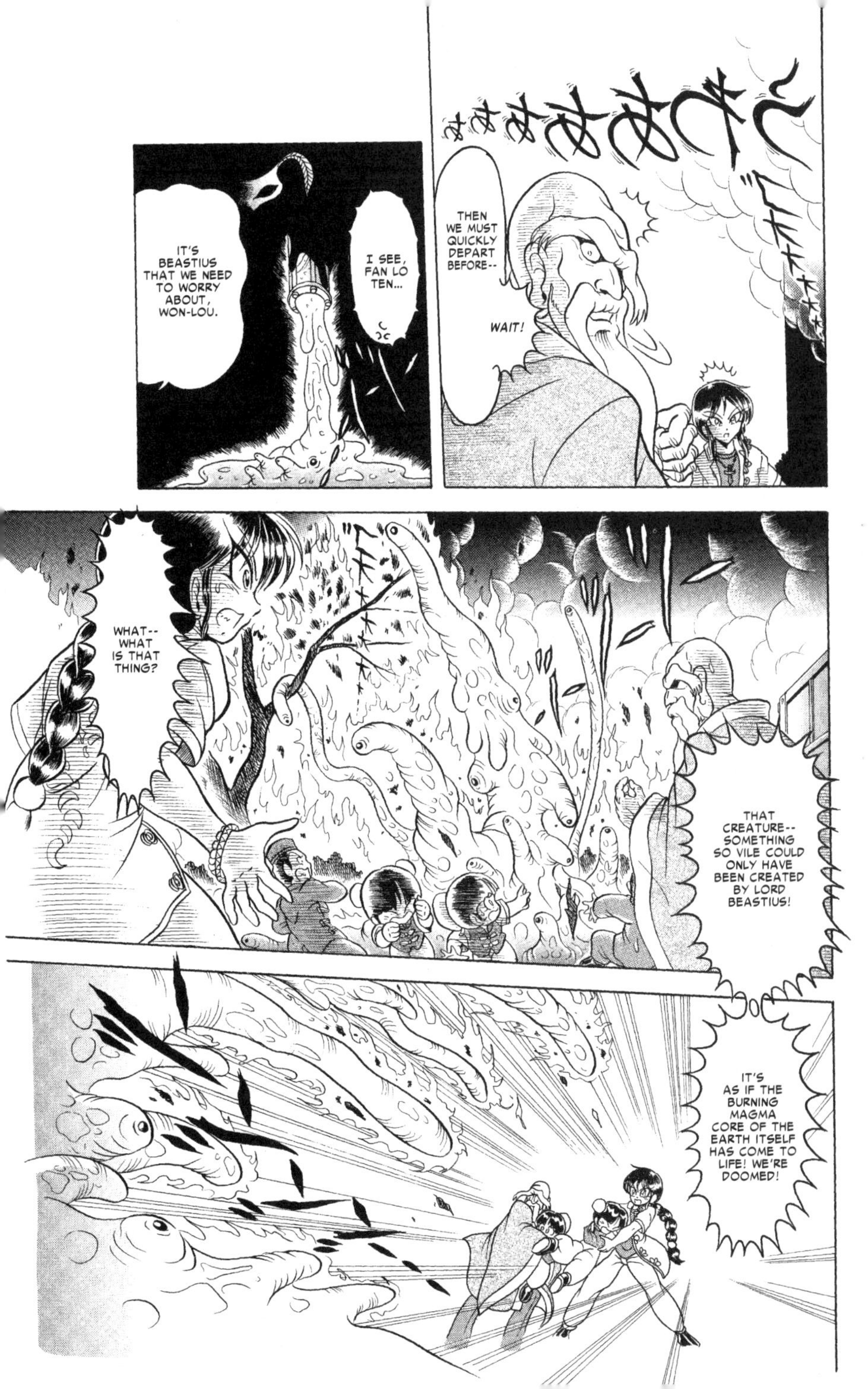
THEN WE MUST QUICKLY DEPART BEFORE--
WAIT!
I SEE, FAN LO TEN...
IT'S BEASTIUS THAT WE NEED TO WORRY ABOUT, WON-LOU.
THAT CREATURE-- SOMETHING SO VILE COULD ONLY HAVE BEEN CREATED BY LORD BEASTIUS!
WHAT-- WHAT IS THAT THING?
IT'S AS IF THE BURNING MAGMA CORE OF THE EARTH ITSELF HAS COME TO LIFE! WE'RE DOOMED!

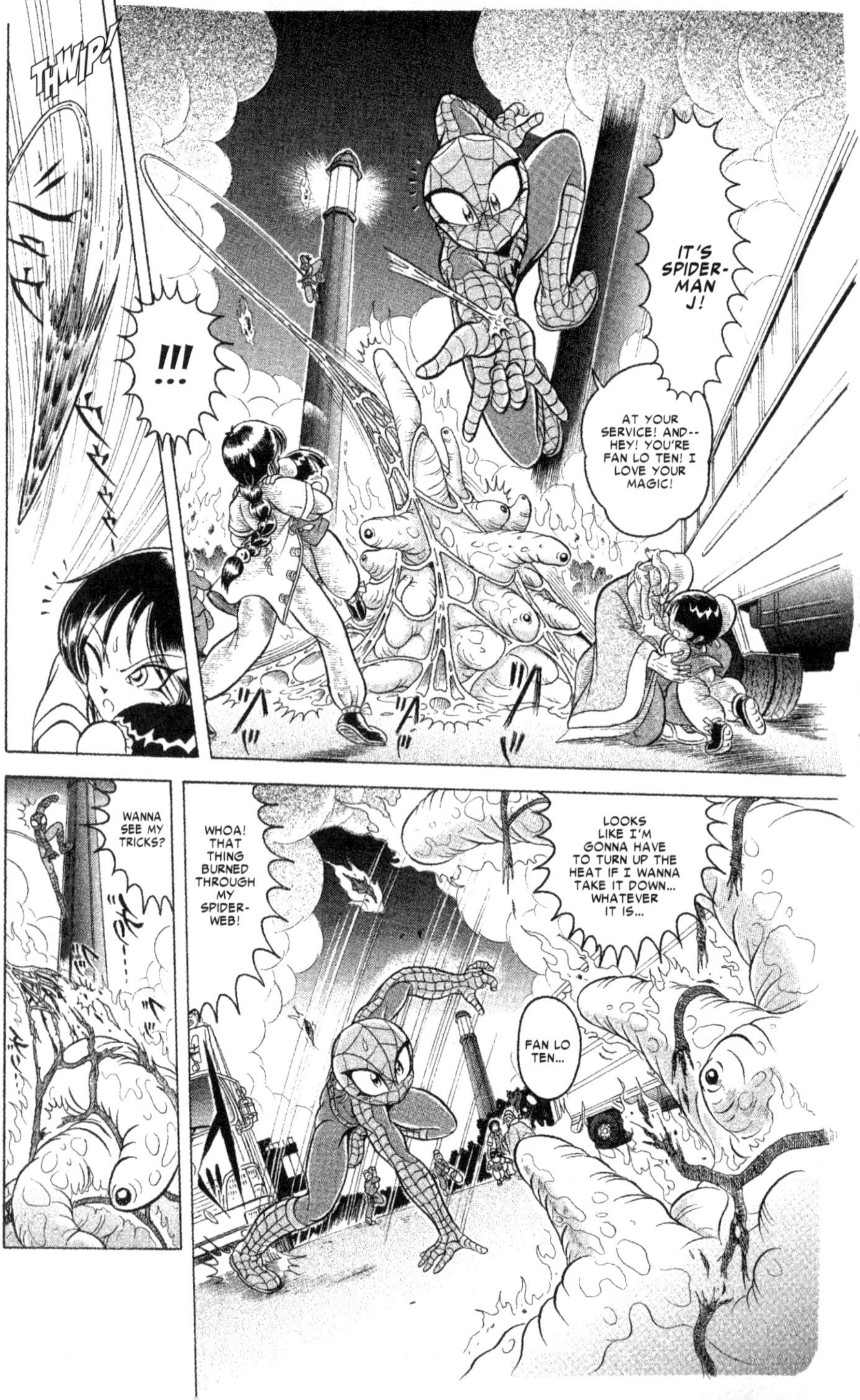
THWIP!
!!!
...
IT'S SPIDER-MAN J!
AT YOUR SERVICE! AND-- HEY! YOU'RE FAN LO TEN! I LOVE YOUR MAGIC!
LOOKS LIKE I'M GONNA HAVE TO TURN UP THE HEAT IF I WANNA TAKE IT DOWN... WHATEVER IT IS...
WHOA! THAT THING BURNED THROUGH MY SPIDER-WEB!
WANNA SEE MY TRICKS?
FAN LO TEN...

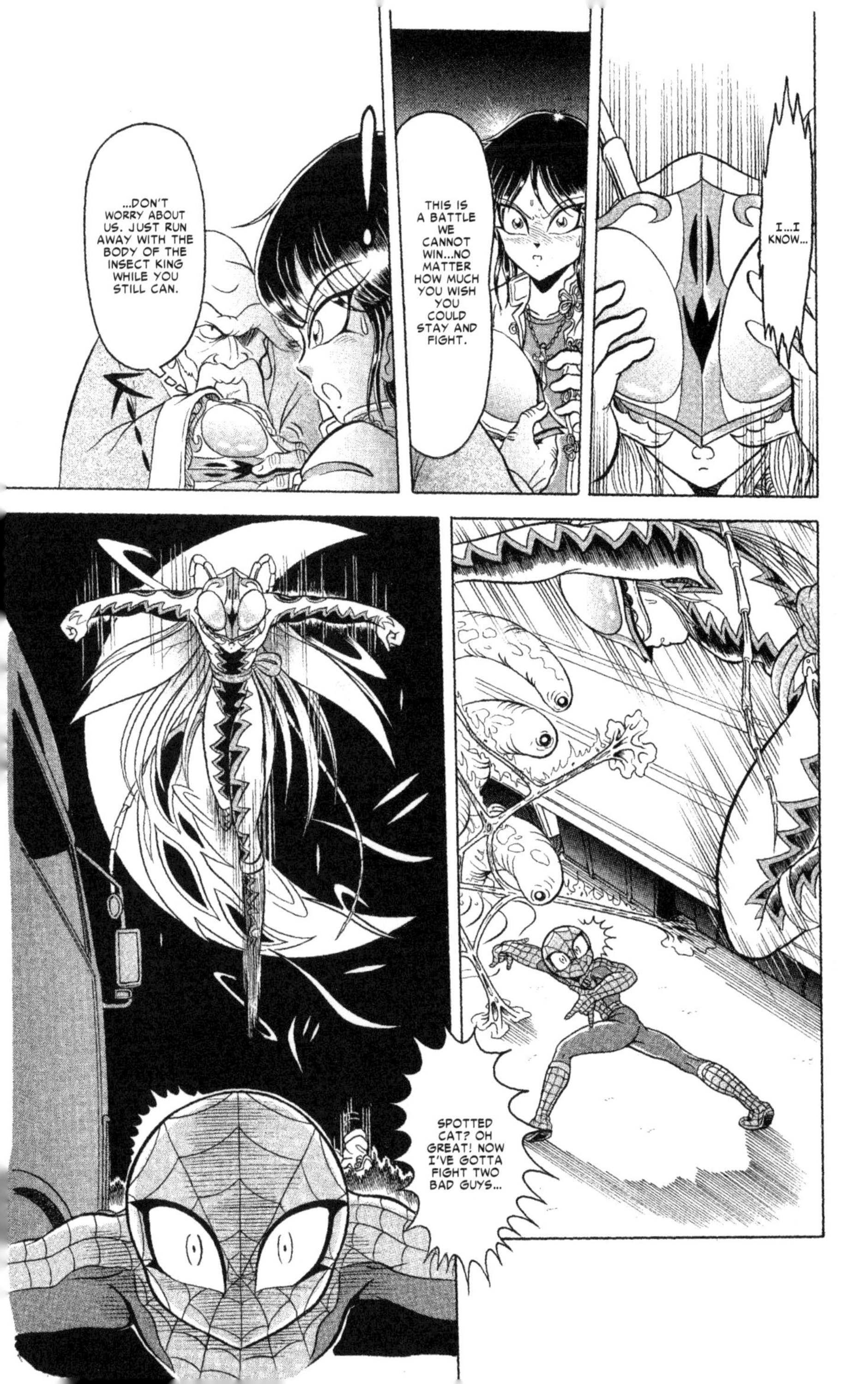
...DON'T WORRY ABOUT US. JUST RUN AWAY WITH THE BODY OF THE INSECT KING WHILE YOU STILL CAN.
THIS IS A BATTLE WE CANNOT WIN...NO MATTER HOW MUCH YOU WISH YOU COULD STAY AND FIGHT.
I...I KNOW...
SPOTTED CAT? OH GREAT! NOW I'VE GOTTA FIGHT TWO BAD GUYS...

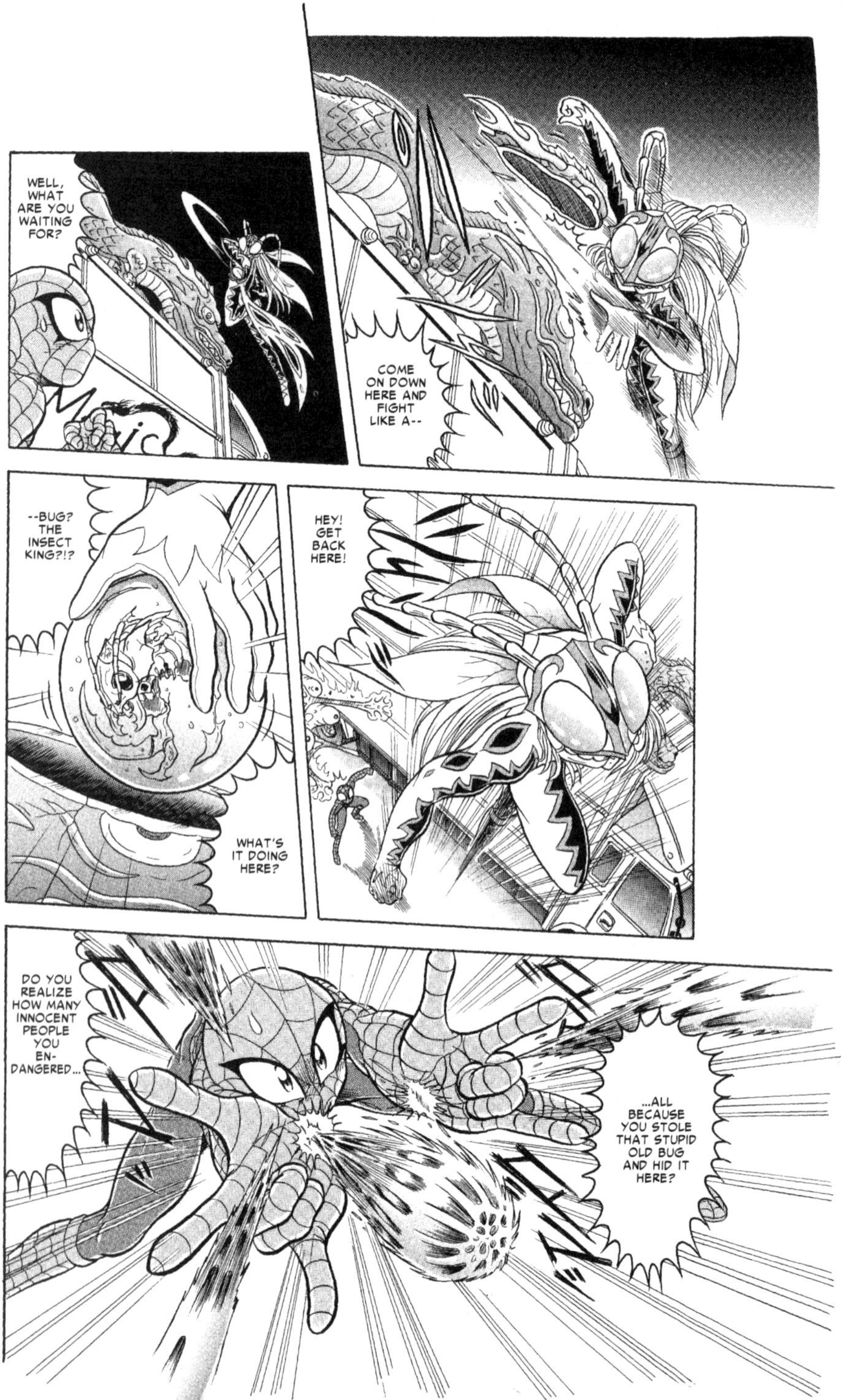

WELL, WHAT ARE YOU WAITING FOR?
COME ON DOWN HERE AND FIGHT LIKE A--
--BUG? THE INSECT KING?!?
WHAT'S IT DOING HERE?
HEY! GET BACK HERE!
DO YOU REALIZE HOW MANY INNOCENT PEOPLE YOU EN-DANGERED...
...ALL BECAUSE YOU STOLE THAT STUPID OLD BUG AND HID IT HERE?

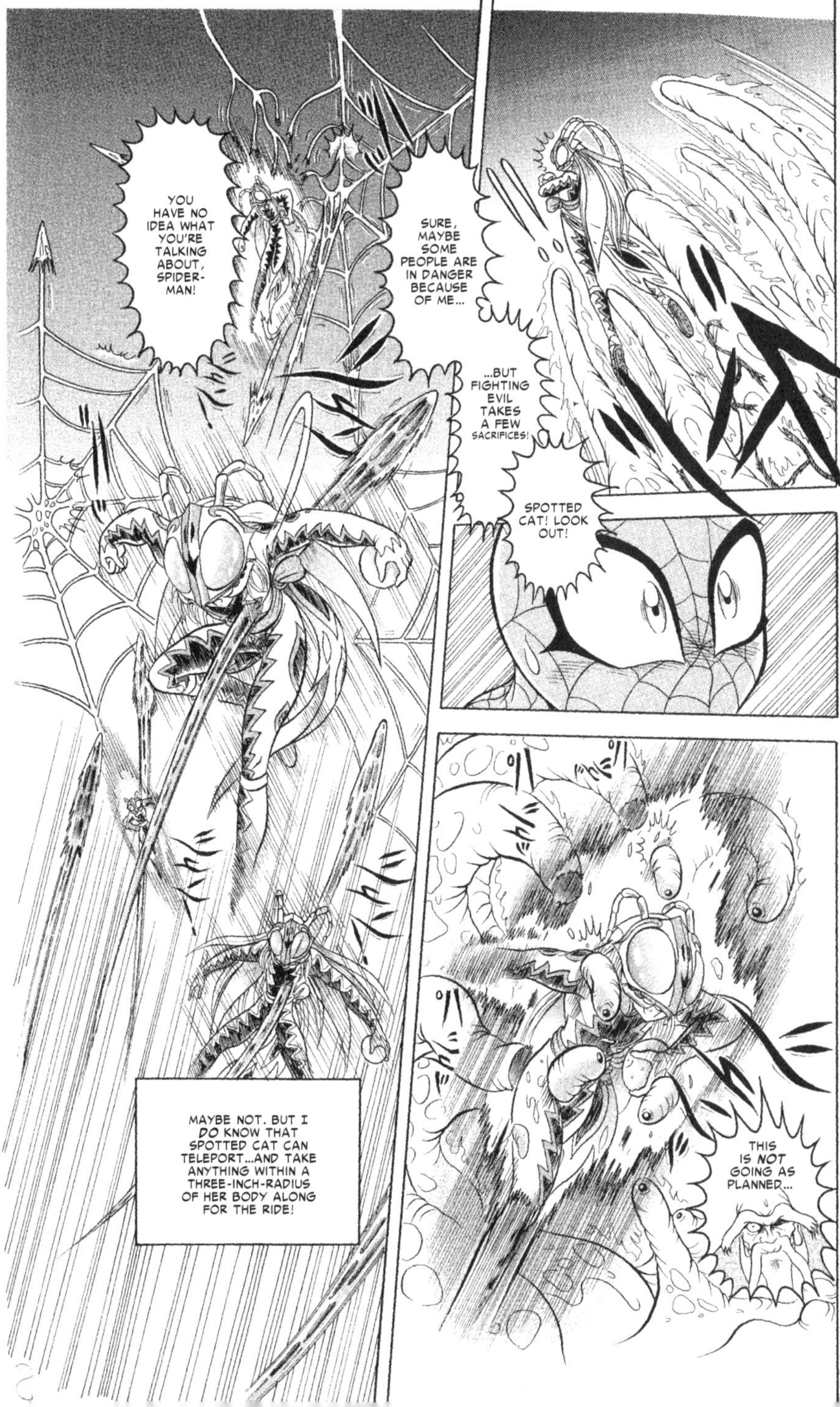
YOU HAVE NO IDEA WHAT YOU'RE TALKING ABOUT, SPIDER-MAN!
SURE, MAYBE SOME PEOPLE ARE IN DANGER BECAUSE OF ME...
...BUT FIGHTING EVIL TAKES A FEW SACRIFICES!
SPOTTED CAT! LOOK OUT!
MAYBE NOT. BUT I DO KNOW THAT SPOTTED CAT CAN TELEPORT...AND TAKE ANYTHING WITHIN A THREE-INCH-RADIUS OF HER BODY ALONG FOR THE RIDE!
THIS IS NOT GOING AS PLANNED...

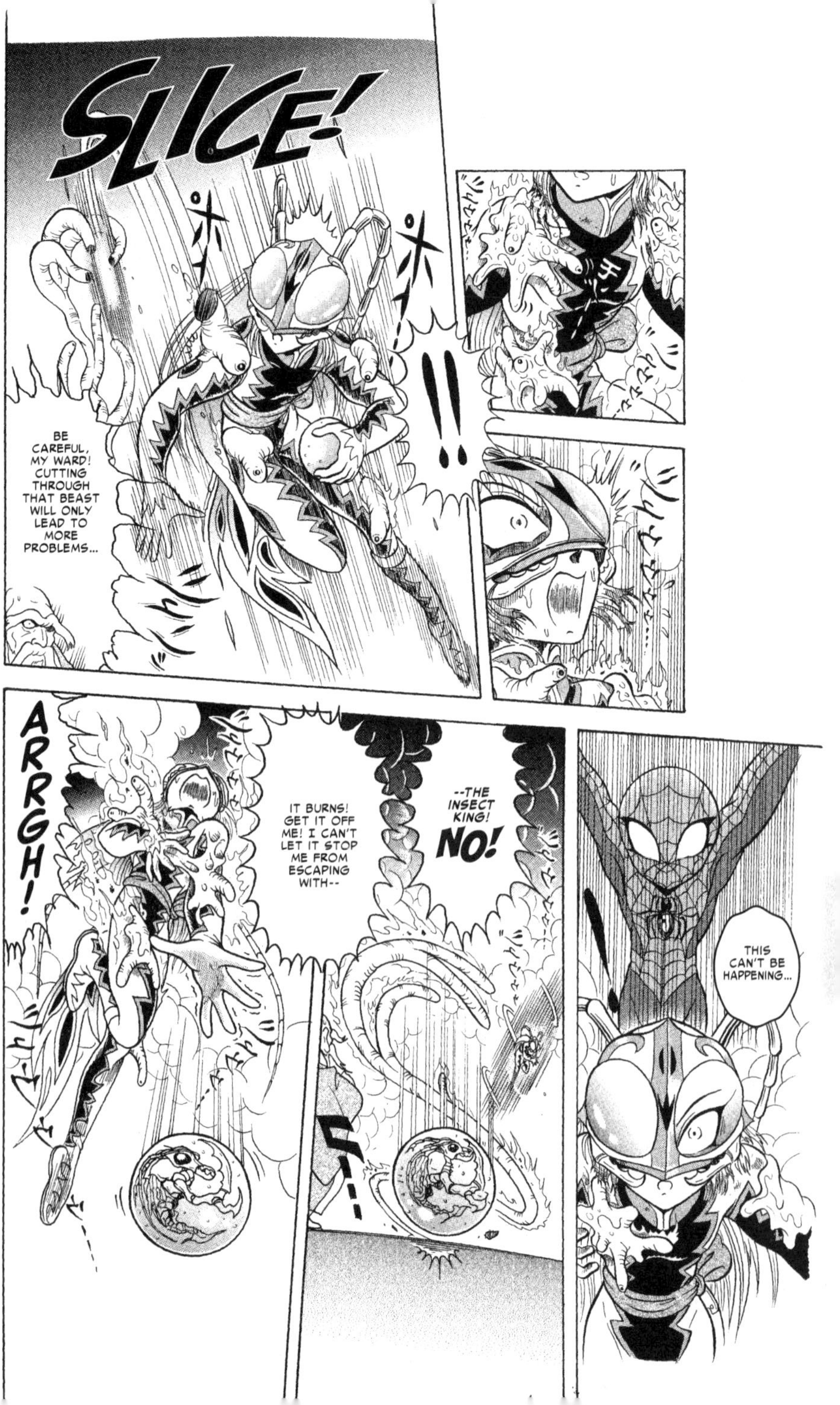
SLICE!
!!
BE CAREFUL, MY WARD! CUTTING THROUGH THAT BEAST WILL ONLY LEAD TO MORE PROBLEMS...
ARRGH!
IT BURNS! GET IT OFF ME! I CAN'T LET IT STOP ME FROM ESCAPING WITH--
--THE INSECT KING! NO!
THIS CAN'T BE HAPPENING...

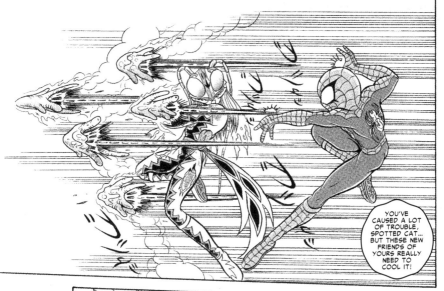

YOU'VE CAUSED A LOT OF TROUBLE, SPOTTED CAT... BUT THESE NEW FRIENDS OF YOURS REALLY NEED TO COOL IT!

GET OUT OF MY WAY!

HEY! I JUST SAVED YOUR LIFE! YOU OWE ME! BESIDES...

...LAST TIME WE MET, YOU SAID IF I CAUGHT YOU--

--YOU WOULD TELL ME EVERYTHING I WANTED TO KNOW. SO START TELLING!

YOU HAVE NO IDEA WHAT OUR POWERS REALLY MEAN, DO YOU?

YOU JUST USE THEM WITHOUT KNOWING WHY?

NO, I... BUT... HUH?

HELP!

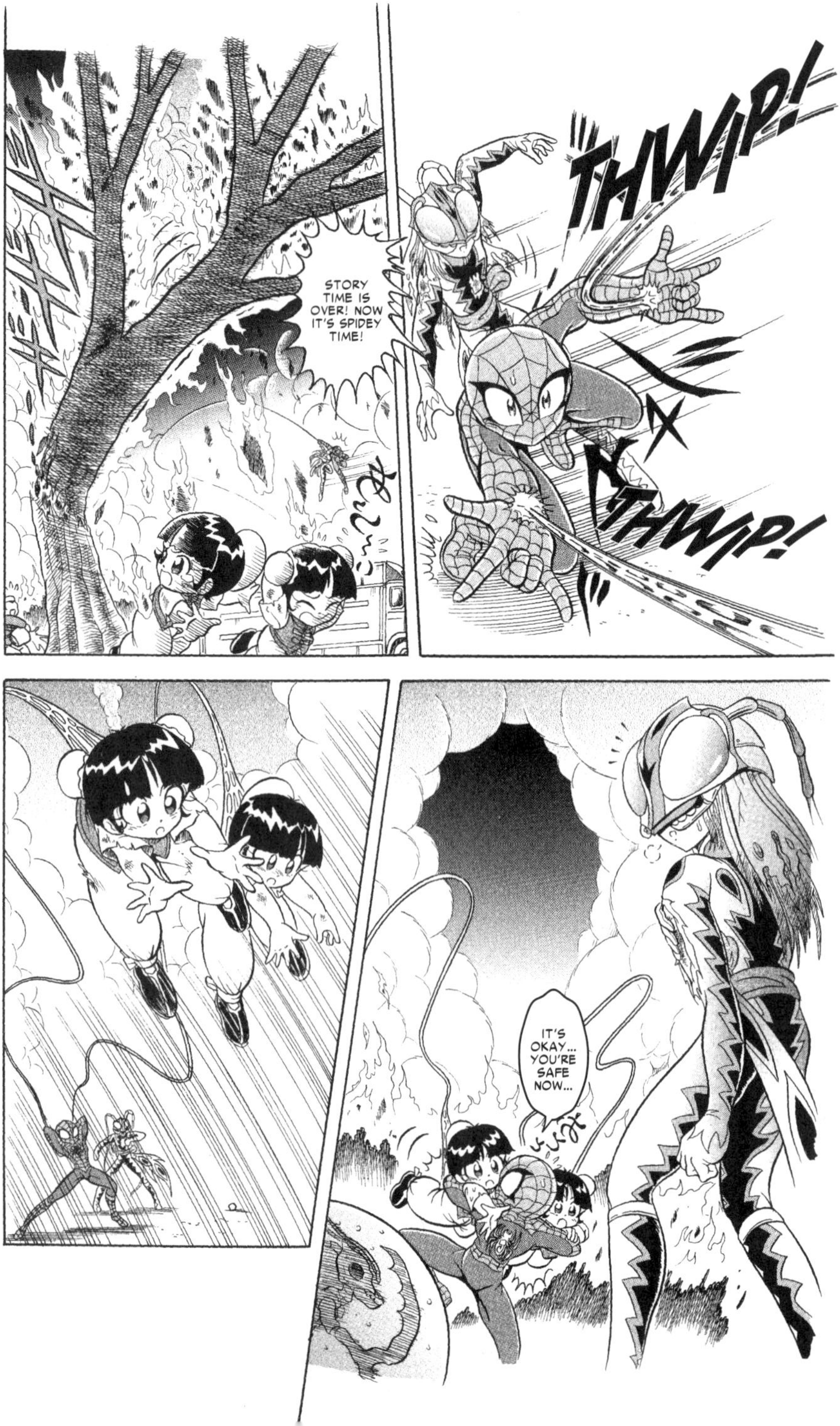
STORY TIME IS OVER! NOW IT'S SPIDEY TIME!
THWIP!
THWIP!
IT'S OKAY... YOU'RE SAFE NOW...

I WAS GOING TO TELL YOU EVERYTHING... BUT YOU CHOSE TO SAVE THOSE KIDS INSTEAD?

HELPING PEOPLE WILL ALWAYS BE MY FIRST PRIORITY! THAT'S WHAT MAKES ME A HERO.

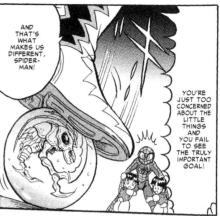

AND THAT'S WHAT MAKES US DIFFERENT, SPIDER-MAN!

YOU'RE JUST TOO CONCERNED ABOUT THE LITTLE THINGS AND YOU FAIL TO SEE THE TRULY IMPORTANT GOAL!

ALL OF THIS IS JUST A GAME TO YOU. AND IT'S A GAME YOU'LL NEVER WIN IF--

--EH?

HANG ON, KIDS! IT'S ABOUT TO GET A LITTLE TOASTY OVER HERE!

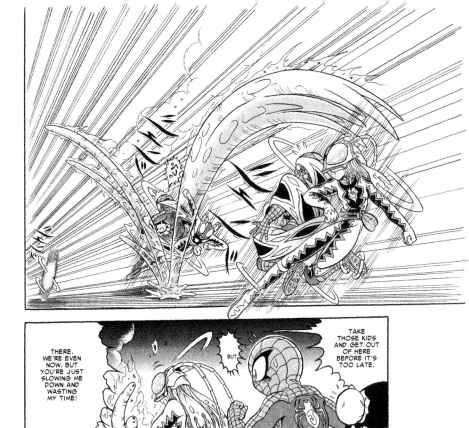

THERE. WE'RE EVEN NOW. BUT YOU'RE JUST SLOWING ME DOWN AND WASTING MY TIME!

BUT

TAKE THOSE KIDS AND GET OUT OF HERE BEFORE IT'S TOO LATE.

I...

NO!

THIS ISN'T A GAME TO ME.

AND THERE'S NO CHANCE I COULD JUST RUN AWAY... EVEN IF I WANTED TO!

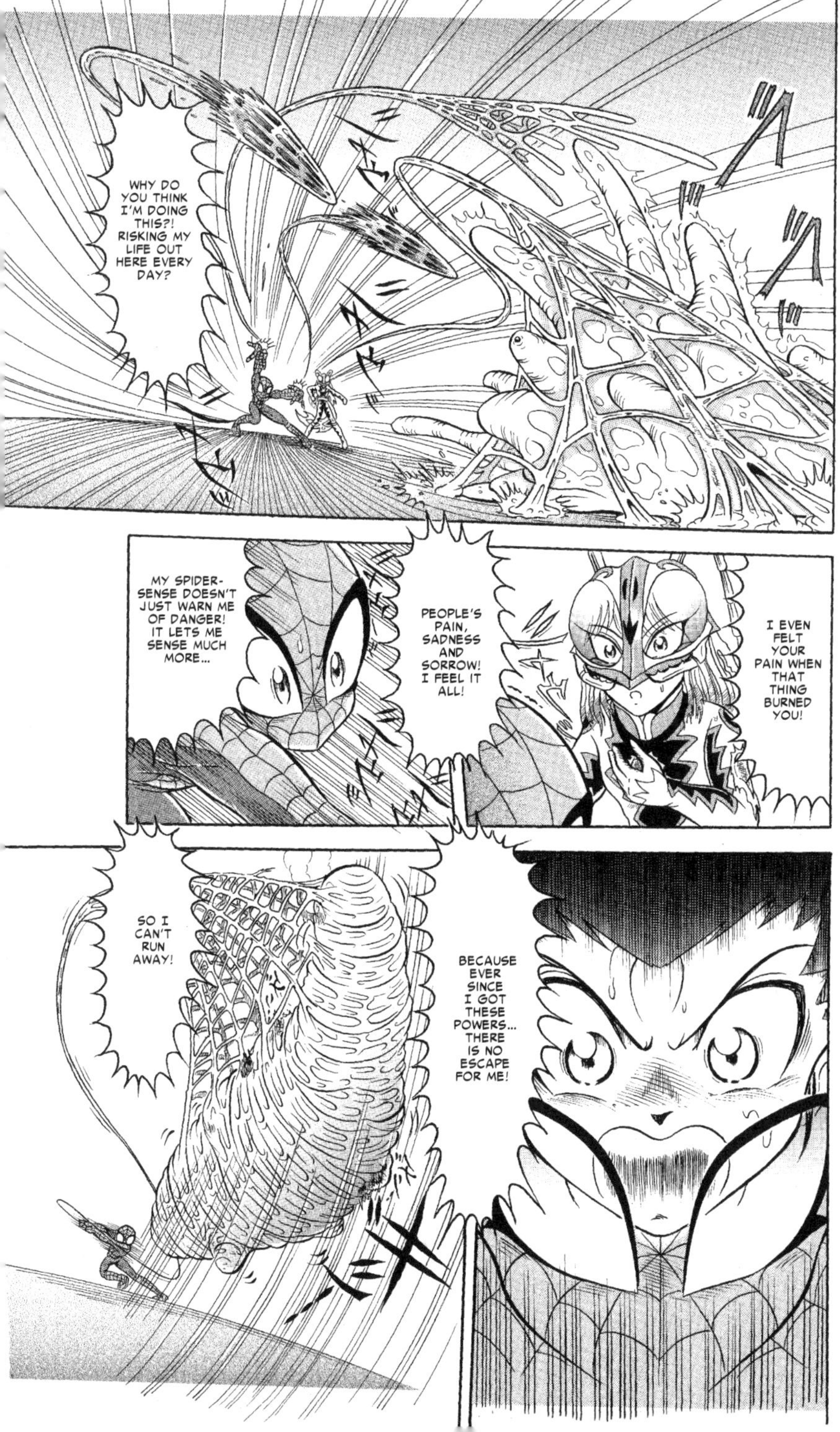
WHY DO YOU THINK I'M DOING THIS?! RISKING MY LIFE OUT HERE EVERY DAY?
MY SPIDER-SENSE DOESN'T JUST WARN ME OF DANGER! IT LETS ME SENSE MUCH MORE...
PEOPLE'S PAIN, SADNESS AND SORROW! I FEEL IT ALL!
I EVEN FELT YOUR PAIN WHEN THAT THING BURNED YOU!
SO I CAN'T RUN AWAY!
BECAUSE EVER SINCE I GOT THESE POWERS... THERE IS NO ESCAPE FOR ME!

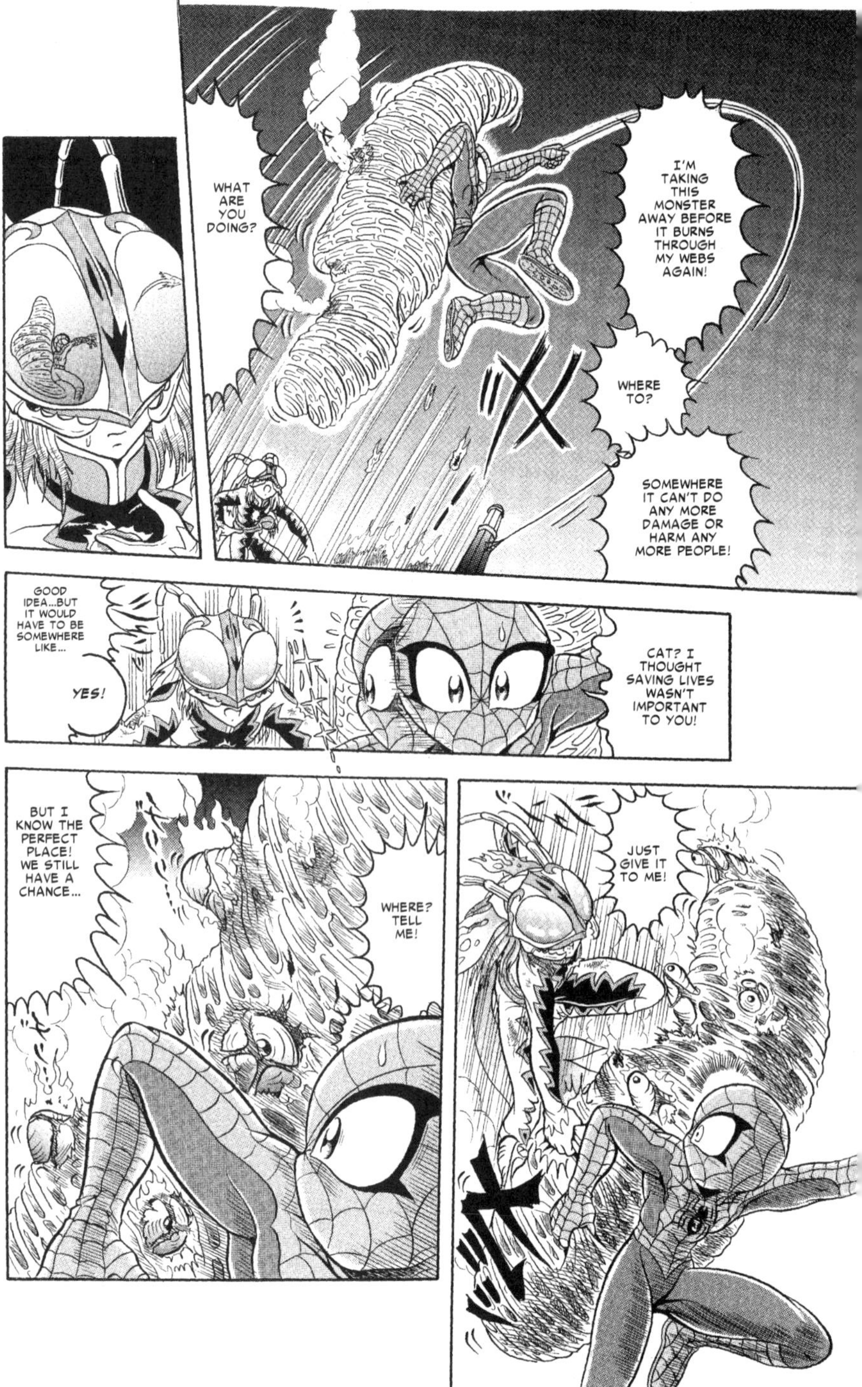

WHAT ARE YOU DOING?
I'M TAKING THIS MONSTER AWAY BEFORE IT BURNS THROUGH MY WEBS AGAIN!
WHERE TO?
SOMEWHERE IT CAN'T DO ANY MORE DAMAGE OR HARM ANY MORE PEOPLE!
GOOD IDEA...BUT IT WOULD HAVE TO BE SOMEWHERE LIKE...
YES!
CAT? I THOUGHT SAVING LIVES WASN'T IMPORTANT TO YOU!
BUT I KNOW THE PERFECT PLACE! WE STILL HAVE A CHANCE...
WHERE? TELL ME!
JUST GIVE IT TO ME!

YOU'RE NOT FAST ENOUGH TO DO THIS ALONE, SPIDER-MAN. LET ME TAKE IT FROM HERE...

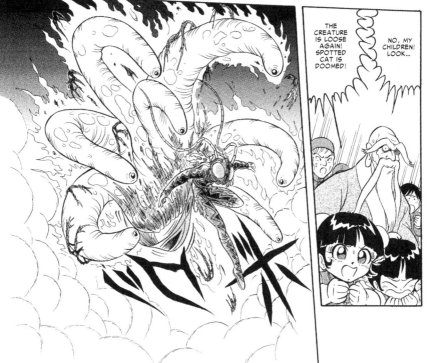

THE CREATURE IS LOOSE AGAIN! SPOTTED CAT IS DOOMED!

NO, MY CHILDREN! LOOK...

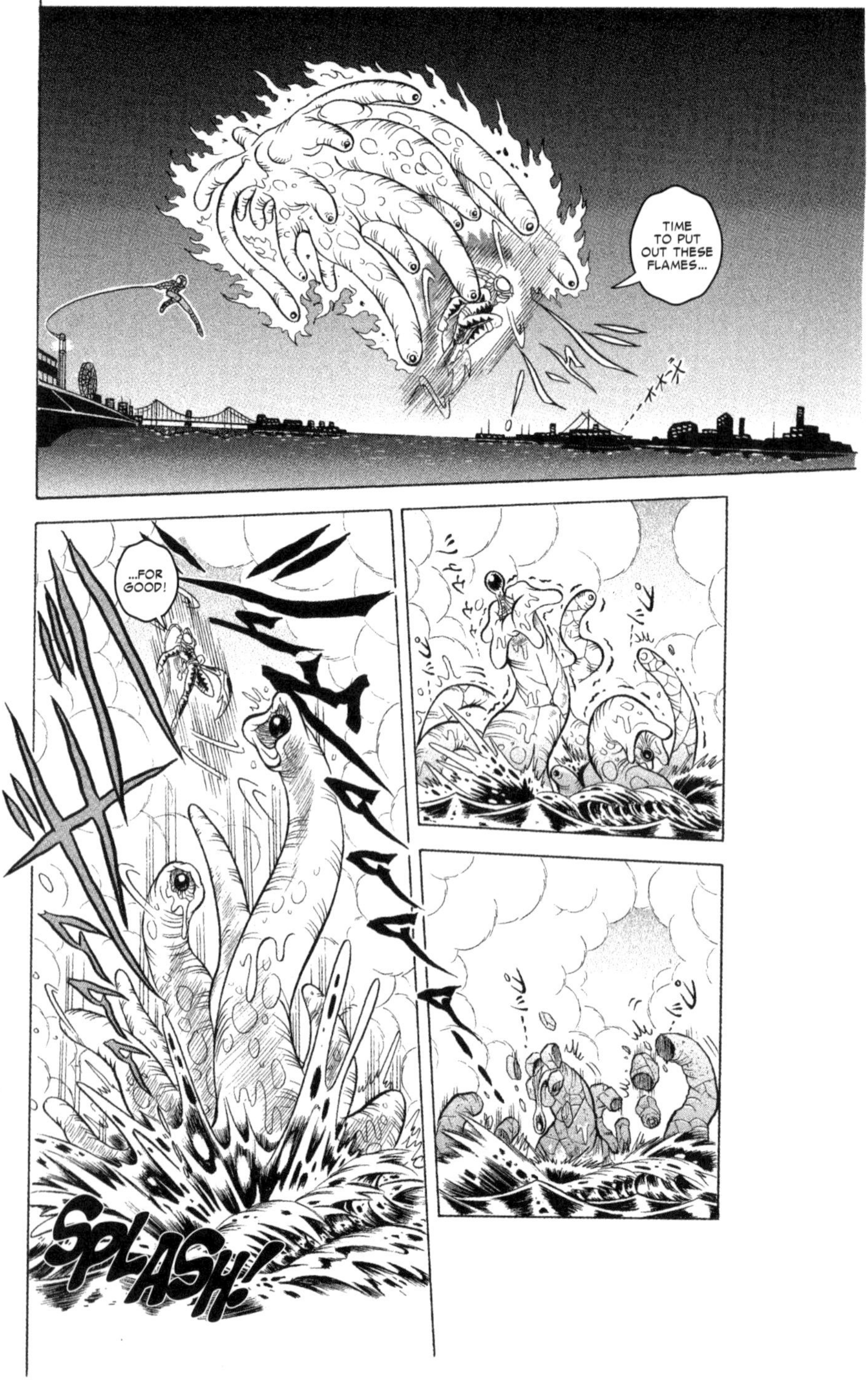
TIME TO PUT OUT THESE FLAMES...
...FOR GOOD!
SPLASH!

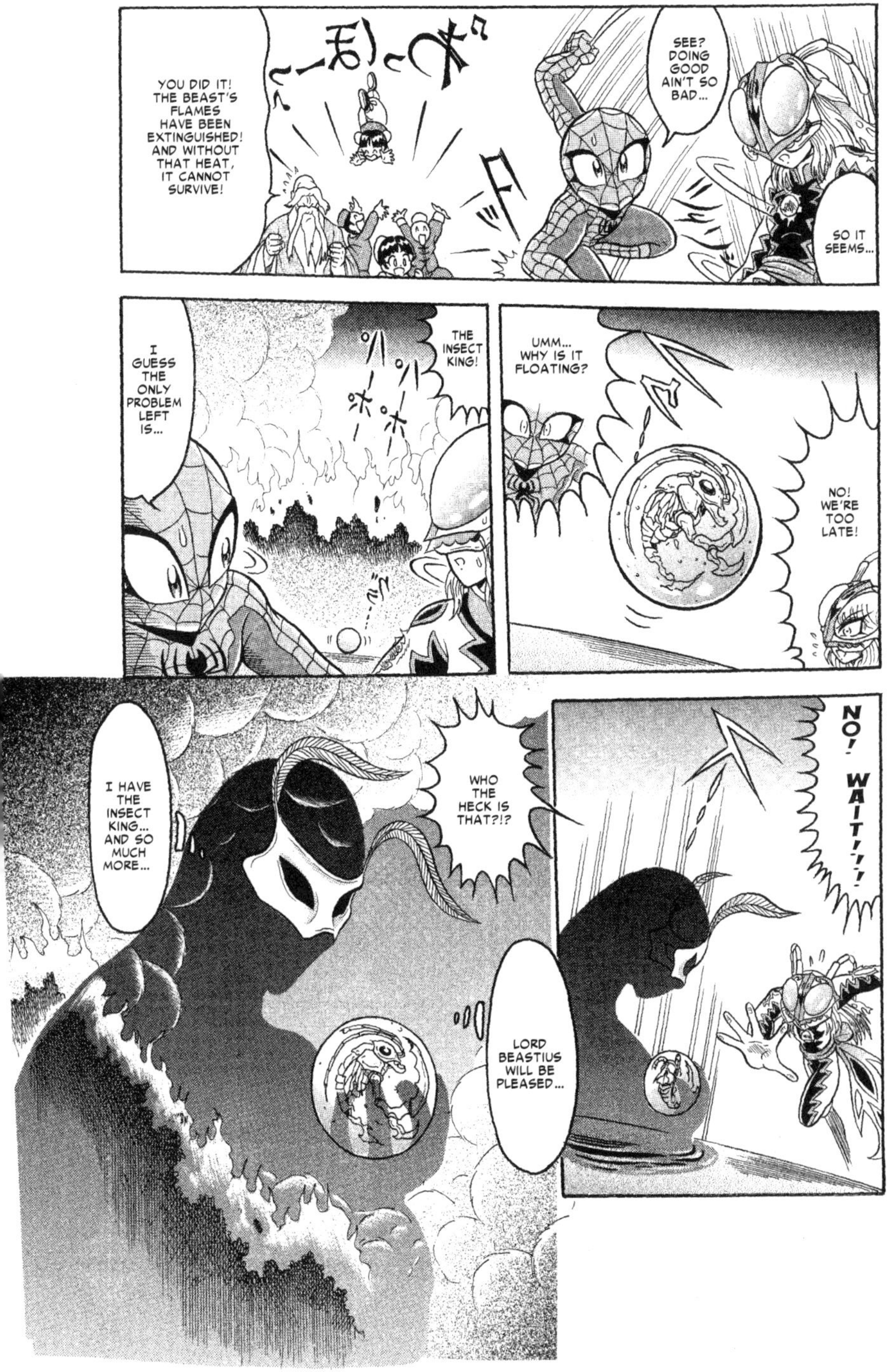
SEE? DOING GOOD AIN'T SO BAD...
SO IT SEEMS...
YOU DID IT! THE BEAST'S FLAMES HAVE BEEN EXTINGUISHED! AND WITHOUT THAT HEAT, IT CANNOT SURVIVE!
UMM... WHY IS IT FLOATING?
NO! WE'RE TOO LATE!
THE INSECT KING!
I GUESS THE ONLY PROBLEM LEFT IS...
NO! WAIT!!!
WHO THE HECK IS THAT?!?
I HAVE THE INSECT KING... AND SO MUCH MORE...
LORD BEASTIUS WILL BE PLEASED...

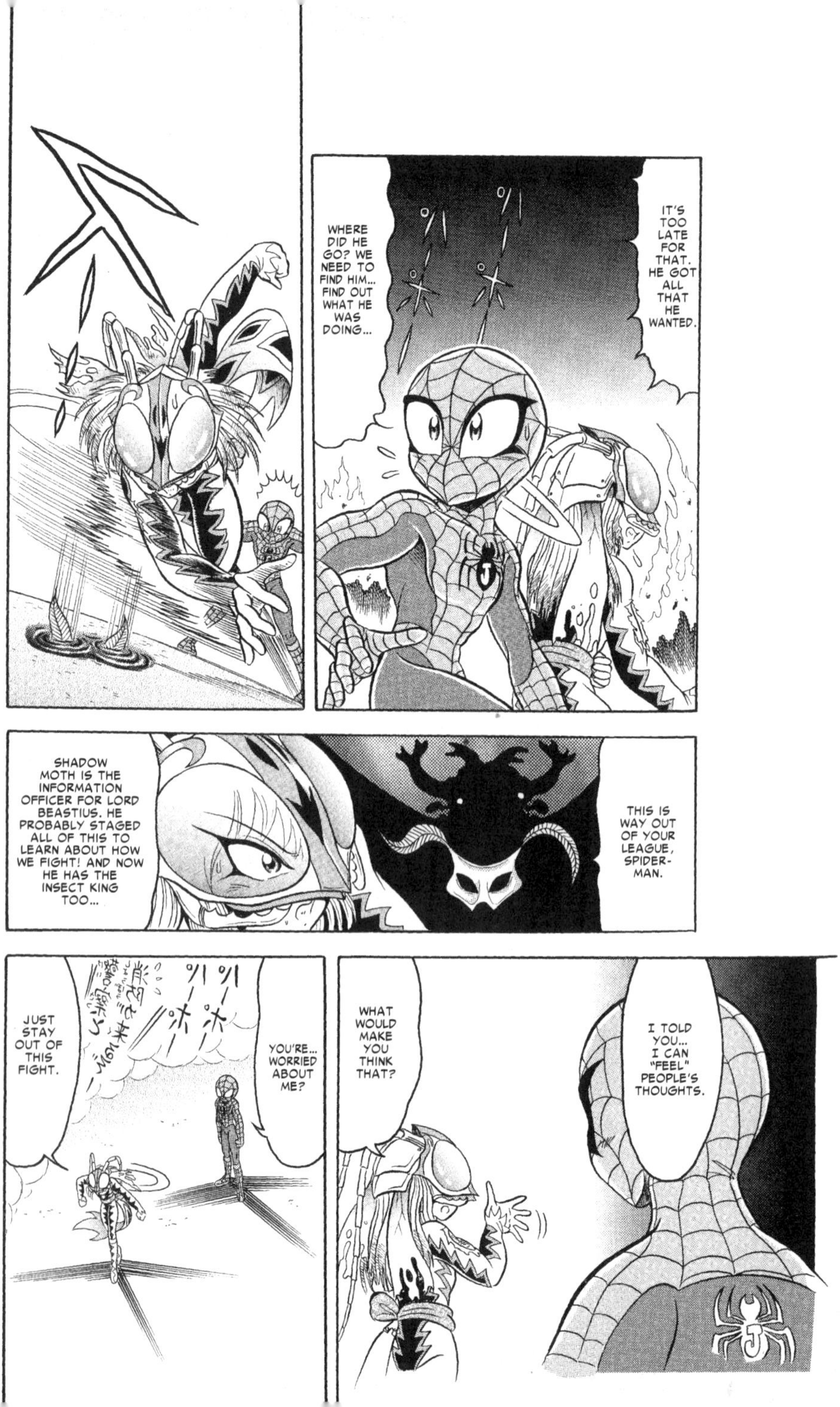
WHERE DID HE GO? WE NEED TO FIND HIM... FIND OUT WHAT HE WAS DOING...
IT'S TOO LATE FOR THAT. HE GOT ALL THAT HE WANTED.
SHADOW MOTH IS THE INFORMATION OFFICER FOR LORD BEASTIUS. HE PROBABLY STAGED ALL OF THIS TO LEARN ABOUT HOW WE FIGHT! AND NOW HE HAS THE INSECT KING TOO...
THIS IS WAY OUT OF YOUR LEAGUE, SPIDER-MAN.
JUST STAY OUT OF THIS FIGHT.
YOU'RE... WORRIED ABOUT ME?
WHAT WOULD MAKE YOU THINK THAT?
I TOLD YOU... I CAN "FEEL" PEOPLE'S THOUGHTS.

I CAN FEEL PEOPLE'S PAIN AND SORROW... BUT ALSO THEIR KINDNESS AND GENEROSITY.

THE ONLY THING YOU'RE GOING TO FEEL NOW...

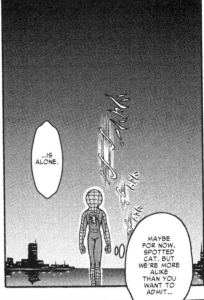

...IS ALONE.

MAYBE FOR NOW, SPOTTED CAT. BUT WE'RE MORE ALIKE THAN YOU WANT TO ADMIT...

AND SOON THE TIME WILL COME...

WE'LL HAVE TO CHOOSE SIDES AGAINST THE ULTIMATE EVIL...

NEITHER OF US MAY BE STRONG ENOUGH TO FACE IT ON OUR OWN... BUT THAT WON'T STOP ME FROM FIGHTING!

I'LL FACE MY DESTINY... WITH OR WITHOUT YOUR HELP!!

END.

CHAPTER 2

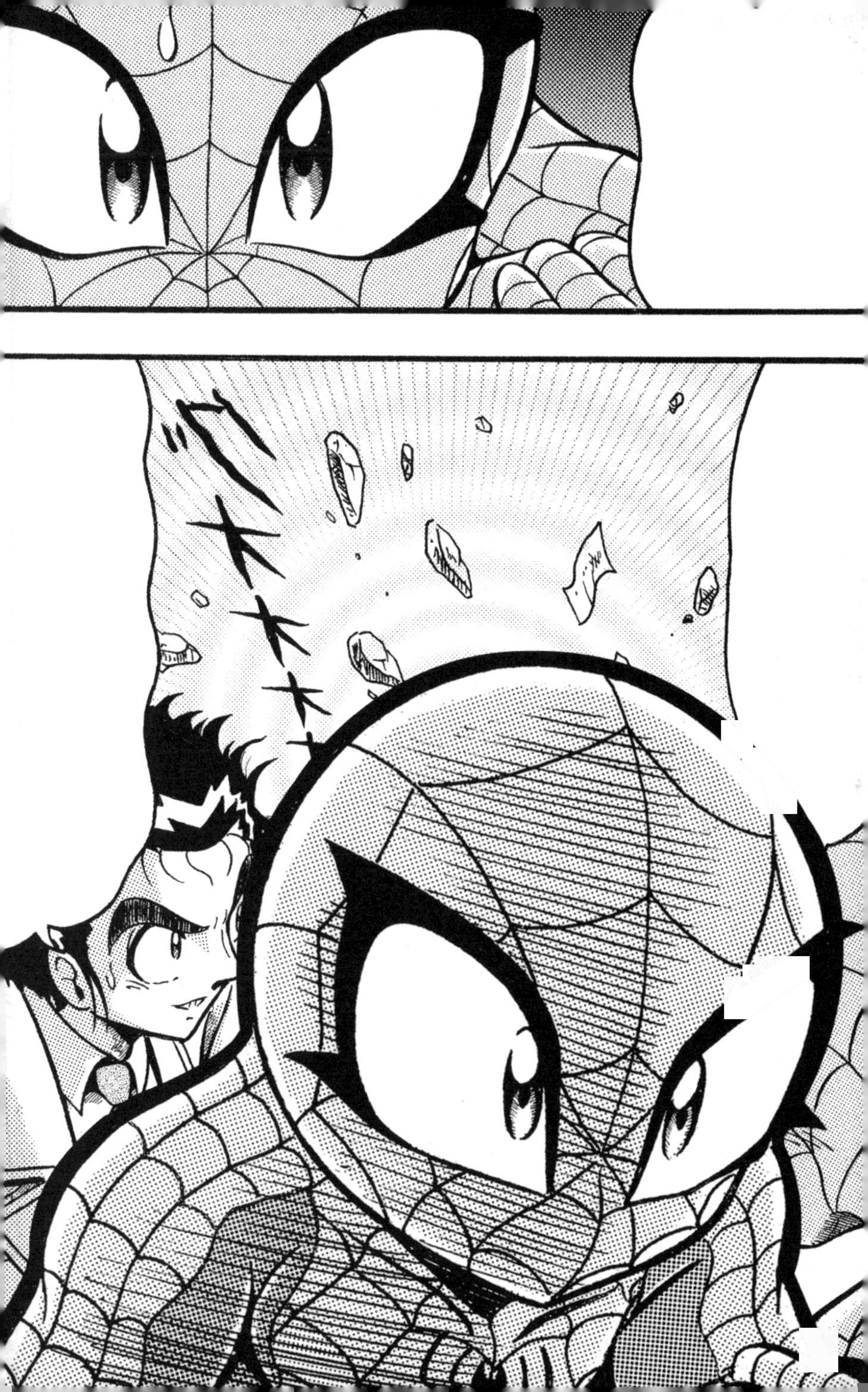

Each corner of the globe has its own unique take on the AMAZING SPIDER-MAN! Direct from Japan, Marvel is proud to present...

SPIDER-MAN J - "The Gravity Of The Situation"

ORIGINAL STORY AND ART BY **YAMANAKA AKIRA**

YUKO FUKAMI	MARC SUMERAK	VC'SJOE CARAMAGNA	JORDAN D. WHITE	NATHAN COSBY & MARK PANICCIA	JOE QUESADA	DAN BUCKLEY
TRANSLATION	ENGLISH ADAPTATION	LETTERING	ASST. EDITOR	EDITORS	EDITOR IN CHIEF	PUBLISHER

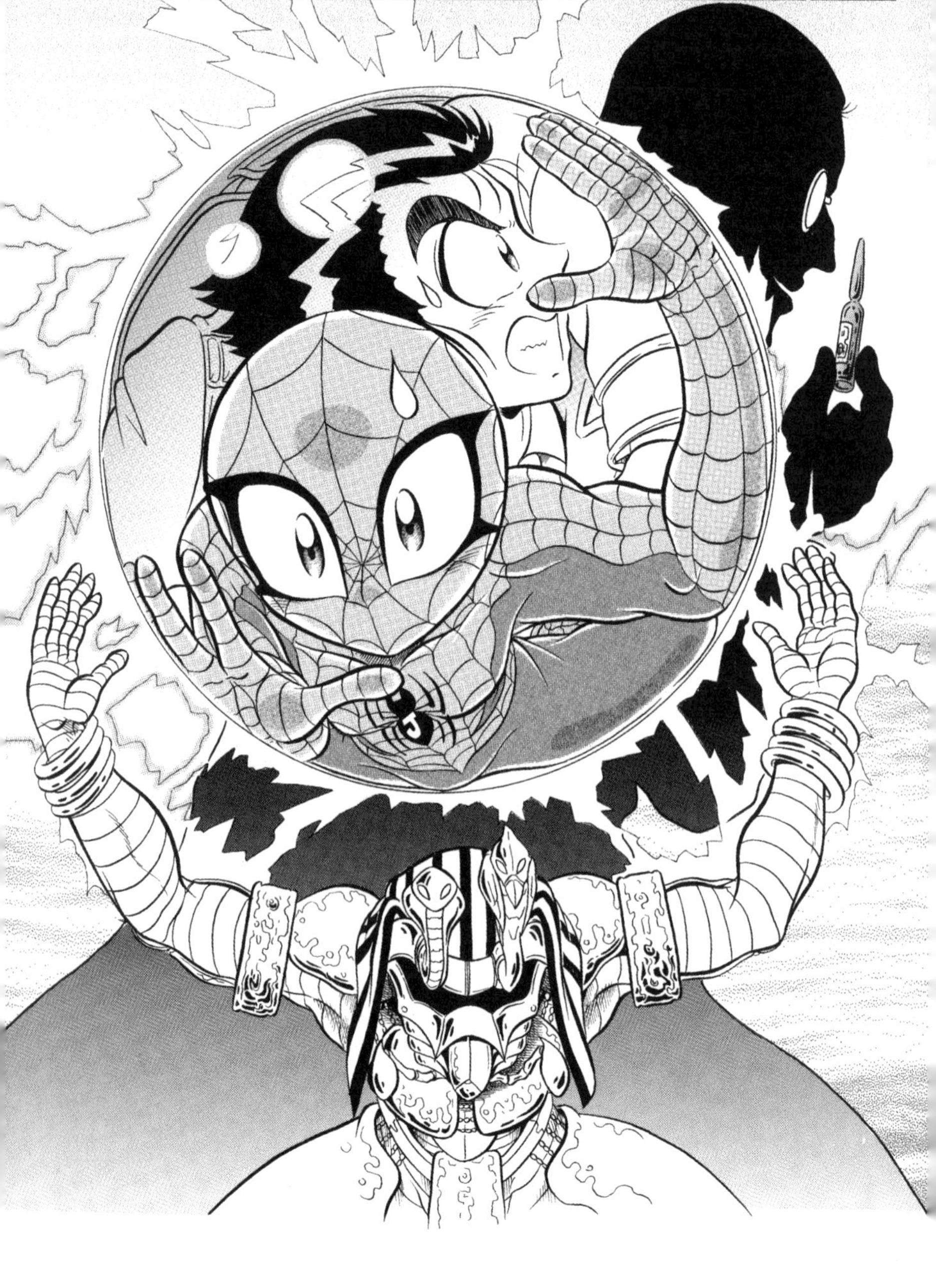

TOKYO. A CITY FULL OF LIFE AND BEAUTY...

HMPH. I JUST DON'T SEE IT.

EVERYONE TOLD ME TOKYO WAS THE GREATEST CITY ON EARTH.

BUT I CAN'T STAND IT HERE. IT'S NO FUN AT ALL!

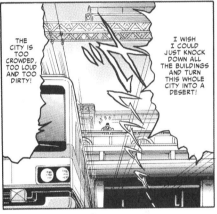

THE CITY IS TOO CROWDED, TOO LOUD AND TOO DIRTY!

I WISH I COULD JUST KNOCK DOWN ALL THE BUILDINGS AND TURN THIS WHOLE CITY INTO A DESERT!

THAT'S A BRILLIANT IDEA! WHY DON'T YOU TRY?

HUH?! WHAT ARE YOU TALKING ABOUT?

TO-GETHER, WE CAN RESHAPE TOKYO HOW-EVER WE WISH!

ALL YOU NEED TO DO IS DRINK FROM THIS VIAL. THE ENHANCED DNA INSIDE WILL GRANT YOU THE POWERS TO MAKE YOUR DREAM A REALITY!

THAT CAN'T BE TRUE...

CAN IT...?

...SO THAT'S THE RUMOR GOING AROUND THE PRECINCT.

A DRINK THAT TURNS YOU INTO A SUPER-VILLAIN? SOUNDS A BIT FAR-FETCHED TO ME, FLYNN.

SAYS THE KID WITH SPIDER POWERS.

IT'S JUST A RUMOR, PETER. BUT I DON'T KNOW...

...AFTER EVERYTHING WE'VE SEEN RECENTLY, ANYTHING IS POSSIBLE! WHAT IF IT'S MADE FROM THAT INSECT KING'S DNA?

IF IT IS, THAT MEANS LORD BEASTIUS IS BEHIND IT...

...AND THAT MEANS MY LIFE JUST GOT A LOT MORE DIFFICULT.

YOUR LIFE?

DON'T FORGET ABOUT THE DETECTIVE THAT'S ALWAYS BRAVELY RISKING HIS LIFE TO HELP YOU WHEN--

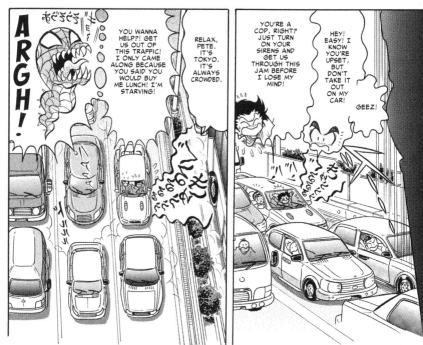

ARGH!

YOU WANNA HELP?! GET US OUT OF THIS TRAFFIC! I ONLY CAME ALONG BECAUSE YOU SAID YOU WOULD BUY ME LUNCH! I'M STARVING!

RELAX, PETE. IT'S TOKYO. IT'S ALWAYS CROWDED.

YOU'RE A COP, RIGHT? JUST TURN ON YOUR SIRENS AND GET US THROUGH THIS JAM BEFORE I LOSE MY MIND!

HEY! EASY! I KNOW YOU'RE UPSET, BUT DON'T TAKE IT OUT ON MY CAR!

GEEZ!

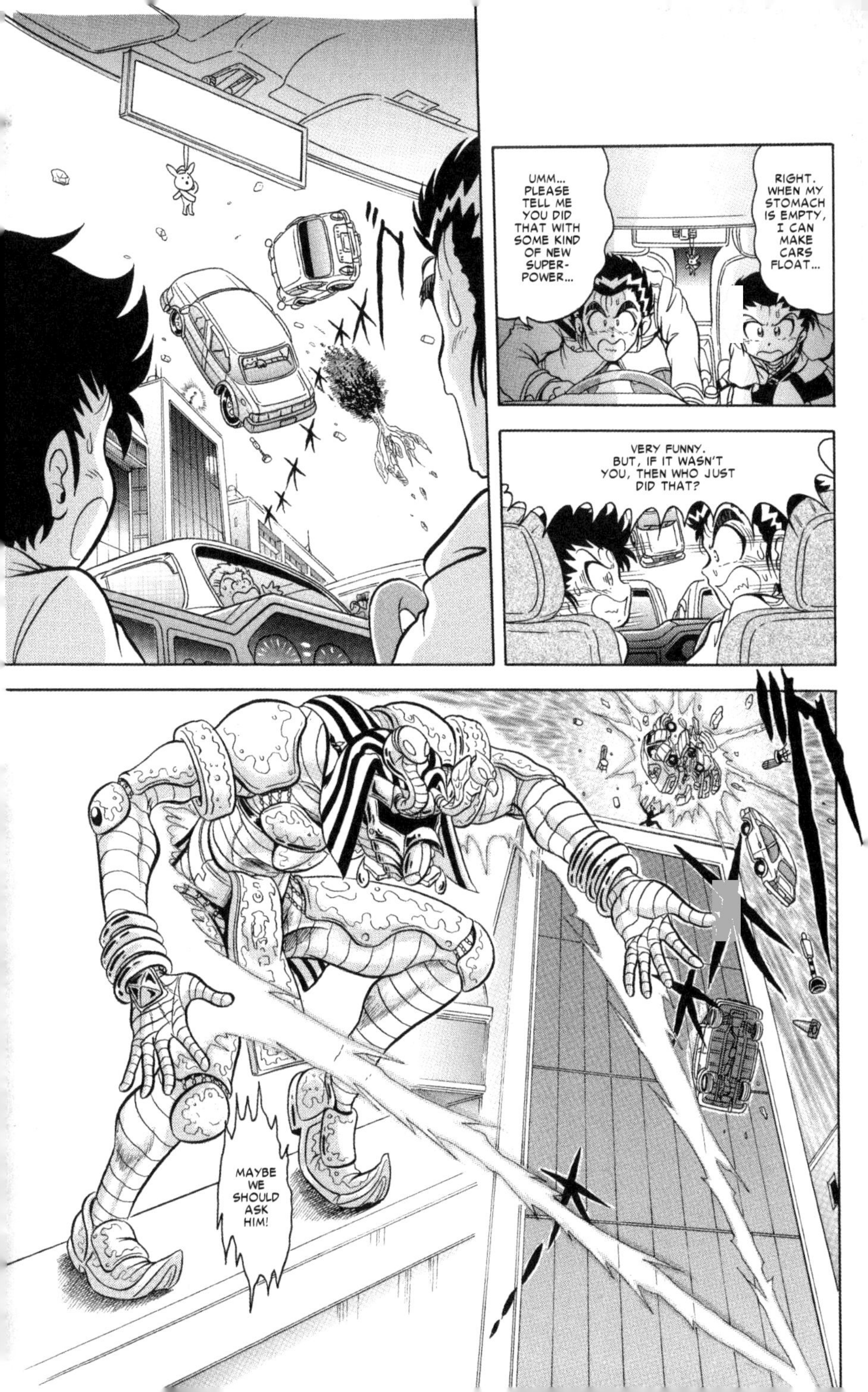
RIGHT. WHEN MY STOMACH IS EMPTY, I CAN MAKE CARS FLOAT...
UMM... PLEASE TELL ME YOU DID THAT WITH SOME KIND OF NEW SUPER-POWER...
VERY FUNNY. BUT, IF IT WASN'T YOU, THEN WHO JUST DID THAT?
MAYBE WE SHOULD ASK HIM!

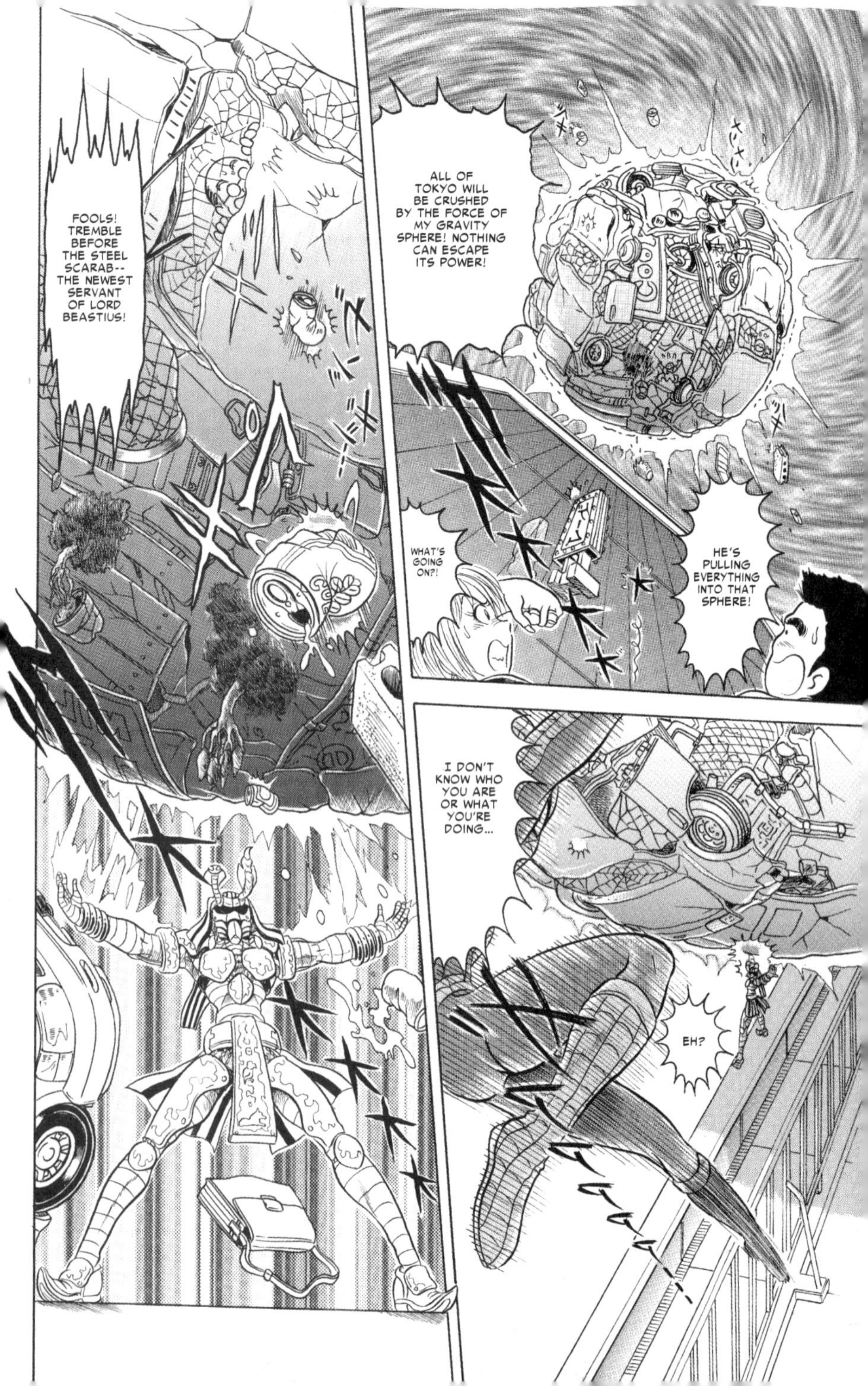
ALL OF TOKYO WILL BE CRUSHED BY THE FORCE OF MY GRAVITY SPHERE! NOTHING CAN ESCAPE ITS POWER!
HE'S PULLING EVERYTHING INTO THAT SPHERE!
WHAT'S GOING ON?!
FOOLS! TREMBLE BEFORE THE STEEL SCARAB-- THE NEWEST SERVANT OF LORD BEASTIUS!
I DON'T KNOW WHO YOU ARE OR WHAT YOU'RE DOING...
EH?

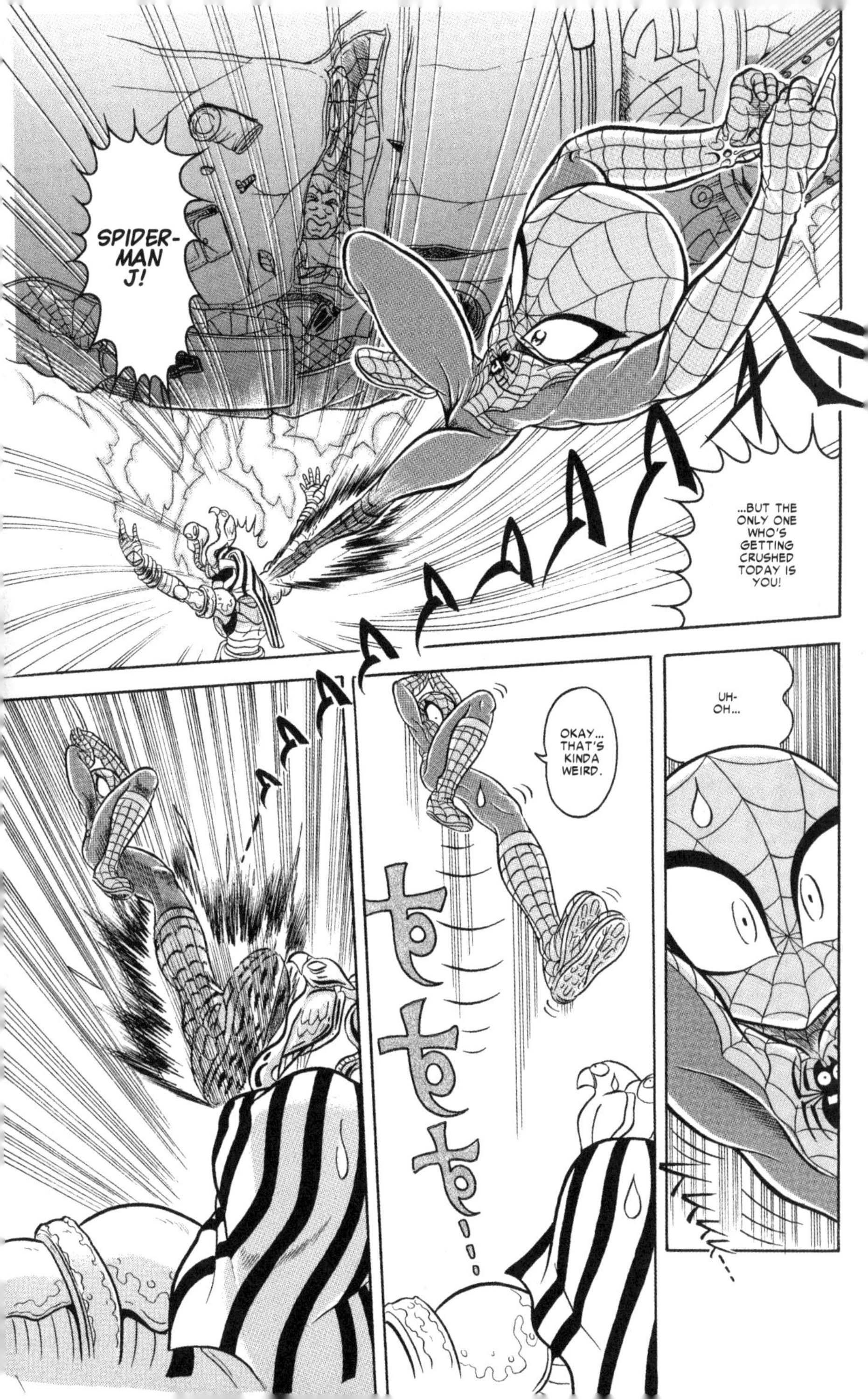
SPIDER-MAN J!
...BUT THE ONLY ONE WHO'S GETTING CRUSHED TODAY IS YOU!
OKAY... THAT'S KINDA WEIRD.
UH-OH...

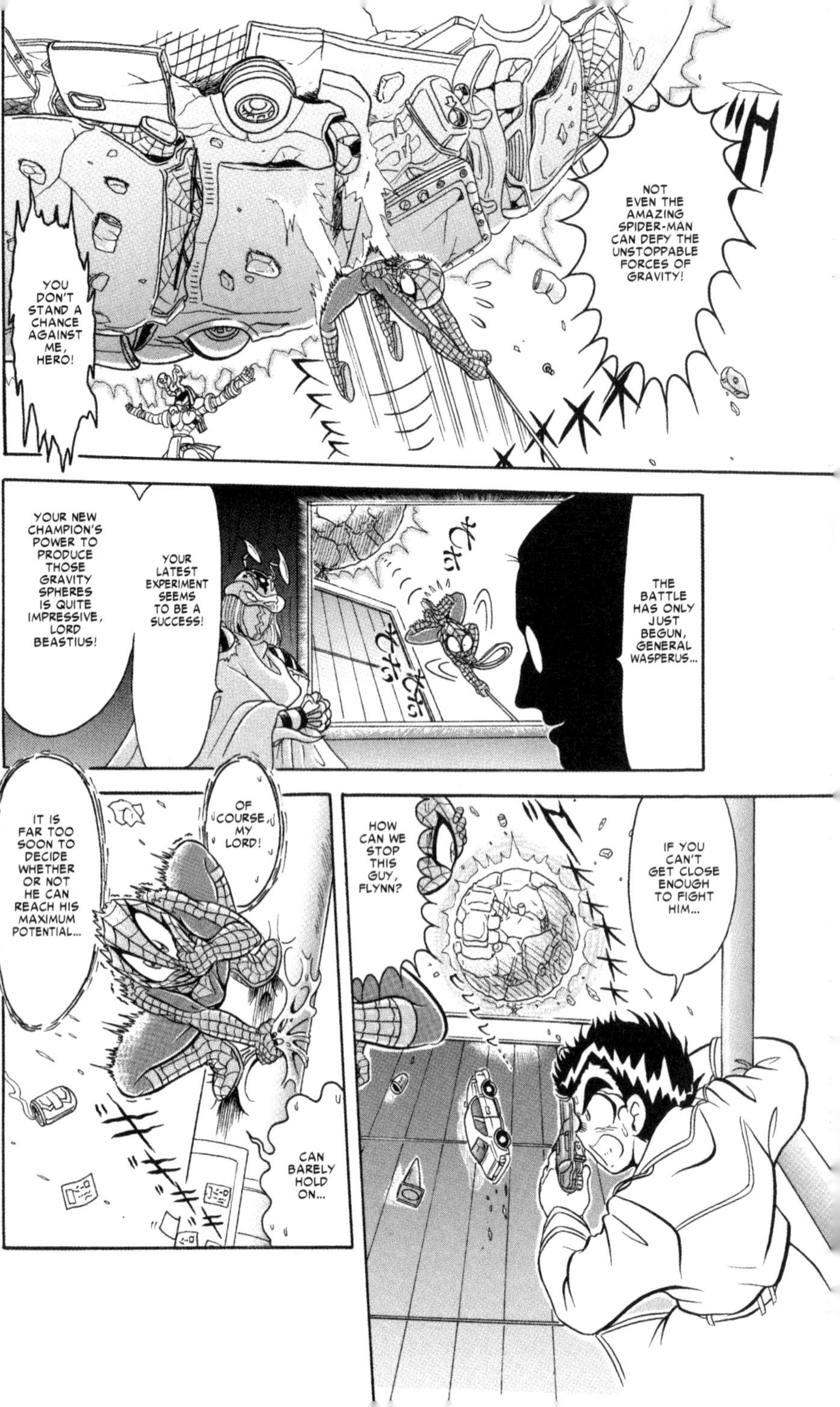
NOT EVEN THE AMAZING SPIDER-MAN CAN DEFY THE UNSTOPPABLE FORCES OF GRAVITY!
YOU DON'T STAND A CHANCE AGAINST ME, HERO!
THE BATTLE HAS ONLY JUST BEGUN, GENERAL WASPERUS...
YOUR LATEST EXPERIMENT SEEMS TO BE A SUCCESS!
YOUR NEW CHAMPION'S POWER TO PRODUCE THOSE GRAVITY SPHERES IS QUITE IMPRESSIVE, LORD BEASTIUS!
OF COURSE, MY LORD!
IT IS FAR TOO SOON TO DECIDE WHETHER OR NOT HE CAN REACH HIS MAXIMUM POTENTIAL...
CAN BARELY HOLD ON...
IF YOU CAN'T GET CLOSE ENOUGH TO FIGHT HIM...
HOW CAN WE STOP THIS GUY, FLYNN?

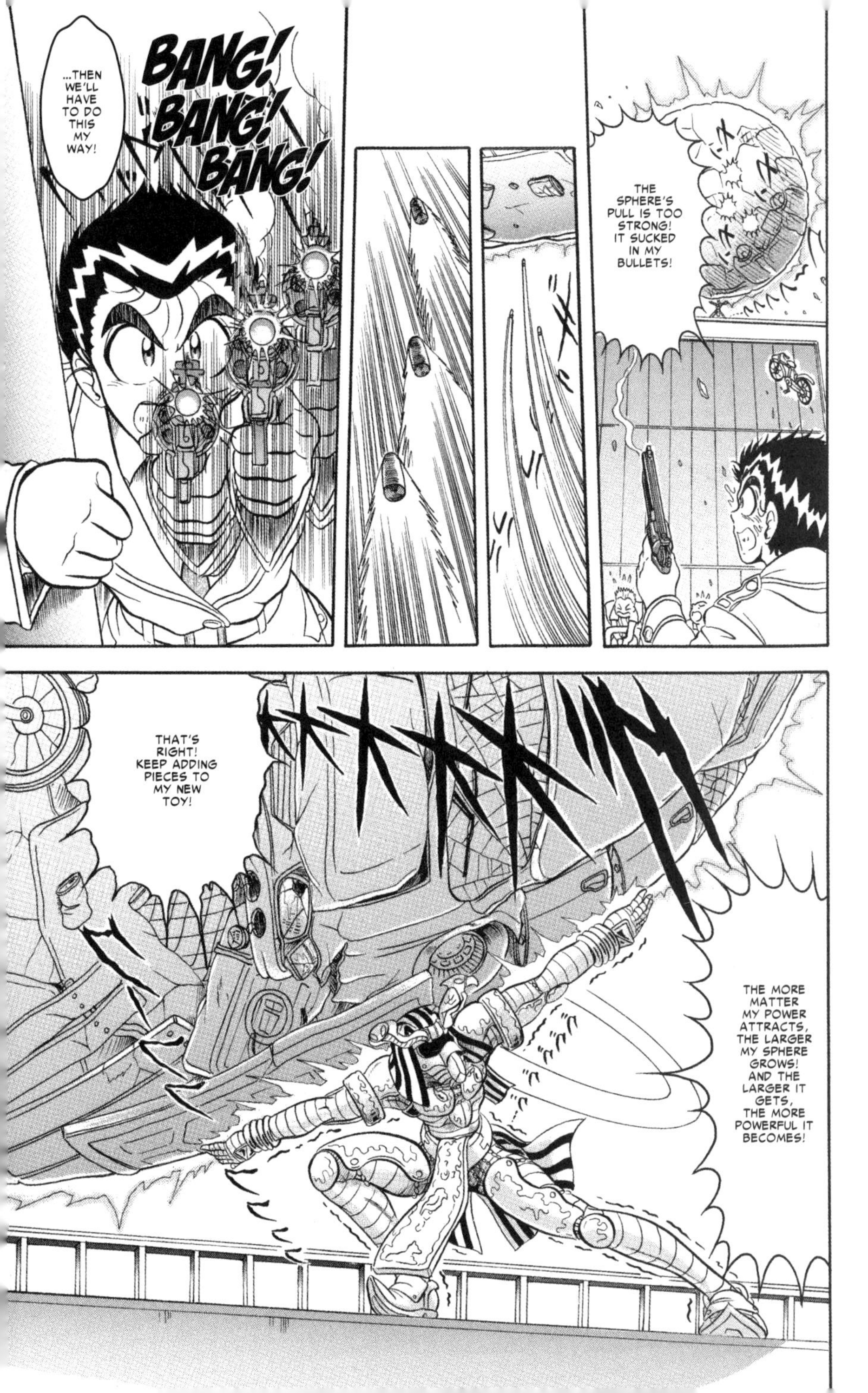
...THEN WE'LL HAVE TO DO THIS MY WAY!
BANG! BANG! BANG!
THE SPHERE'S PULL IS TOO STRONG! IT SUCKED IN MY BULLETS!
THAT'S RIGHT! KEEP ADDING PIECES TO MY NEW TOY!
THE MORE MATTER MY POWER ATTRACTS, THE LARGER MY SPHERE GROWS! AND THE LARGER IT GETS, THE MORE POWERFUL IT BECOMES!

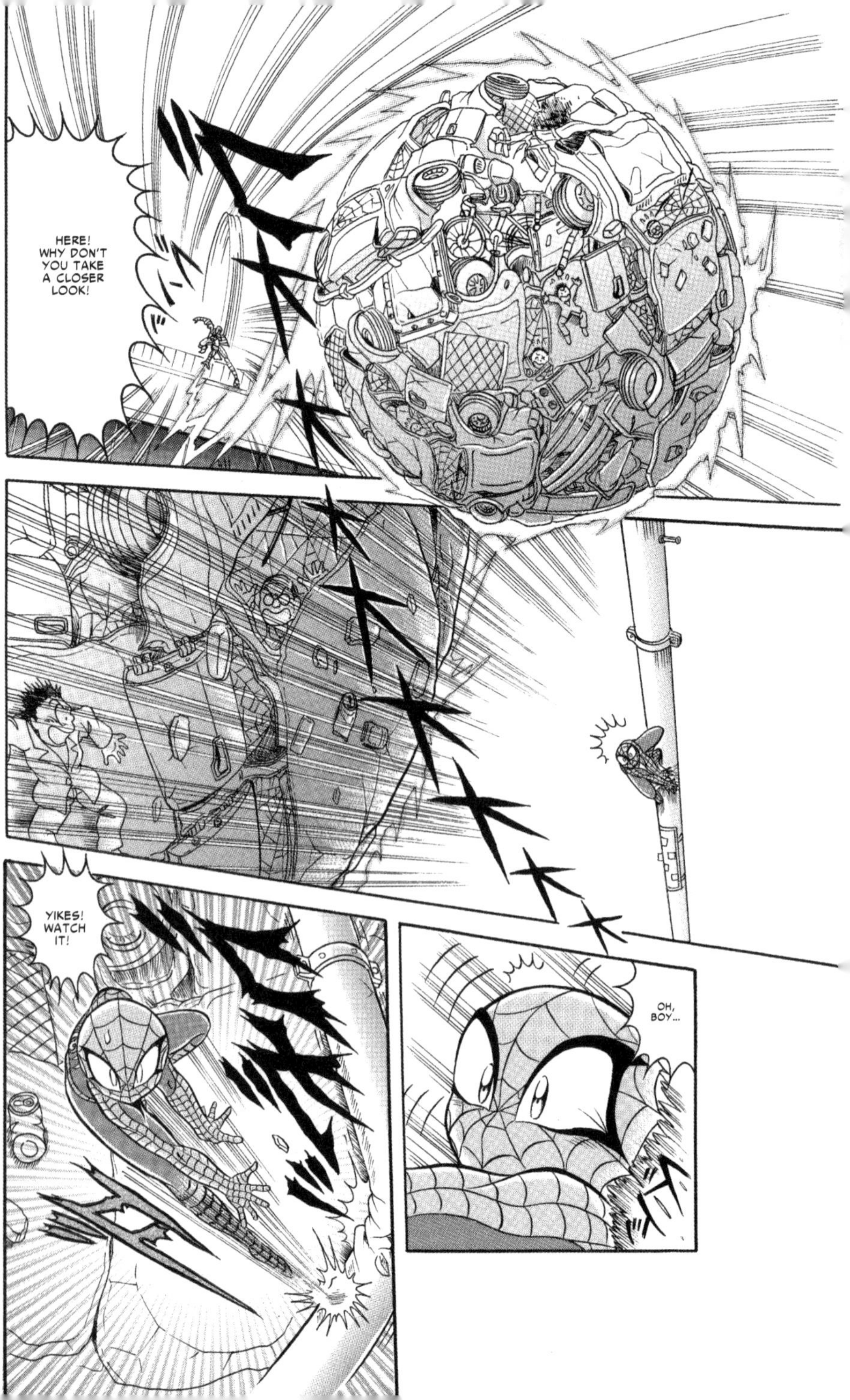
HERE! WHY DON'T YOU TAKE A CLOSER LOOK!
YIKES! WATCH IT!
OH, BOY...

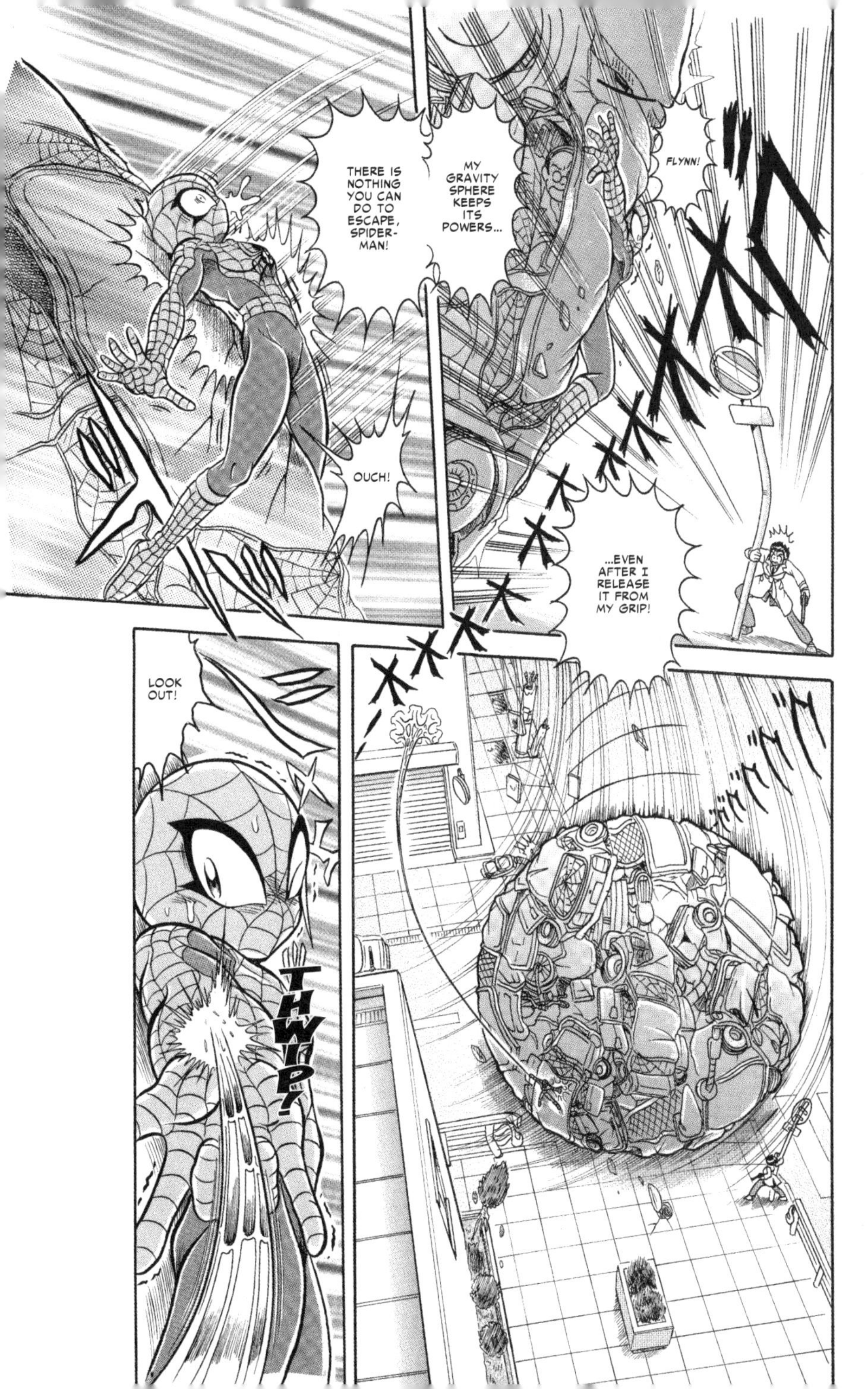
THERE IS NOTHING YOU CAN DO TO ESCAPE, SPIDER-MAN!
OUCH!
MY GRAVITY SPHERE KEEPS ITS POWERS...
FLYNN!
...EVEN AFTER I RELEASE IT FROM MY GRIP!
LOOK OUT!
THWIP!

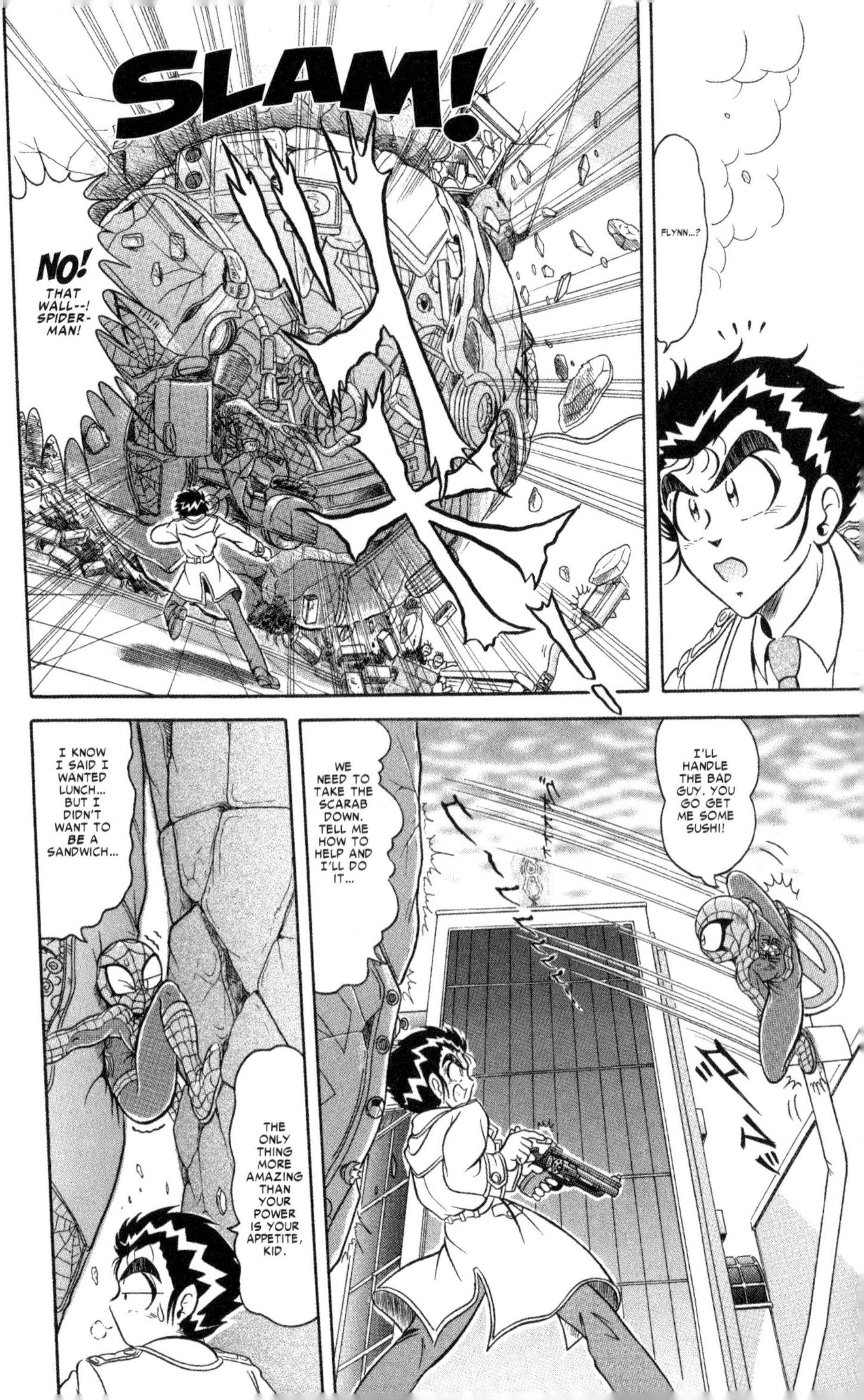
SLAM!
NO! THAT WALL--! SPIDER-MAN!
FLYNN...?
I'LL HANDLE THE BAD GUY. YOU GO GET ME SOME SUSHI!
WE NEED TO TAKE THE SCARAB DOWN. TELL ME HOW TO HELP AND I'LL DO IT...
I KNOW I SAID I WANTED LUNCH... BUT I DIDN'T WANT TO BE A SANDWICH...
THE ONLY THING MORE AMAZING THAN YOUR POWER IS YOUR APPETITE, KID.

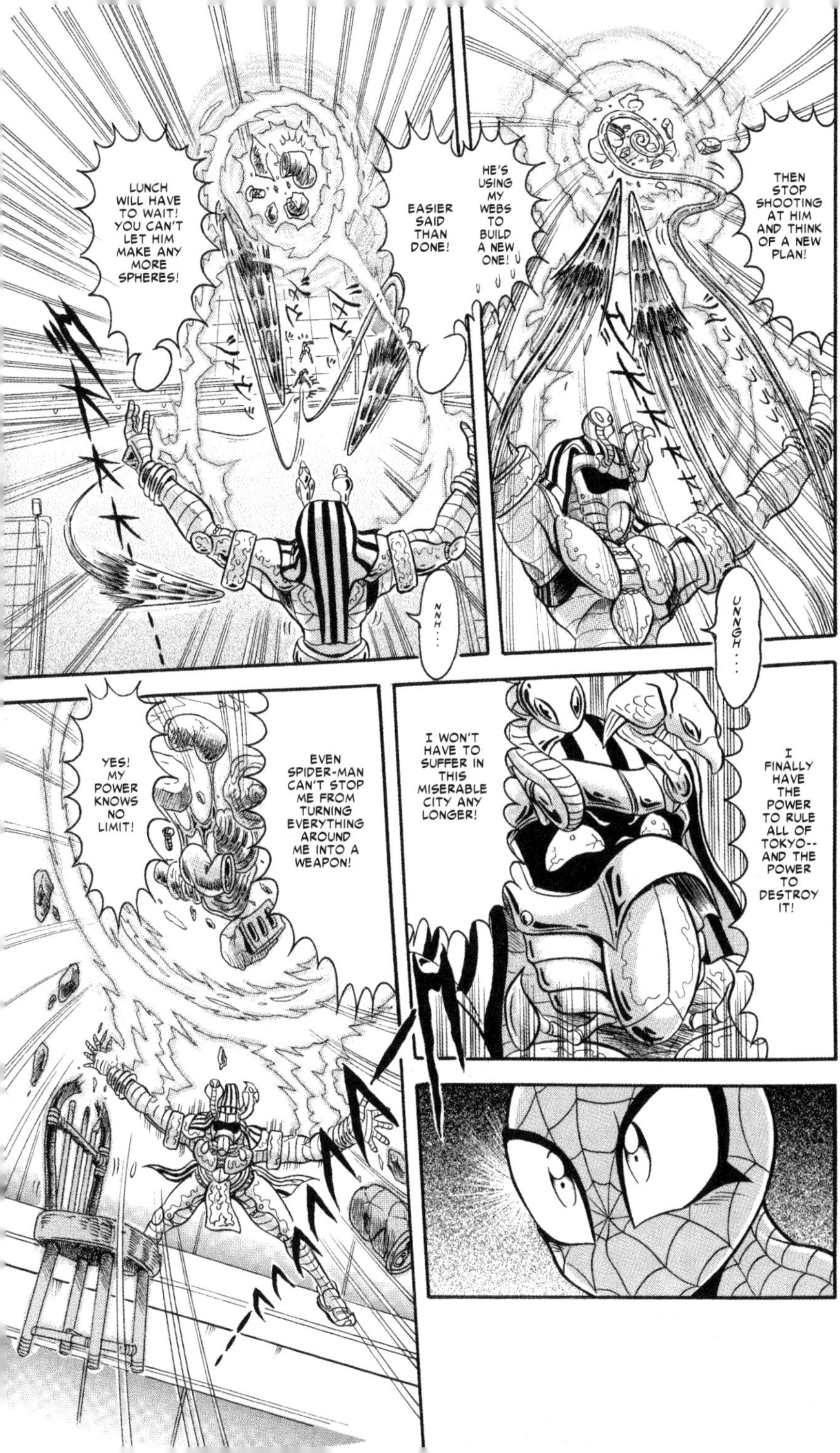
LUNCH WILL HAVE TO WAIT! YOU CAN'T LET HIM MAKE ANY MORE SPHERES!
EASIER SAID THAN DONE!
HE'S USING MY WEBS TO BUILD A NEW ONE!
THEN STOP SHOOTING AT HIM AND THINK OF A NEW PLAN!
NNH...
UNNGH...
YES! MY POWER KNOWS NO LIMIT!
EVEN SPIDER-MAN CAN'T STOP ME FROM TURNING EVERYTHING AROUND ME INTO A WEAPON!
I WON'T HAVE TO SUFFER IN THIS MISERABLE CITY ANY LONGER!
I FINALLY HAVE THE POWER TO RULE ALL OF TOKYO-- AND THE POWER TO DESTROY IT!

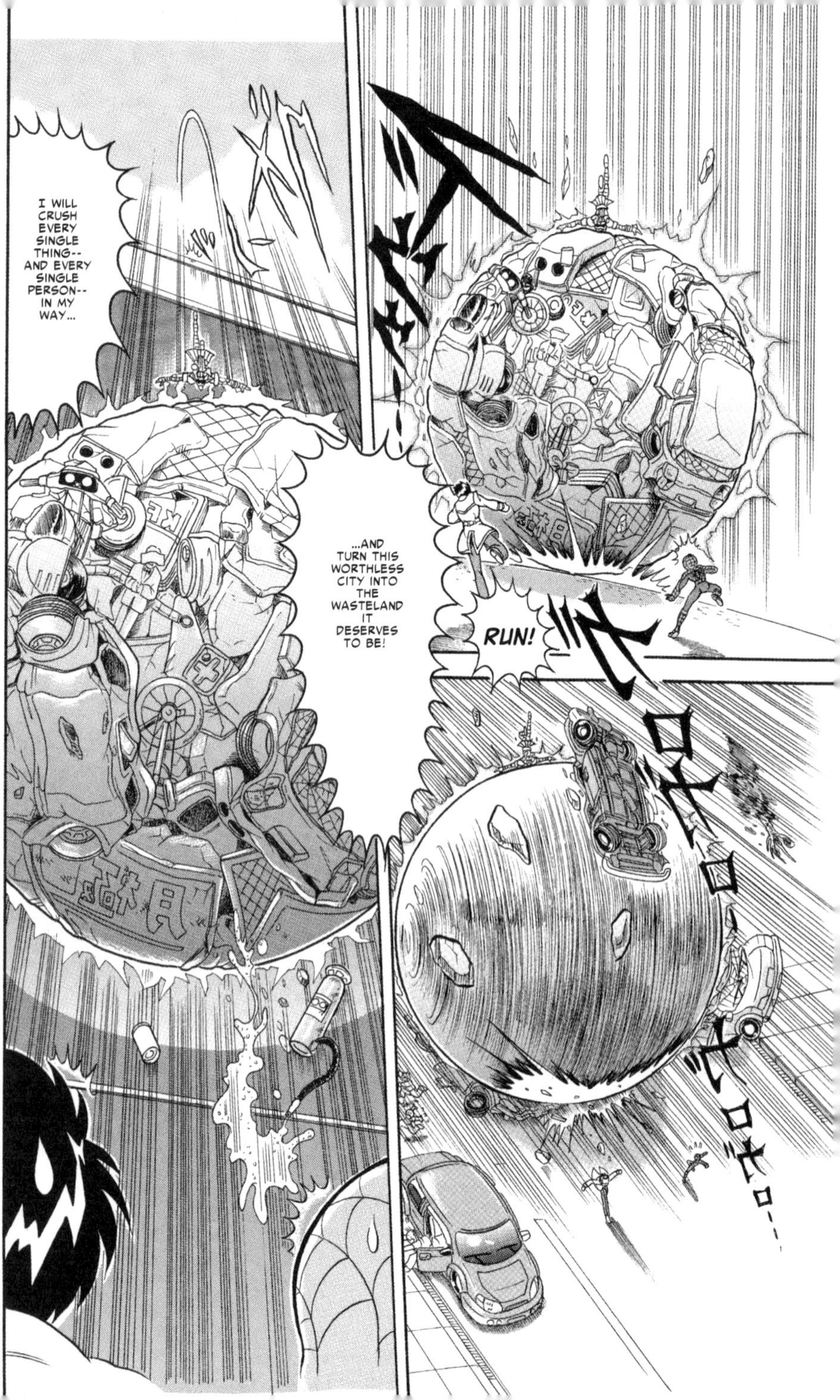
RUN!
I WILL CRUSH EVERY SINGLE THING-- AND EVERY SINGLE PERSON-- IN MY WAY...
...AND TURN THIS WORTHLESS CITY INTO THE WASTELAND IT DESERVES TO BE!

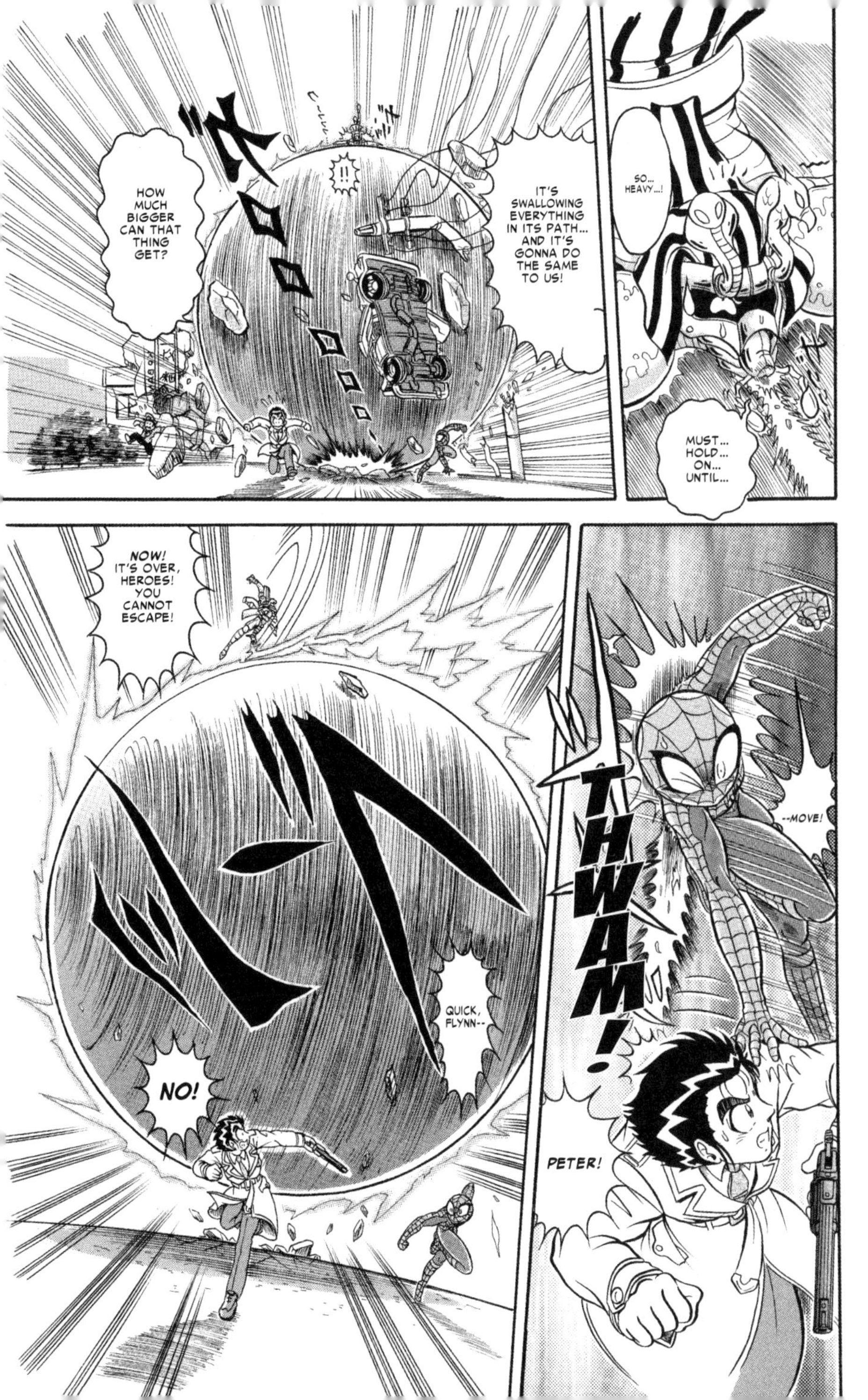
HOW MUCH BIGGER CAN THAT THING GET?
!!
IT'S SWALLOWING EVERYTHING IN ITS PATH... AND IT'S GONNA DO THE SAME TO US!
SO... HEAVY...!
MUST... HOLD... ON... UNTIL...
NOW! IT'S OVER, HEROES! YOU CANNOT ESCAPE!
QUICK, FLYNN--
NO!
THWAM!
--MOVE!
PETER!

YOU...YOU SAVED ME! BUT YOU'RE HURT! WE NEED TO GET YOU AWAY FROM THIS MANIAC BEFORE--

NO. IT'S NOT HIS FAULT!

WHAT?

HE'S JUST INTOXICATED BY HIS NEW POWER, SO HE'S LASHING OUT AT THE WORLD WITH IT.

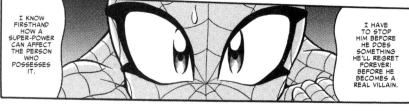

I KNOW FIRSTHAND HOW A SUPER-POWER CAN AFFECT THE PERSON WHO POSSESSES IT.

I HAVE TO STOP HIM BEFORE HE DOES SOMETHING HE'LL REGRET FOREVER! BEFORE HE BECOMES A REAL VILLAIN.

YOU'RE RIGHT... BUT HOW DO WE STOP HIM? HIS ABILITY TO PRODUCE THOSE SPHERES SEEMS TO BE ENDLESS.

YEAH, I KNOW. BUT SOMETHING DOESN'T SEEM QUITE RIGHT...

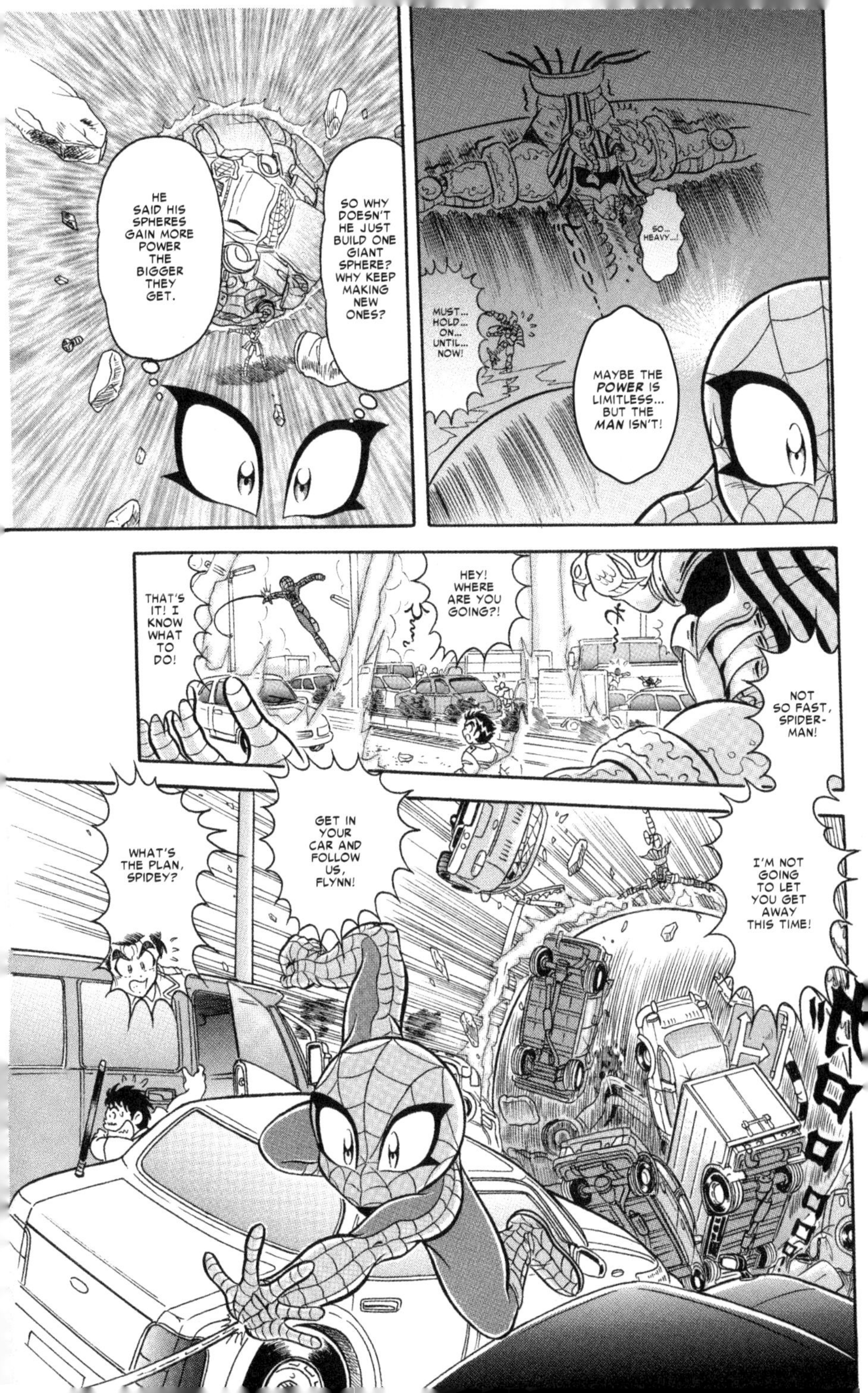
HE SAID HIS SPHERES GAIN MORE POWER THE BIGGER THEY GET.
SO WHY DOESN'T HE JUST BUILD ONE GIANT SPHERE? WHY KEEP MAKING NEW ONES?
SO... HEAVY...!
MUST... HOLD... ON... UNTIL... NOW!
MAYBE THE POWER IS LIMITLESS... BUT THE MAN ISN'T!
THAT'S IT! I KNOW WHAT TO DO!
HEY! WHERE ARE YOU GOING?!
NOT SO FAST, SPIDER-MAN!
WHAT'S THE PLAN, SPIDEY?
GET IN YOUR CAR AND FOLLOW US, FLYNN!
I'M NOT GOING TO LET YOU GET AWAY THIS TIME!

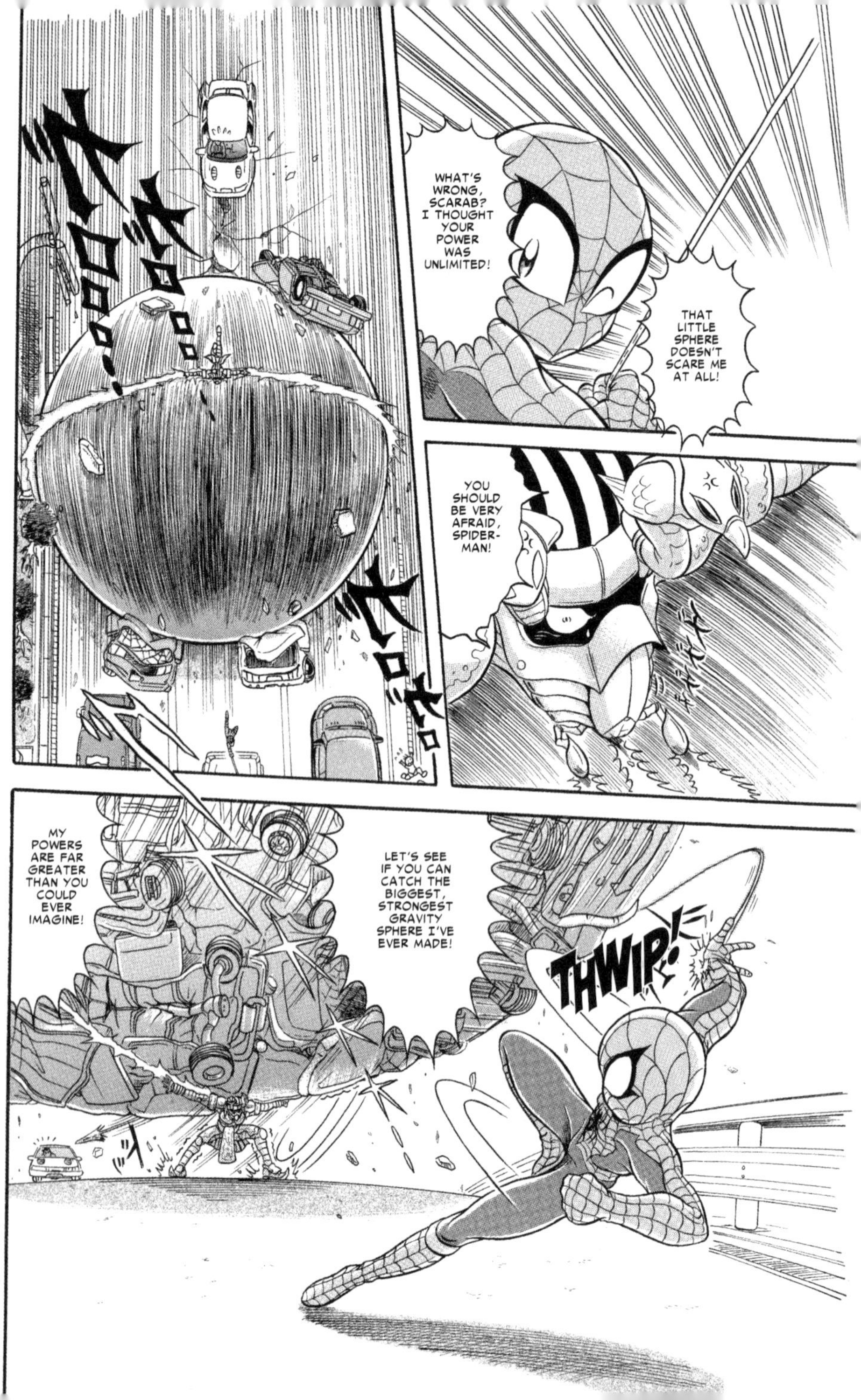
WHAT'S WRONG, SCARAB? I THOUGHT YOUR POWER WAS UNLIMITED!
THAT LITTLE SPHERE DOESN'T SCARE ME AT ALL!
YOU SHOULD BE VERY AFRAID, SPIDER-MAN!
MY POWERS ARE FAR GREATER THAN YOU COULD EVER IMAGINE!
LET'S SEE IF YOU CAN CATCH THE BIGGEST, STRONGEST GRAVITY SPHERE I'VE EVER MADE!
THWIP!

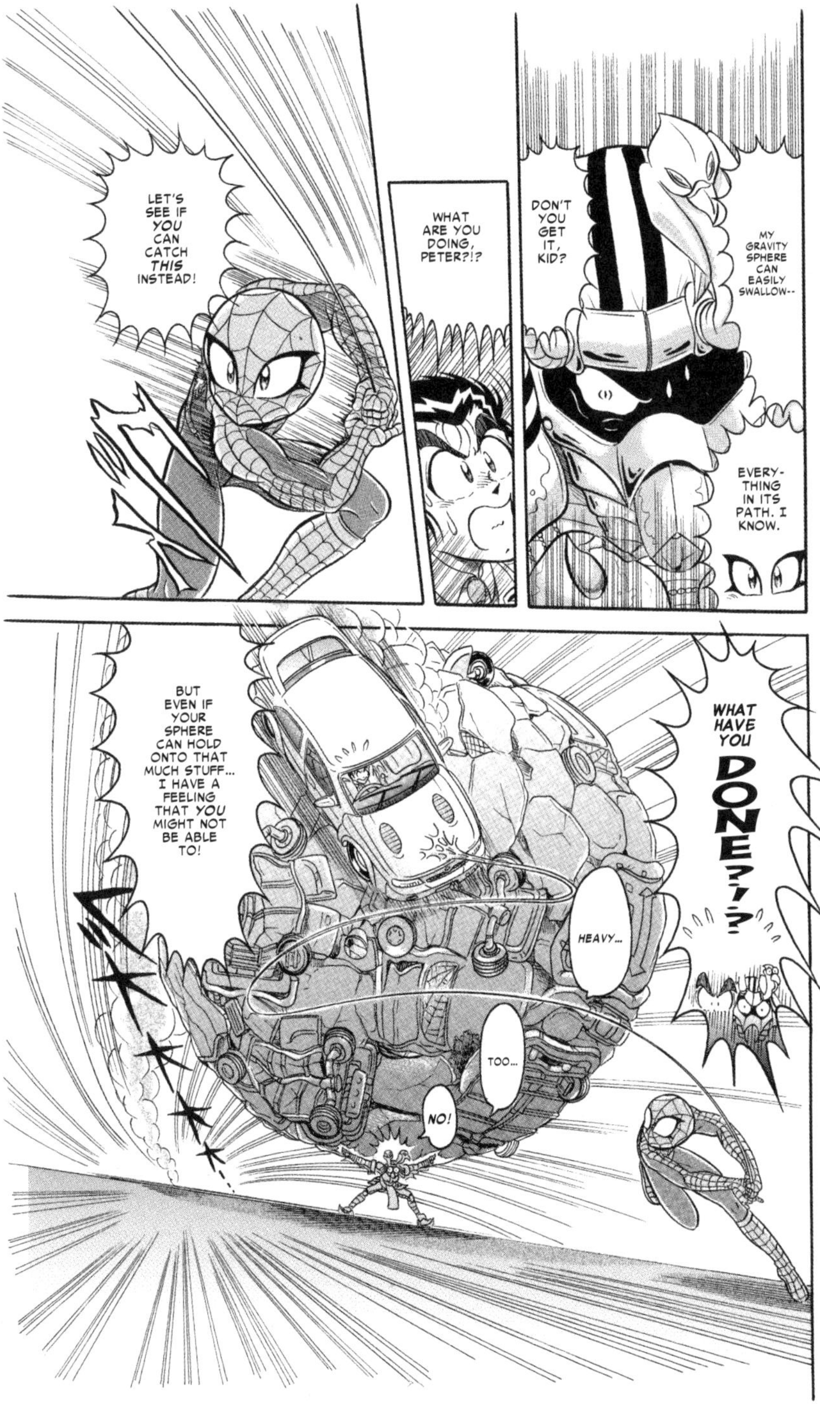
LET'S SEE IF *YOU* CAN CATCH *THIS* INSTEAD!
WHAT ARE YOU DOING, PETER?!?
DON'T YOU GET IT, KID?
MY GRAVITY SPHERE CAN EASILY SWALLOW--
EVERY-THING IN ITS PATH. I KNOW.
BUT EVEN IF YOUR SPHERE CAN HOLD ONTO THAT MUCH STUFF... I HAVE A FEELING THAT *YOU* MIGHT NOT BE ABLE TO!
WHAT HAVE YOU DONE?!?
HEAVY...
TOO...
NO!

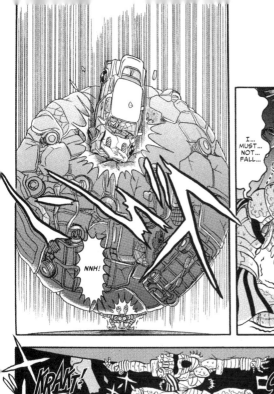

NNH!

I... MUST... NOT... FALL...

HUH. NOT BAD! I GUESS YOU REALLY ARE MORE POWERFUL THAN I THOUGHT.

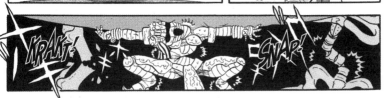

Ғ₭РДДТ!

SNAP!

THEN AGAIN... MAYBE NOT!

SMASH!

!!!

YOUR NEW MINION HAS FAILED US, MY LORD.

NO... NOT QUITE, GENERAL...

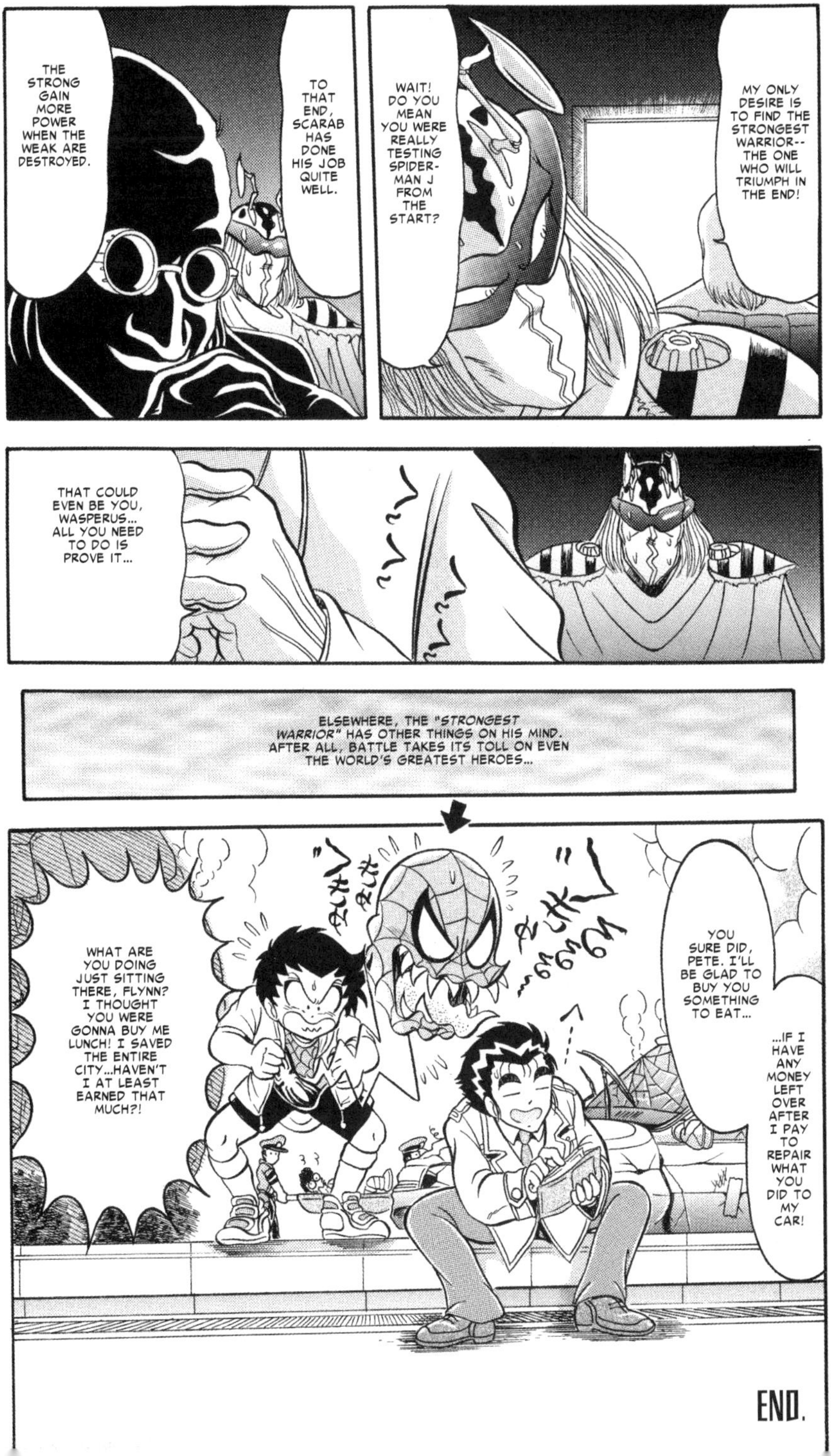
THE STRONG GAIN MORE POWER WHEN THE WEAK ARE DESTROYED.
TO THAT END, SCARAB HAS DONE HIS JOB QUITE WELL.
WAIT! DO YOU MEAN YOU WERE REALLY TESTING SPIDER-MAN J FROM THE START?
MY ONLY DESIRE IS TO FIND THE STRONGEST WARRIOR-- THE ONE WHO WILL TRIUMPH IN THE END!
THAT COULD EVEN BE YOU, WASPERUS... ALL YOU NEED TO DO IS PROVE IT...
ELSEWHERE, THE "STRONGEST WARRIOR" HAS OTHER THINGS ON HIS MIND. AFTER ALL, BATTLE TAKES ITS TOLL ON EVEN THE WORLD'S GREATEST HEROES...
WHAT ARE YOU DOING JUST SITTING THERE, FLYNN? I THOUGHT YOU WERE GONNA BUY ME LUNCH! I SAVED THE ENTIRE CITY...HAVEN'T I AT LEAST EARNED THAT MUCH?!
YOU SURE DID, PETE. I'LL BE GLAD TO BUY YOU SOMETHING TO EAT...
...IF I HAVE ANY MONEY LEFT OVER AFTER I PAY TO REPAIR WHAT YOU DID TO MY CAR!
END.

CHAPTER 3

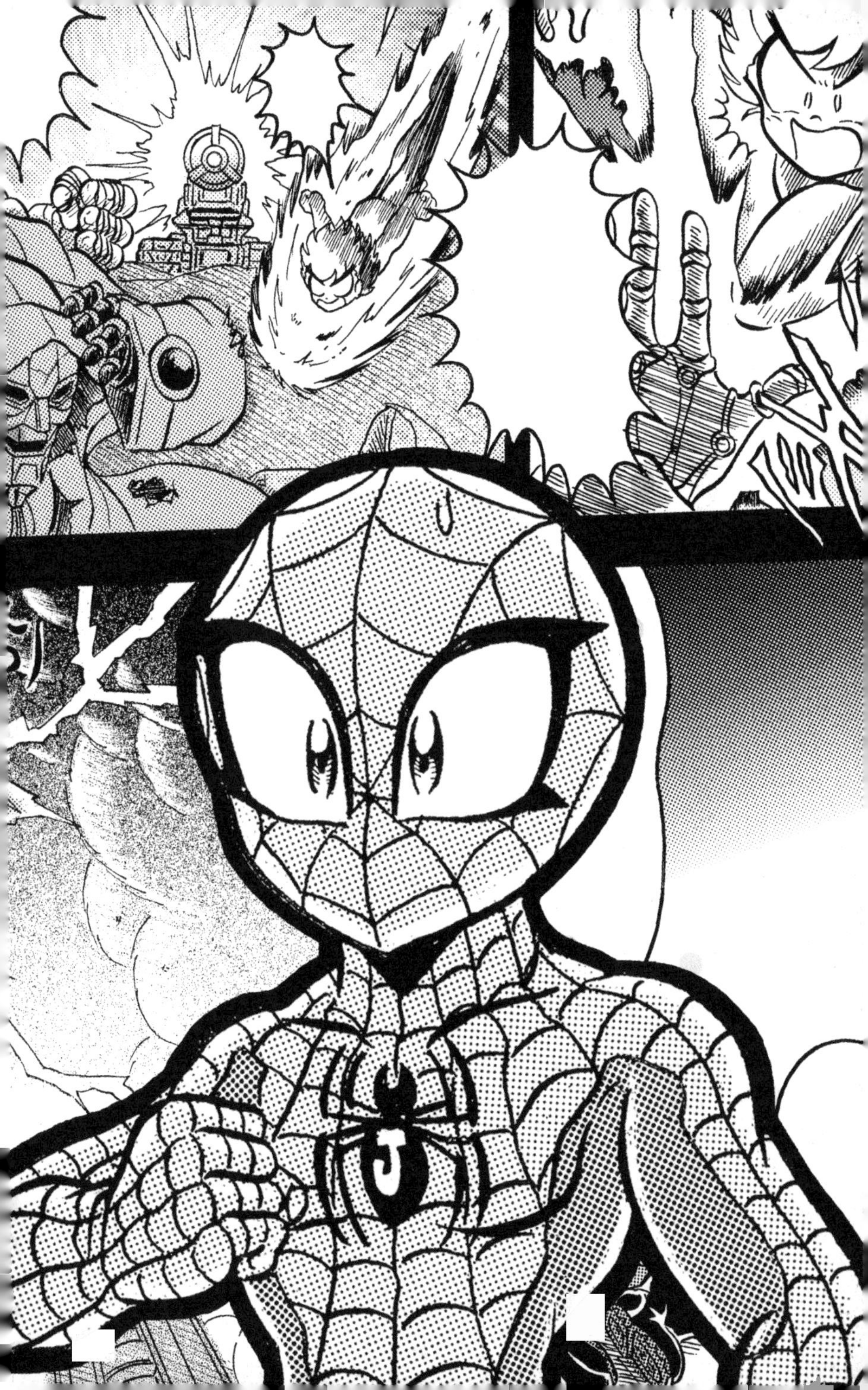

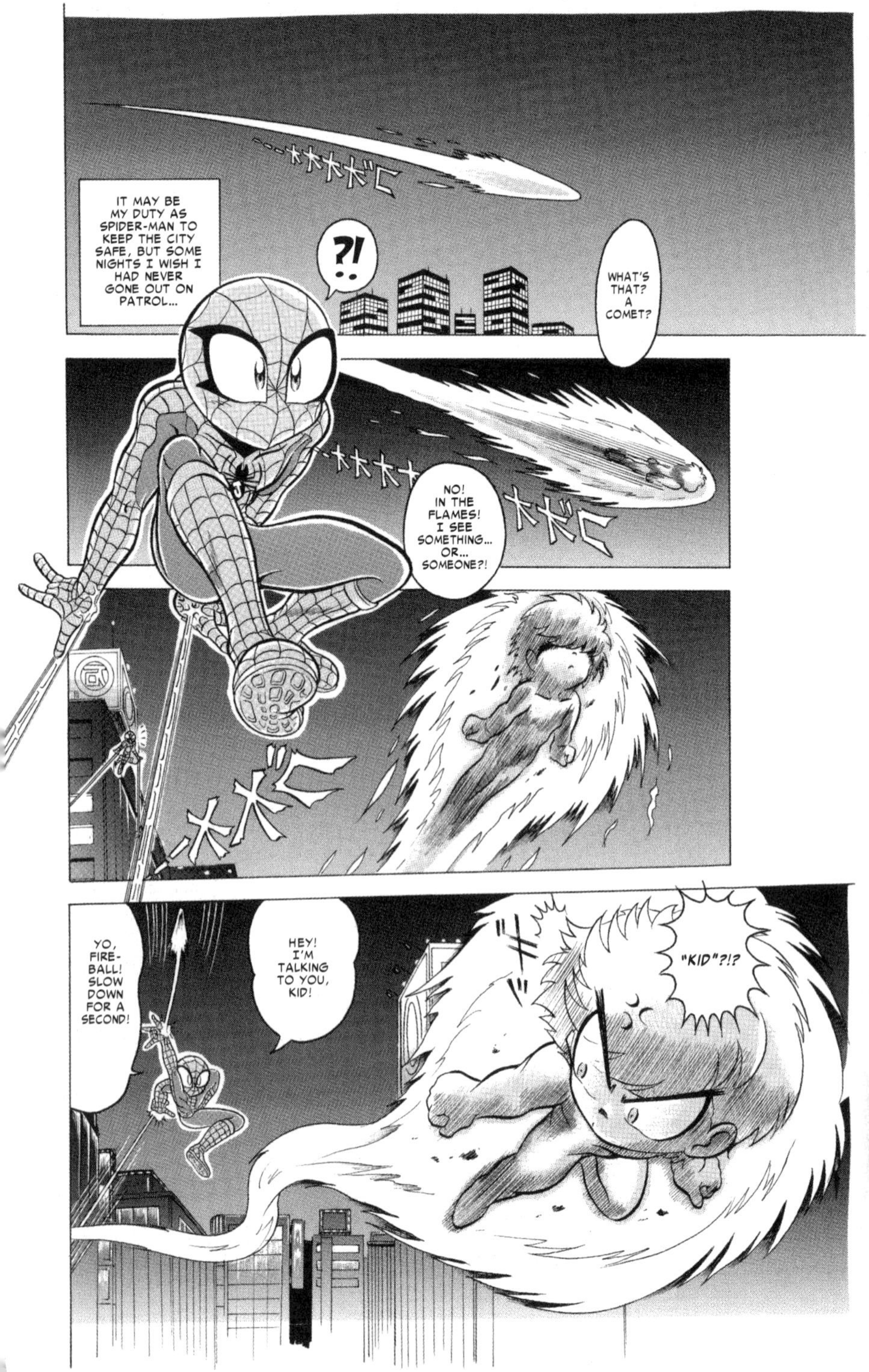
IT MAY BE MY DUTY AS SPIDER-MAN TO KEEP THE CITY SAFE, BUT SOME NIGHTS I WISH I HAD NEVER GONE OUT ON PATROL...
?!
WHAT'S THAT? A COMET?
NO! IN THE FLAMES! I SEE SOMETHING... OR... SOMEONE?!
YO, FIRE-BALL! SLOW DOWN FOR A SECOND!
HEY! I'M TALKING TO YOU, KID!
"KID"?!?

Each corner of the globe has its own unique take on the AMAZING SPIDER-MAN! Direct from Japan, Marvel is proud to present...

SPIDER-MAN J "IMPENDING DOOM"

ORIGINAL STORY AND ART BY YAMANAKA AKIRA

YUKO FUKAMI TRANSLATION | MARC SUMERAK ENGLISH ADAPTATION | VC'SJOE CARAMAGNA LETTERING | JORDAN D. WHITE ASST. EDITOR | NATE COSBY & MARK PANICCIA EDITORS | JOE QUESADA EDITOR IN CHIEF | DAN BUCKLEY PUBLISHER

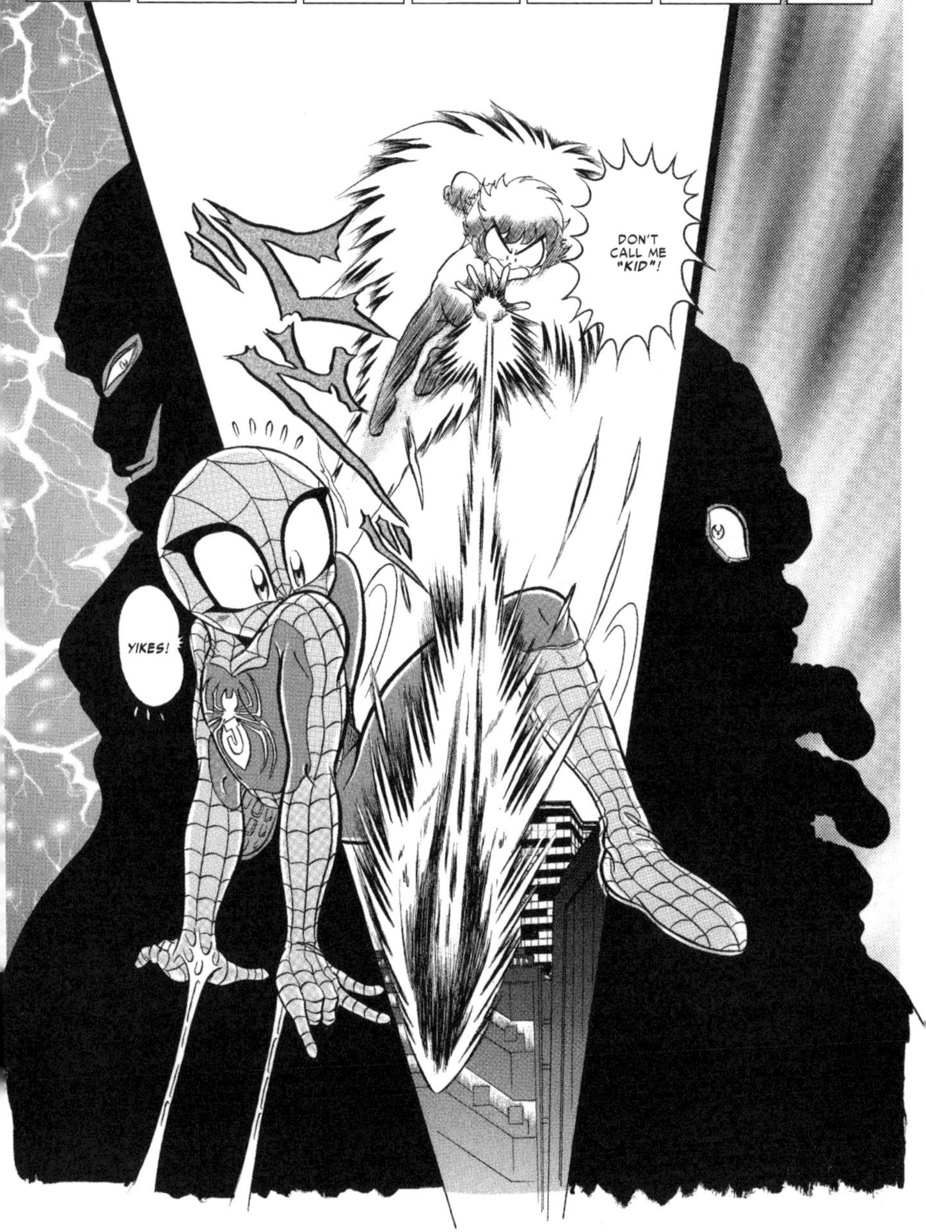
DON'T CALL ME "KID"!
YIKES!

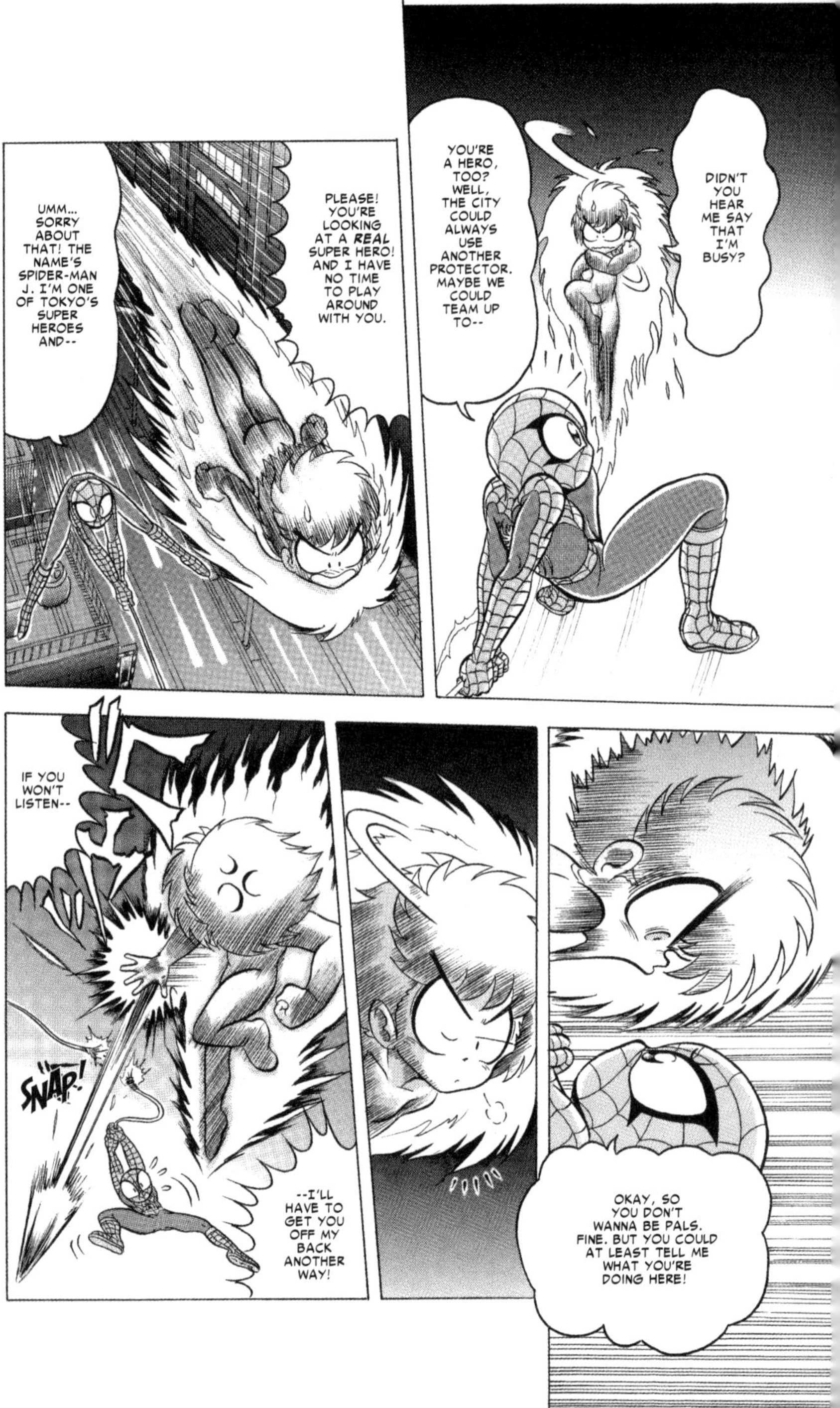

UMM... SORRY ABOUT THAT! THE NAME'S SPIDER-MAN J. I'M ONE OF TOKYO'S SUPER HEROES AND--
PLEASE! YOU'RE LOOKING AT A **REAL** SUPER HERO! AND I HAVE NO TIME TO PLAY AROUND WITH YOU.
YOU'RE A HERO, TOO? WELL, THE CITY COULD ALWAYS USE ANOTHER PROTECTOR. MAYBE WE COULD TEAM UP TO--
DIDN'T YOU HEAR ME SAY THAT I'M BUSY?
IF YOU WON'T LISTEN--
SNAP!
--I'LL HAVE TO GET YOU OFF MY BACK ANOTHER WAY!
OKAY, SO YOU DON'T WANNA BE PALS. FINE. BUT YOU COULD AT LEAST TELL ME WHAT YOU'RE DOING HERE!

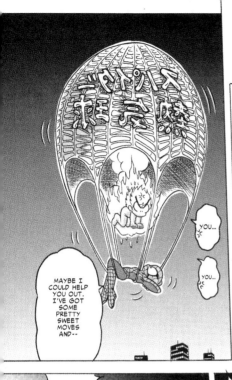

YOU...

YOU...

MAYBE I COULD HELP YOU OUT. I'VE GOT SOME PRETTY SWEET MOVES AND--

YOU HAVE NO IDEA WHO YOU'RE MESSING WITH!

I GUESS NOT...

THEN WHY DON'T YOU COOL DOWN FOR A WHILE AND FILL ME IN?

YEAH, RIGHT!

I'M AS HOT AS THEY COME! I DON'T COOL DOWN FOR ANYONE!

THWIP!

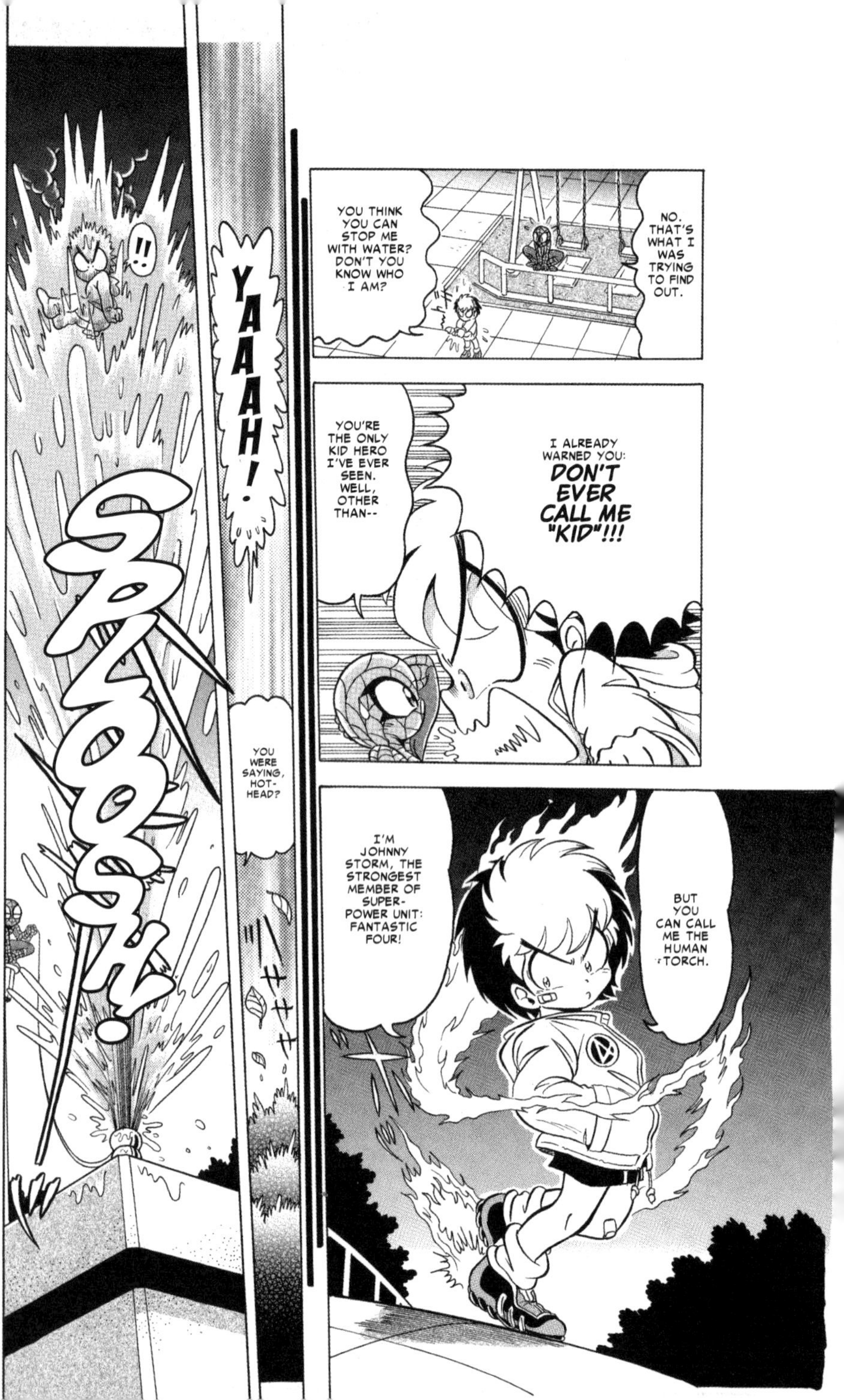
!!
SPLOOOSH!
YAAAH!
YOU WERE SAYING, HOT-HEAD?
YOU THINK YOU CAN STOP ME WITH WATER? DON'T YOU KNOW WHO I AM?
NO. THAT'S WHAT I WAS TRYING TO FIND OUT.
YOU'RE THE ONLY KID HERO I'VE EVER SEEN. WELL, OTHER THAN--
I ALREADY WARNED YOU: DON'T EVER CALL ME "KID"!!!
I'M JOHNNY STORM, THE STRONGEST MEMBER OF SUPER-POWER UNIT: FANTASTIC FOUR!
BUT YOU CAN CALL ME THE HUMAN TORCH.

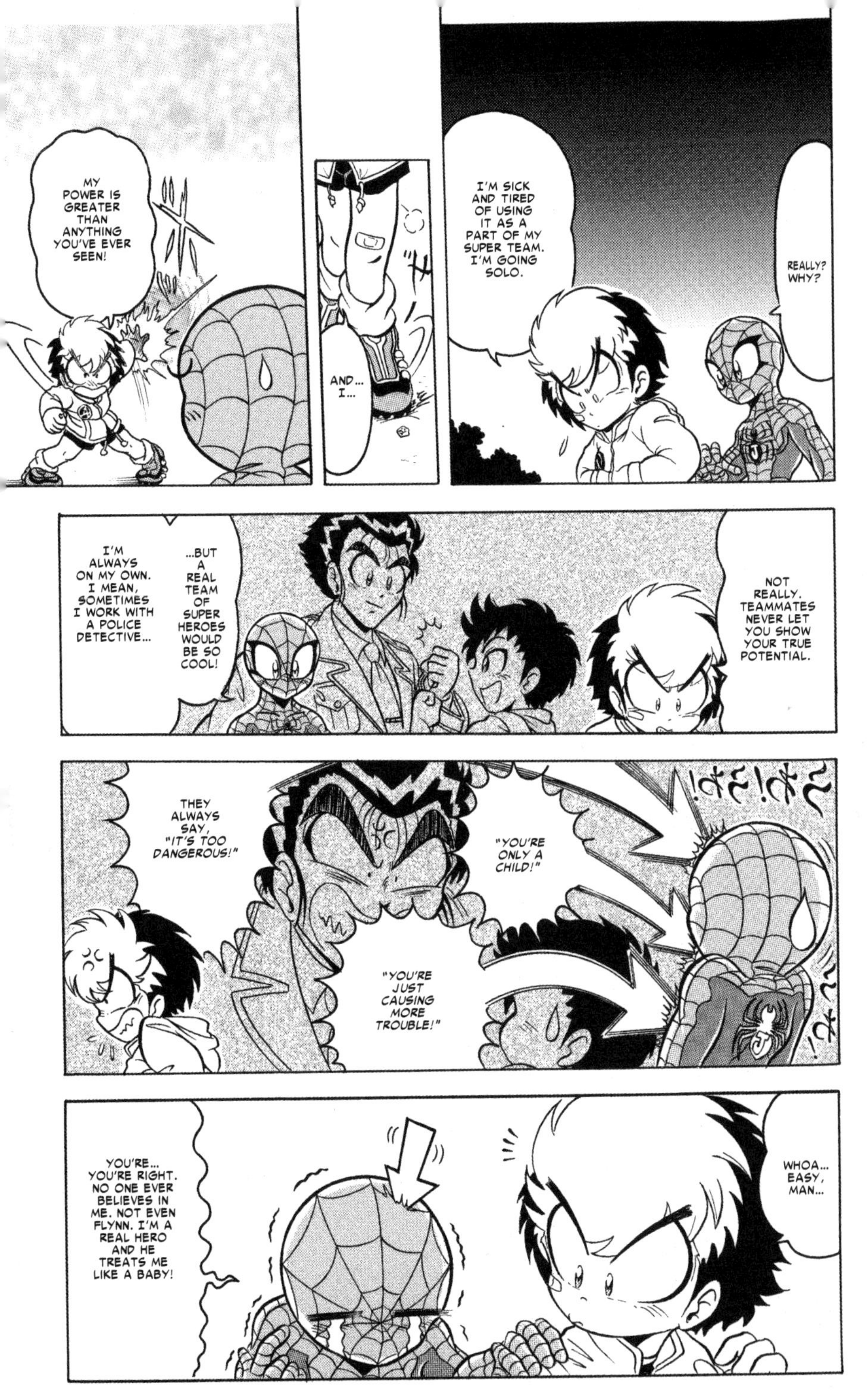
MY POWER IS GREATER THAN ANYTHING YOU'VE EVER SEEN!
AND... I...
I'M SICK AND TIRED OF USING IT AS A PART OF MY SUPER TEAM. I'M GOING SOLO.
REALLY? WHY?
I'M ALWAYS ON MY OWN. I MEAN, SOMETIMES I WORK WITH A POLICE DETECTIVE...
...BUT A REAL TEAM OF SUPER HEROES WOULD BE SO COOL!
NOT REALLY. TEAMMATES NEVER LET YOU SHOW YOUR TRUE POTENTIAL.
THEY ALWAYS SAY, "IT'S TOO DANGEROUS!"
"YOU'RE ONLY A CHILD!"
"YOU'RE JUST CAUSING MORE TROUBLE!"
YOU'RE... YOU'RE RIGHT. NO ONE EVER BELIEVES IN ME. NOT EVEN FLYNN. I'M A REAL HERO AND HE TREATS ME LIKE A BABY!
WHOA... EASY, MAN...

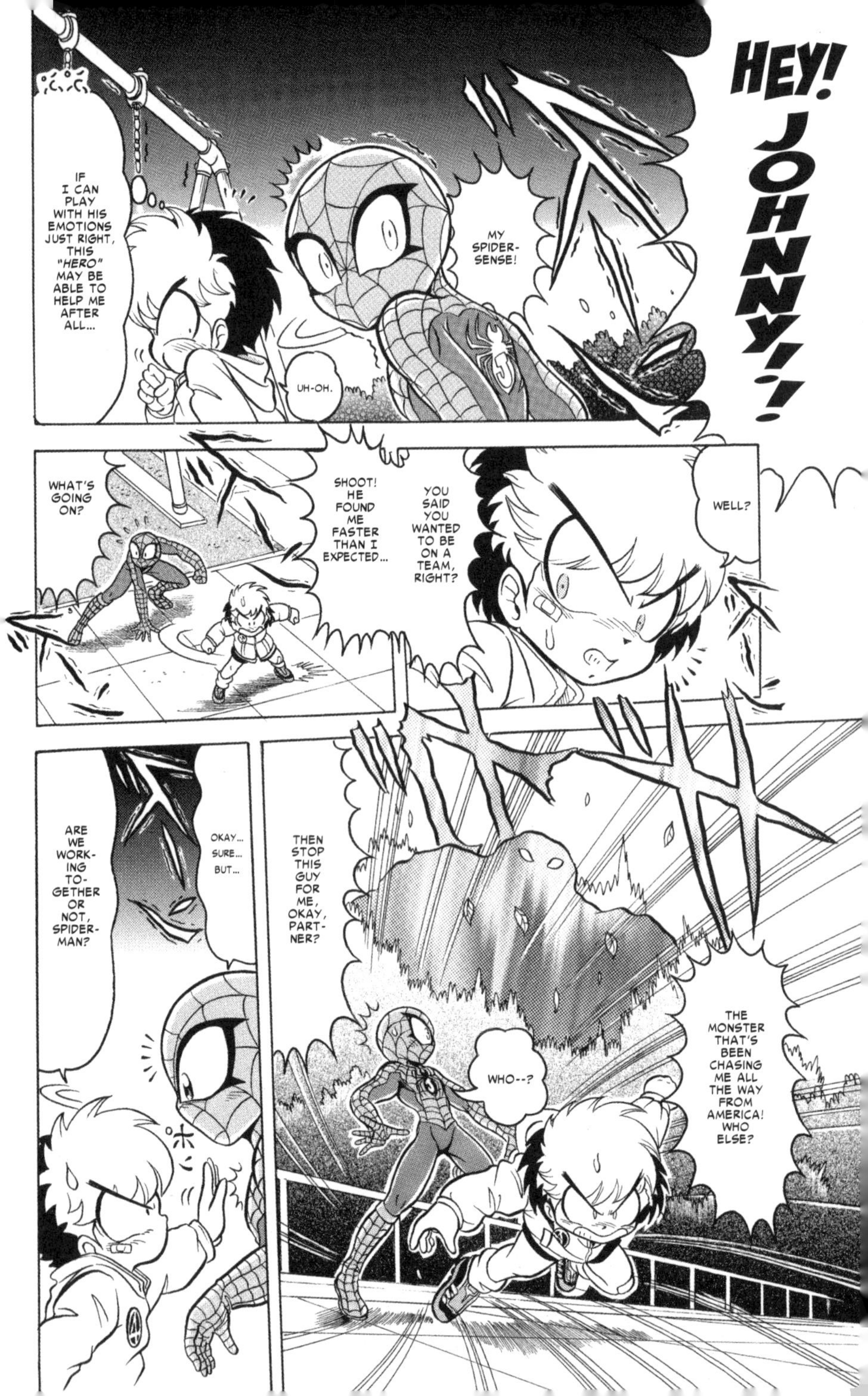

HEY! JOHNNY!!
MY SPIDER-SENSE!
IF I CAN PLAY WITH HIS EMOTIONS JUST RIGHT, THIS "HERO" MAY BE ABLE TO HELP ME AFTER ALL...
UH-OH.
WELL?
YOU SAID YOU WANTED TO BE ON A TEAM, RIGHT?
SHOOT! HE FOUND ME FASTER THAN I EXPECTED...
WHAT'S GOING ON?
THEN STOP THIS GUY FOR ME, OKAY, PARTNER?
OKAY... SURE... BUT...
ARE WE WORKING TOGETHER OR NOT, SPIDER-MAN?
THE MONSTER THAT'S BEEN CHASING ME ALL THE WAY FROM AMERICA! WHO ELSE?
WHO--?

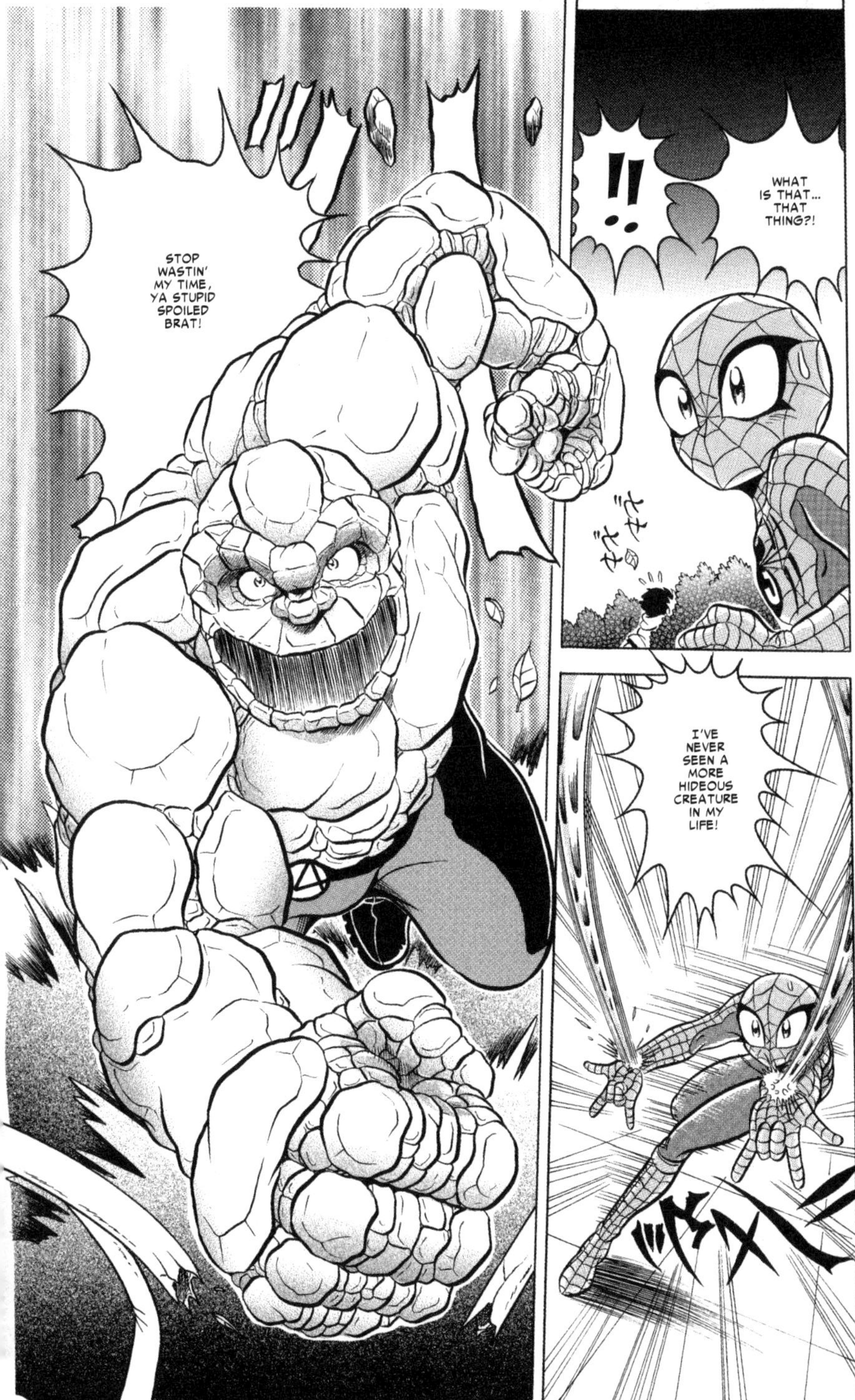
STOP WASTIN' MY TIME, YA STUPID SPOILED BRAT!
!!
WHAT IS THAT... THAT THING?!
I'VE NEVER SEEN A MORE HIDEOUS CREATURE IN MY LIFE!

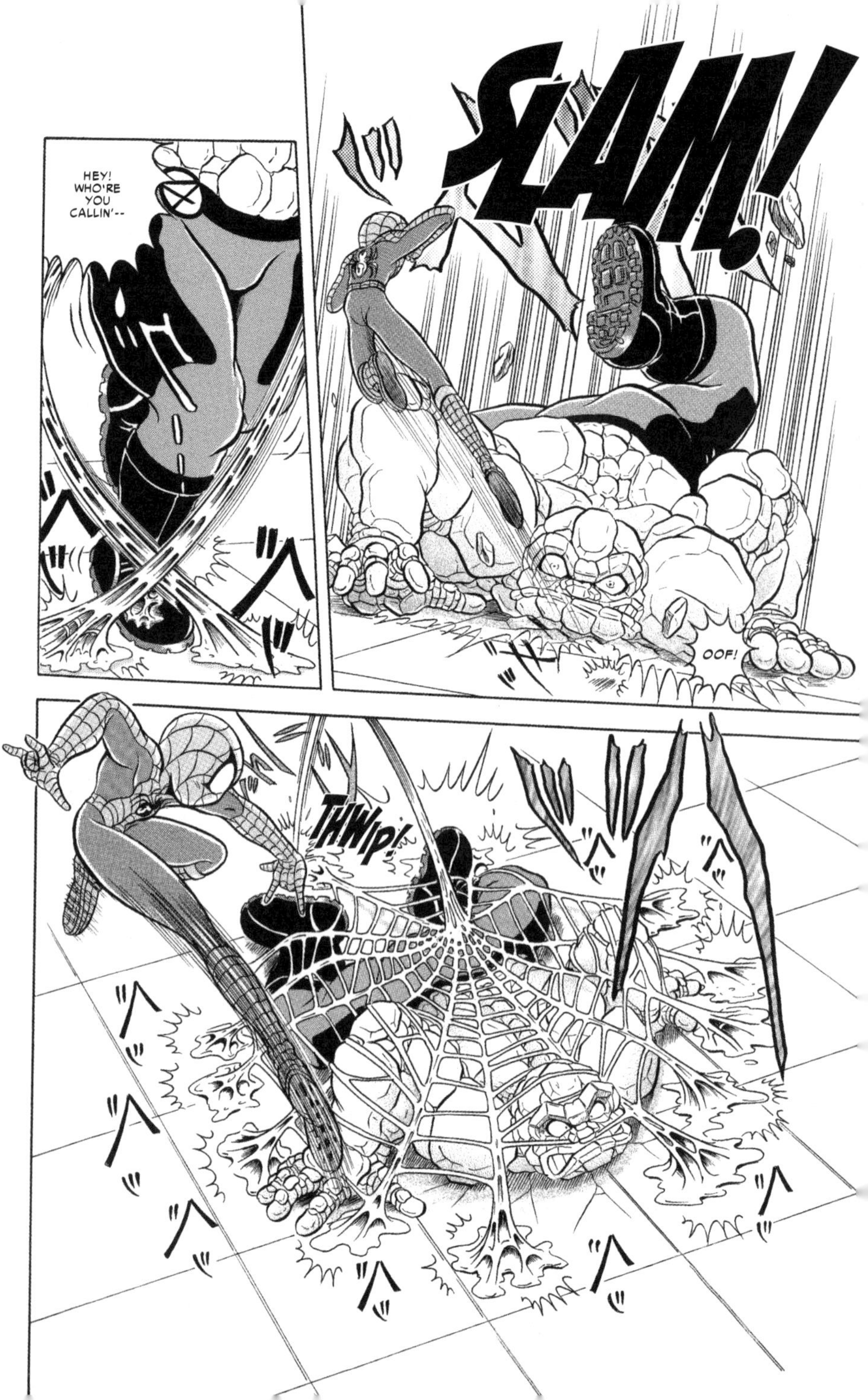
HEY! WHO'RE YOU CALLIN'--
SLAM!
OOF!
THWIP!

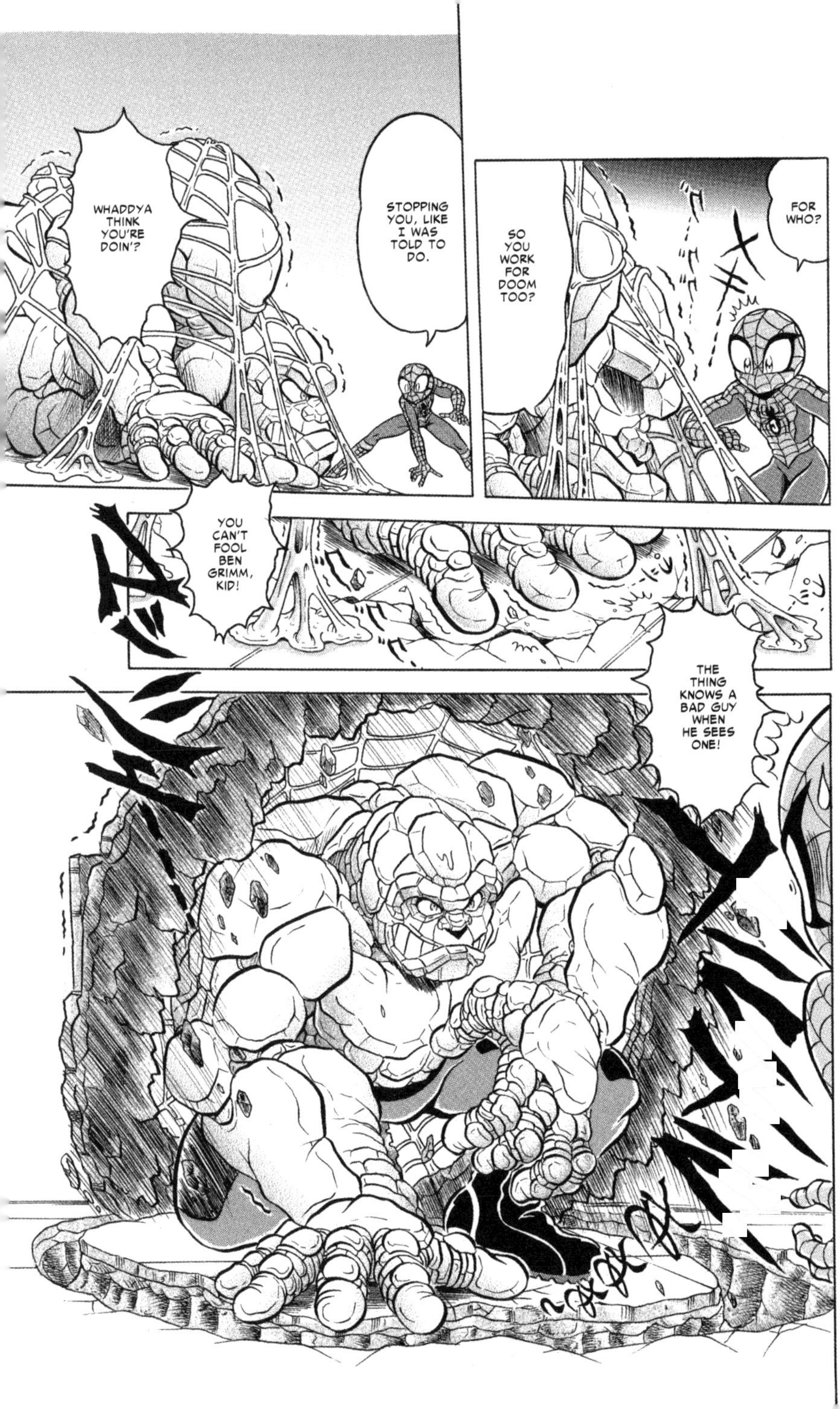
WHADDYA THINK YOU'RE DOIN'?
STOPPING YOU, LIKE I WAS TOLD TO DO.
FOR WHO?
SO YOU WORK FOR DOOM TOO?
YOU CAN'T FOOL BEN GRIMM, KID!
THE THING KNOWS A BAD GUY WHEN HE SEES ONE!

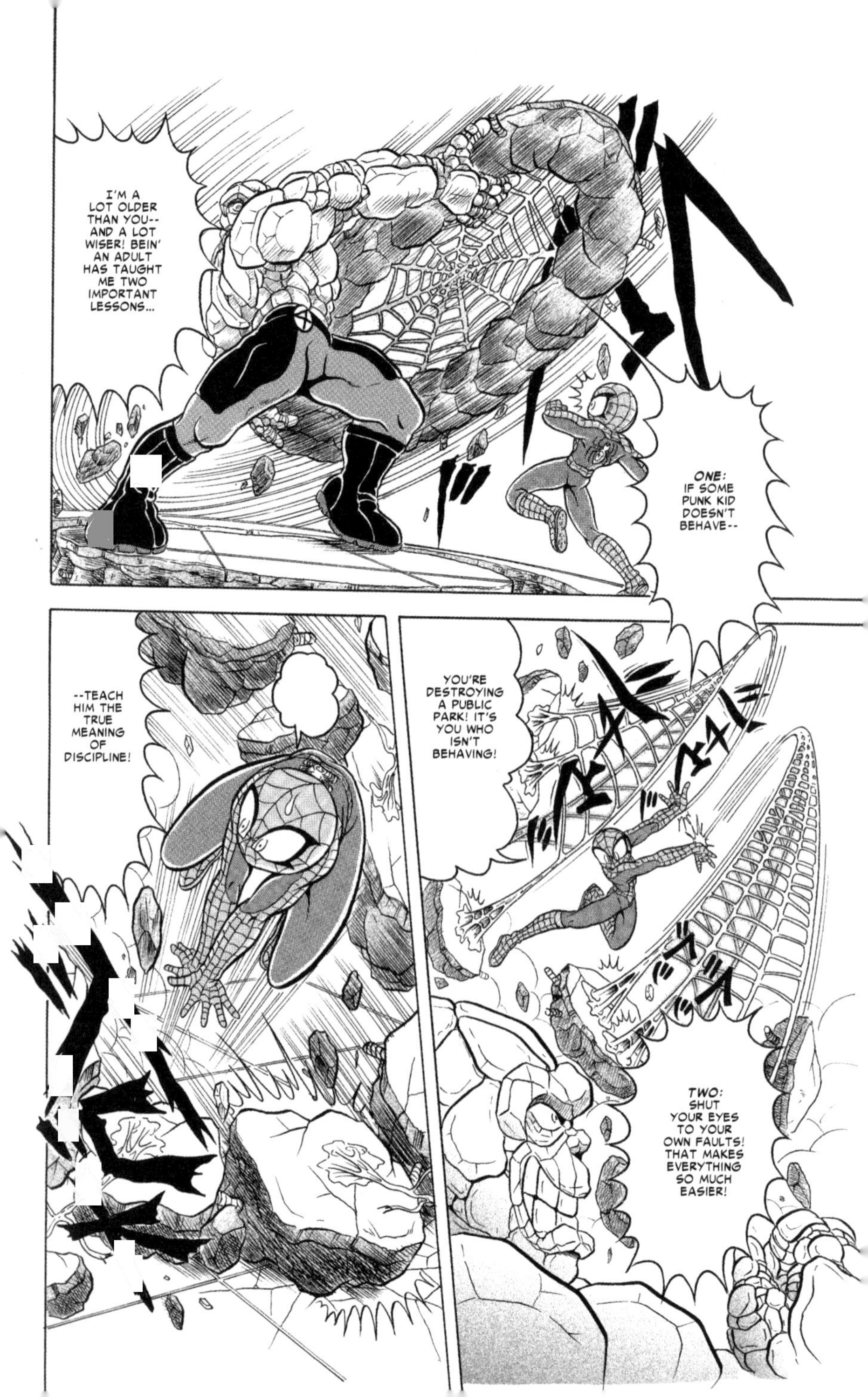
I'M A LOT OLDER THAN YOU--AND A LOT WISER! BEIN' AN ADULT HAS TAUGHT ME TWO IMPORTANT LESSONS...
ONE: IF SOME PUNK KID DOESN'T BEHAVE--
--TEACH HIM THE TRUE MEANING OF DISCIPLINE!
YOU'RE DESTROYING A PUBLIC PARK! IT'S YOU WHO ISN'T BEHAVING!
TWO: SHUT YOUR EYES TO YOUR OWN FAULTS! THAT MAKES EVERYTHING SO MUCH EASIER!

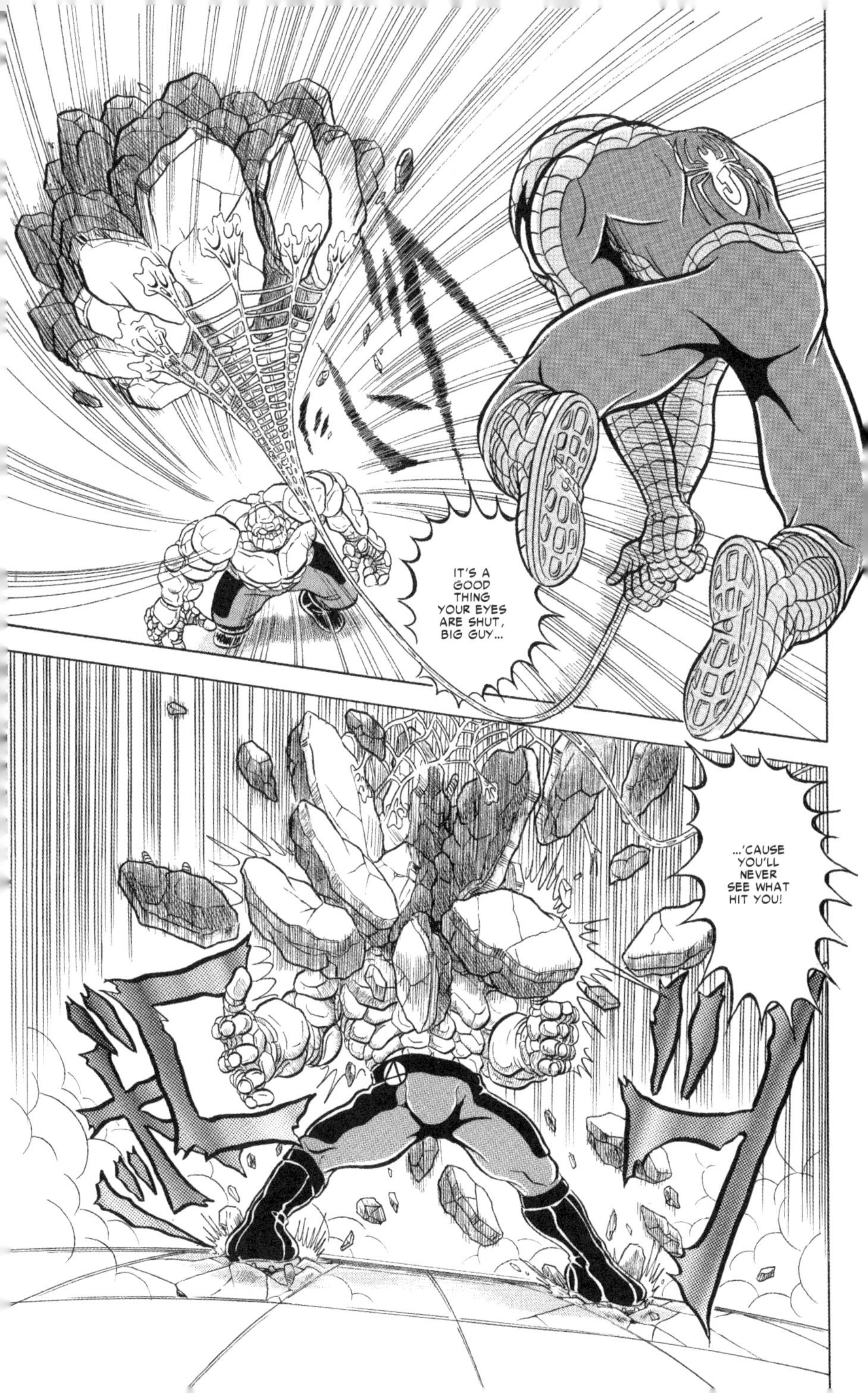
IT'S A GOOD THING YOUR EYES ARE SHUT, BIG GUY...
...'CAUSE YOU'LL NEVER SEE WHAT HIT YOU!

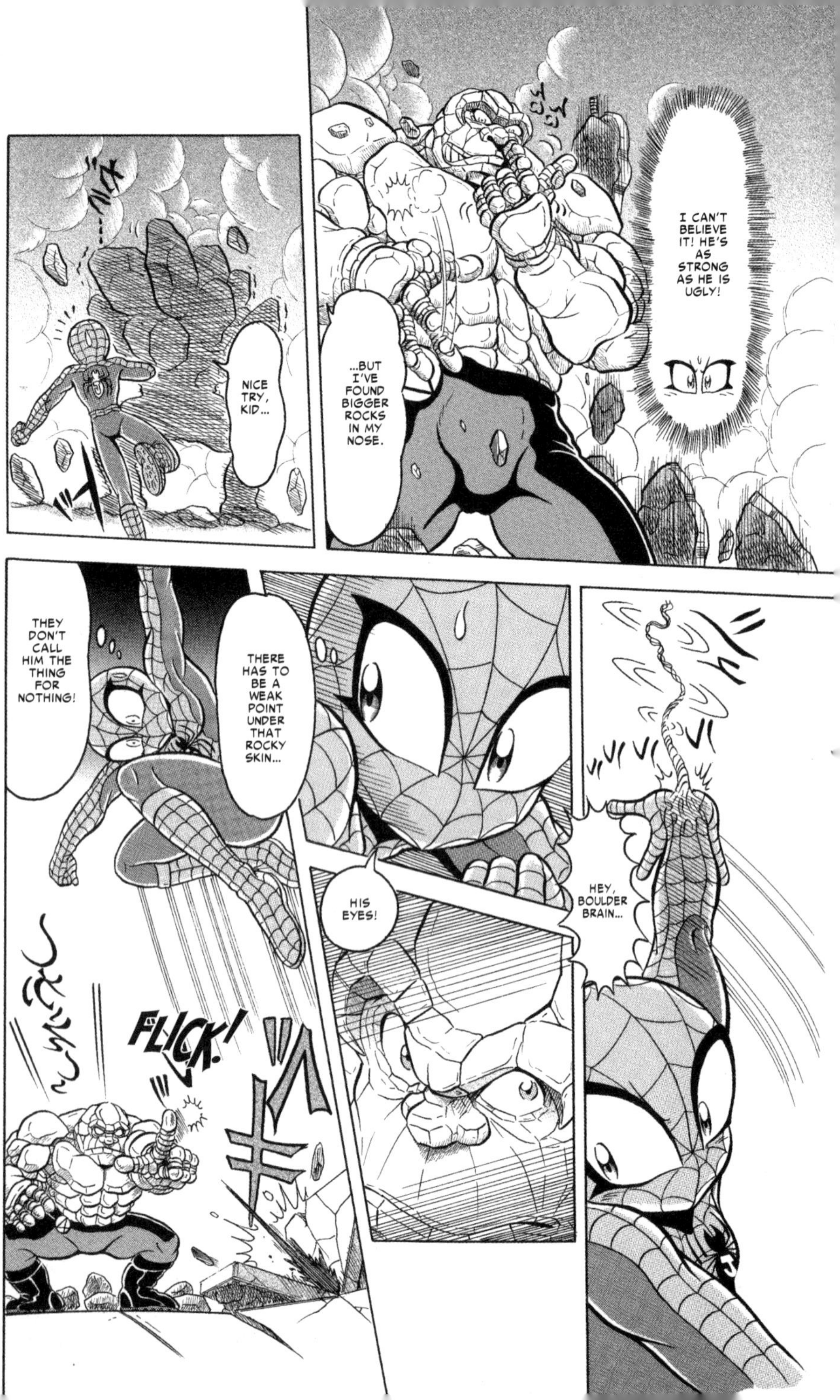
NICE TRY, KID...
...BUT I'VE FOUND BIGGER ROCKS IN MY NOSE.
I CAN'T BELIEVE IT! HE'S AS STRONG AS HE IS UGLY!
THEY DON'T CALL HIM THE THING FOR NOTHING!
THERE HAS TO BE A WEAK POINT UNDER THAT ROCKY SKIN...
HIS EYES!
HEY, BOULDER BRAIN...
FLICK!

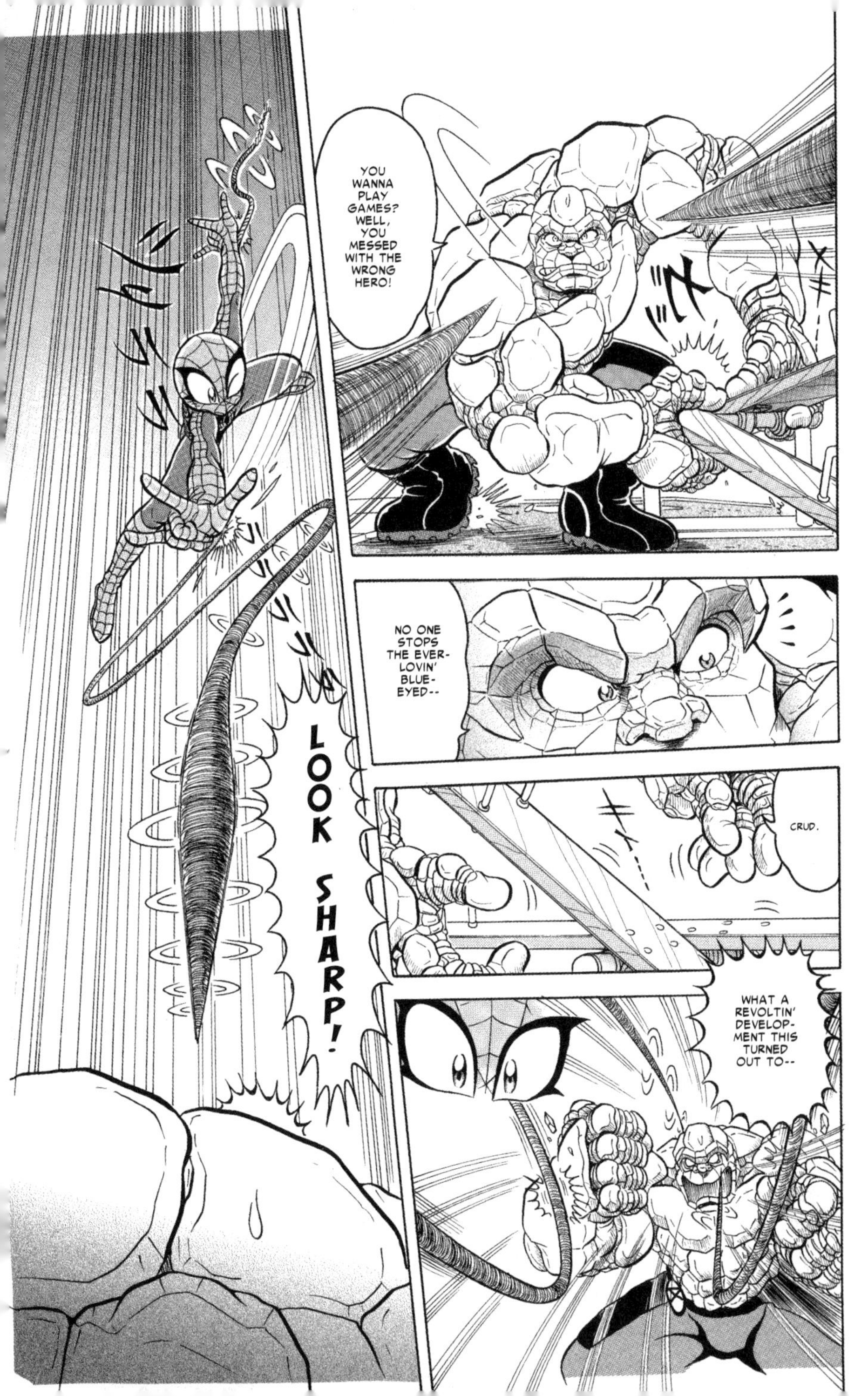

YOU WANNA PLAY GAMES? WELL, YOU MESSED WITH THE WRONG HERO!
LOOK SHARP!
NO ONE STOPS THE EVER-LOVIN' BLUE-EYED--
CRUD.
WHAT A REVOLTIN' DEVELOPMENT THIS TURNED OUT TO--

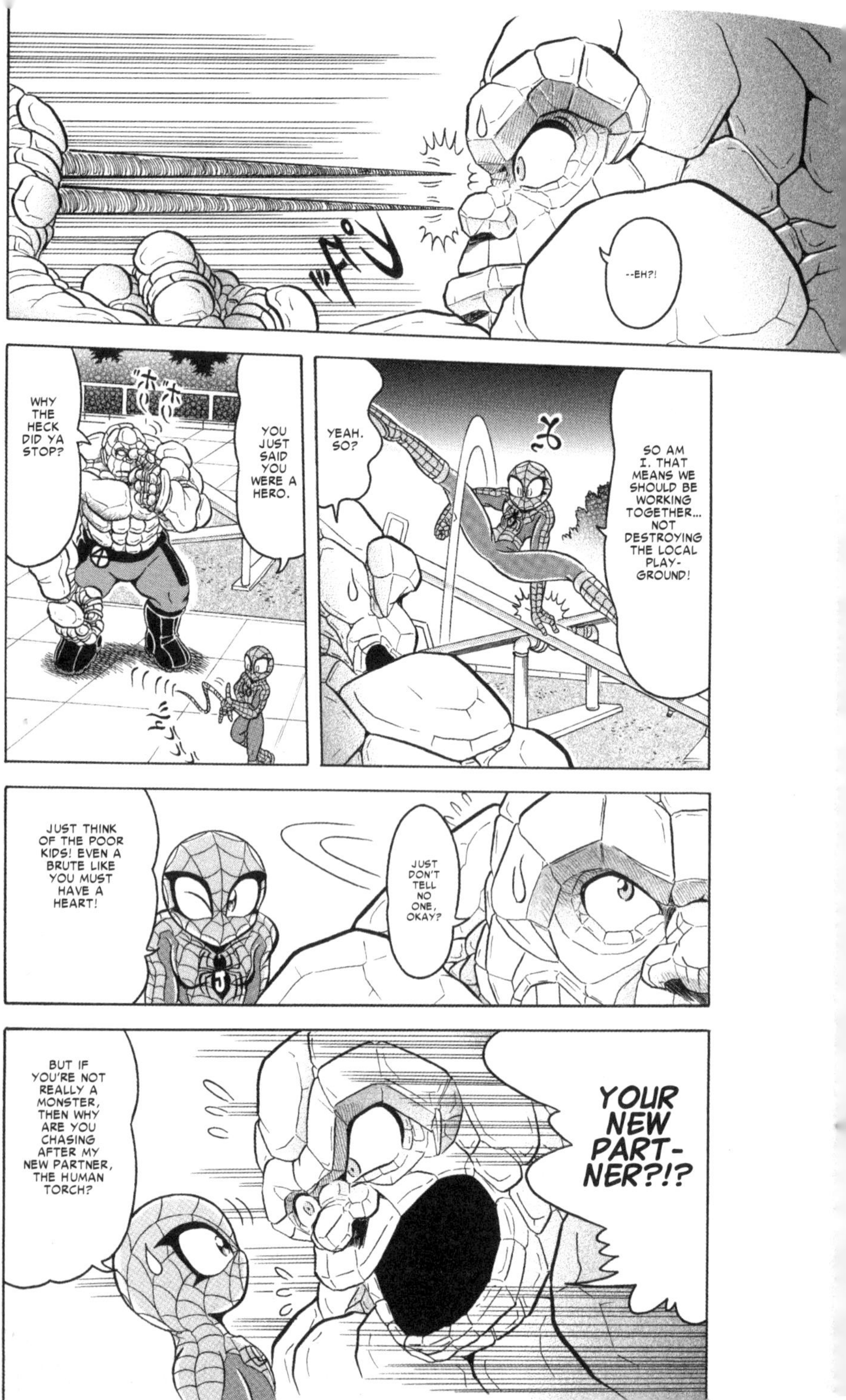
--EH?!
WHY THE HECK DID YA STOP?
YOU JUST SAID YOU WERE A HERO.
YEAH. SO?
SO AM I. THAT MEANS WE SHOULD BE WORKING TOGETHER... NOT DESTROYING THE LOCAL PLAY-GROUND!
JUST THINK OF THE POOR KIDS! EVEN A BRUTE LIKE YOU MUST HAVE A HEART!
JUST DON'T TELL NO ONE, OKAY?
BUT IF YOU'RE NOT REALLY A MONSTER, THEN WHY ARE YOU CHASING AFTER MY NEW PARTNER, THE HUMAN TORCH?
YOUR NEW PART-NER?!?

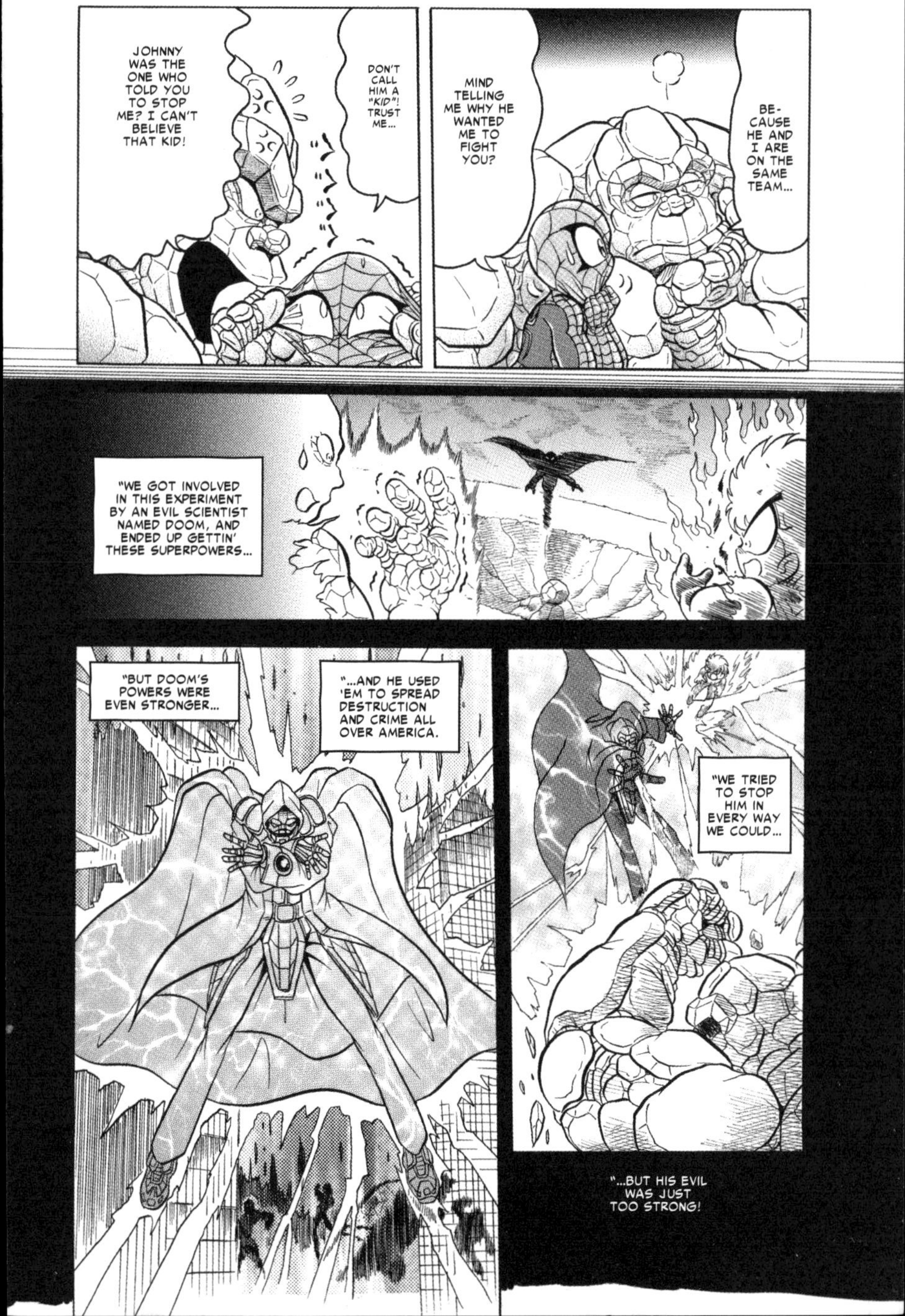

JOHNNY WAS THE ONE WHO TOLD YOU TO STOP ME? I CAN'T BELIEVE THAT KID!
DON'T CALL HIM A "KID"! TRUST ME...
MIND TELLING ME WHY HE WANTED ME TO FIGHT YOU?
BE-CAUSE HE AND I ARE ON THE SAME TEAM...
"WE GOT INVOLVED IN THIS EXPERIMENT BY AN EVIL SCIENTIST NAMED DOOM, AND ENDED UP GETTIN' THESE SUPERPOWERS...
"BUT DOOM'S POWERS WERE EVEN STRONGER...
"...AND HE USED 'EM TO SPREAD DESTRUCTION AND CRIME ALL OVER AMERICA.
"WE TRIED TO STOP HIM IN EVERY WAY WE COULD...
"...BUT HIS EVIL WAS JUST TOO STRONG!

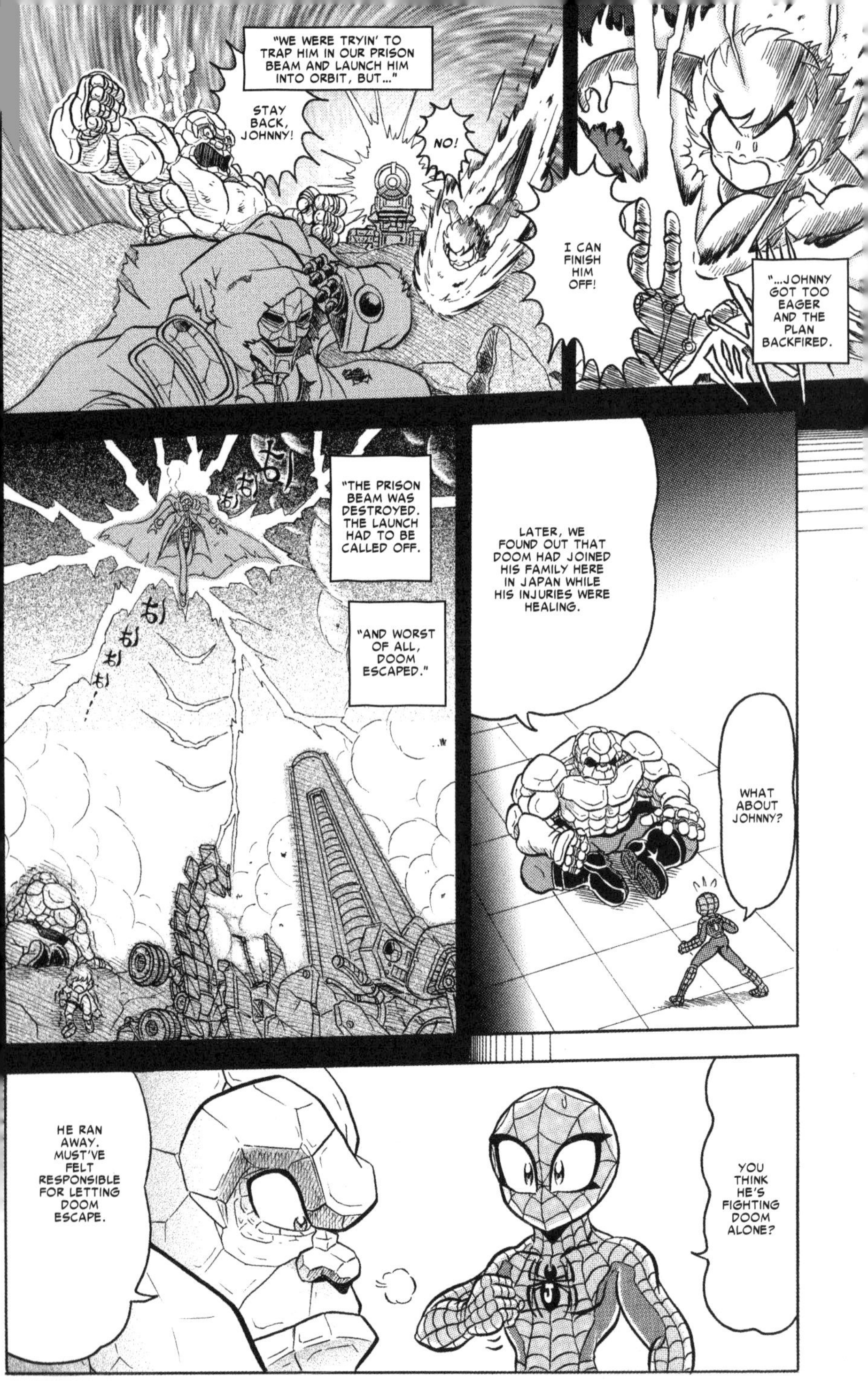
"WE WERE TRYIN' TO TRAP HIM IN OUR PRISON BEAM AND LAUNCH HIM INTO ORBIT, BUT..."
STAY BACK, JOHNNY!
NO!
I CAN FINISH HIM OFF!
"...JOHNNY GOT TOO EAGER AND THE PLAN BACKFIRED.
"THE PRISON BEAM WAS DESTROYED. THE LAUNCH HAD TO BE CALLED OFF.
"AND WORST OF ALL, DOOM ESCAPED."
LATER, WE FOUND OUT THAT DOOM HAD JOINED HIS FAMILY HERE IN JAPAN WHILE HIS INJURIES WERE HEALING.
WHAT ABOUT JOHNNY?
HE RAN AWAY. MUST'VE FELT RESPONSIBLE FOR LETTING DOOM ESCAPE.
YOU THINK HE'S FIGHTING DOOM ALONE?

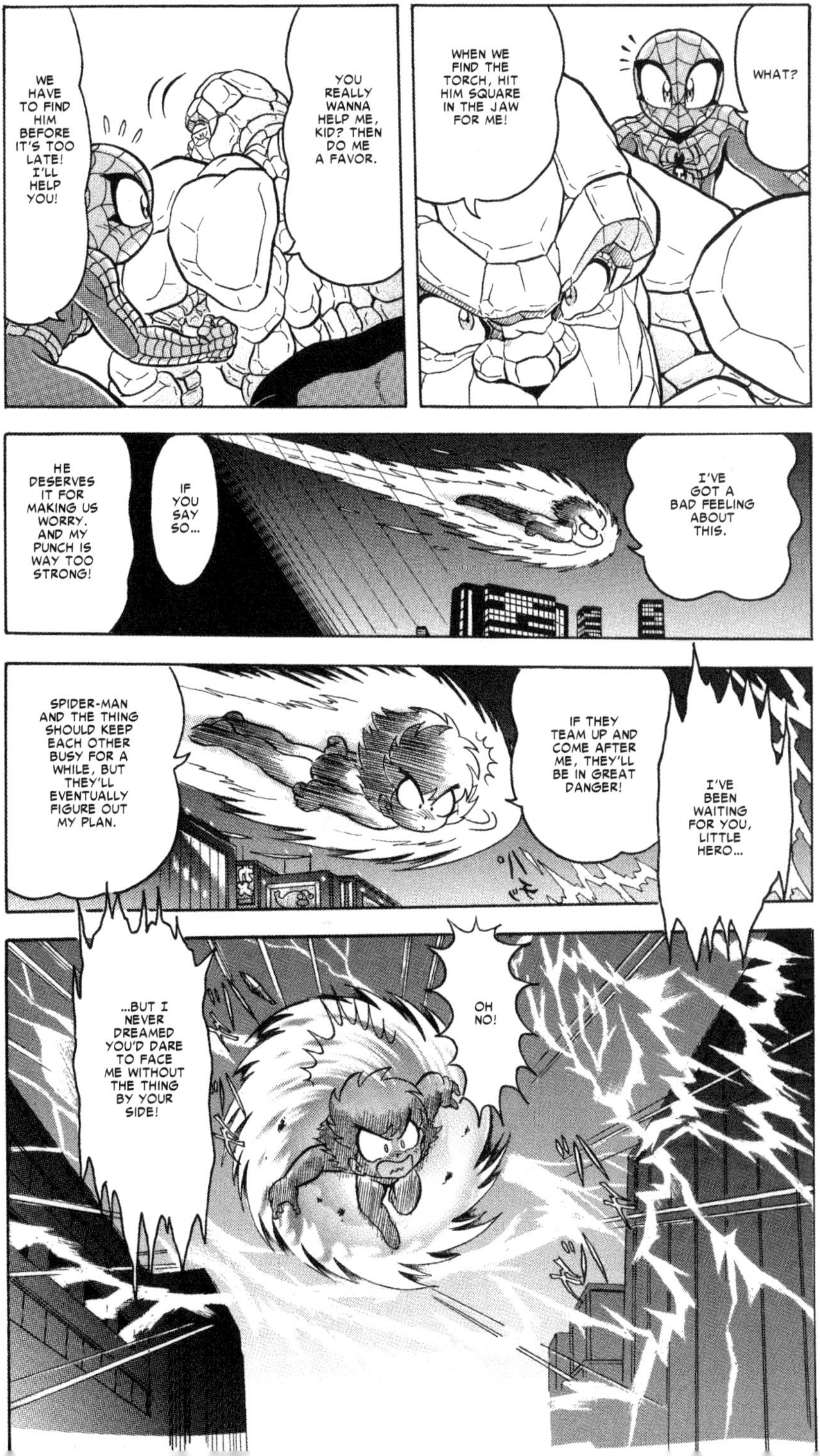
WE HAVE TO FIND HIM BEFORE IT'S TOO LATE! I'LL HELP YOU!
YOU REALLY WANNA HELP ME, KID? THEN DO ME A FAVOR.
WHEN WE FIND THE TORCH, HIT HIM SQUARE IN THE JAW FOR ME!
WHAT?
HE DESERVES IT FOR MAKING US WORRY. AND MY PUNCH IS WAY TOO STRONG!
IF YOU SAY SO...
I'VE GOT A BAD FEELING ABOUT THIS.
SPIDER-MAN AND THE THING SHOULD KEEP EACH OTHER BUSY FOR A WHILE, BUT THEY'LL EVENTUALLY FIGURE OUT MY PLAN.
IF THEY TEAM UP AND COME AFTER ME, THEY'LL BE IN GREAT DANGER!
I'VE BEEN WAITING FOR YOU, LITTLE HERO...
...BUT I NEVER DREAMED YOU'D DARE TO FACE ME WITHOUT THE THING BY YOUR SIDE!
OH NO!

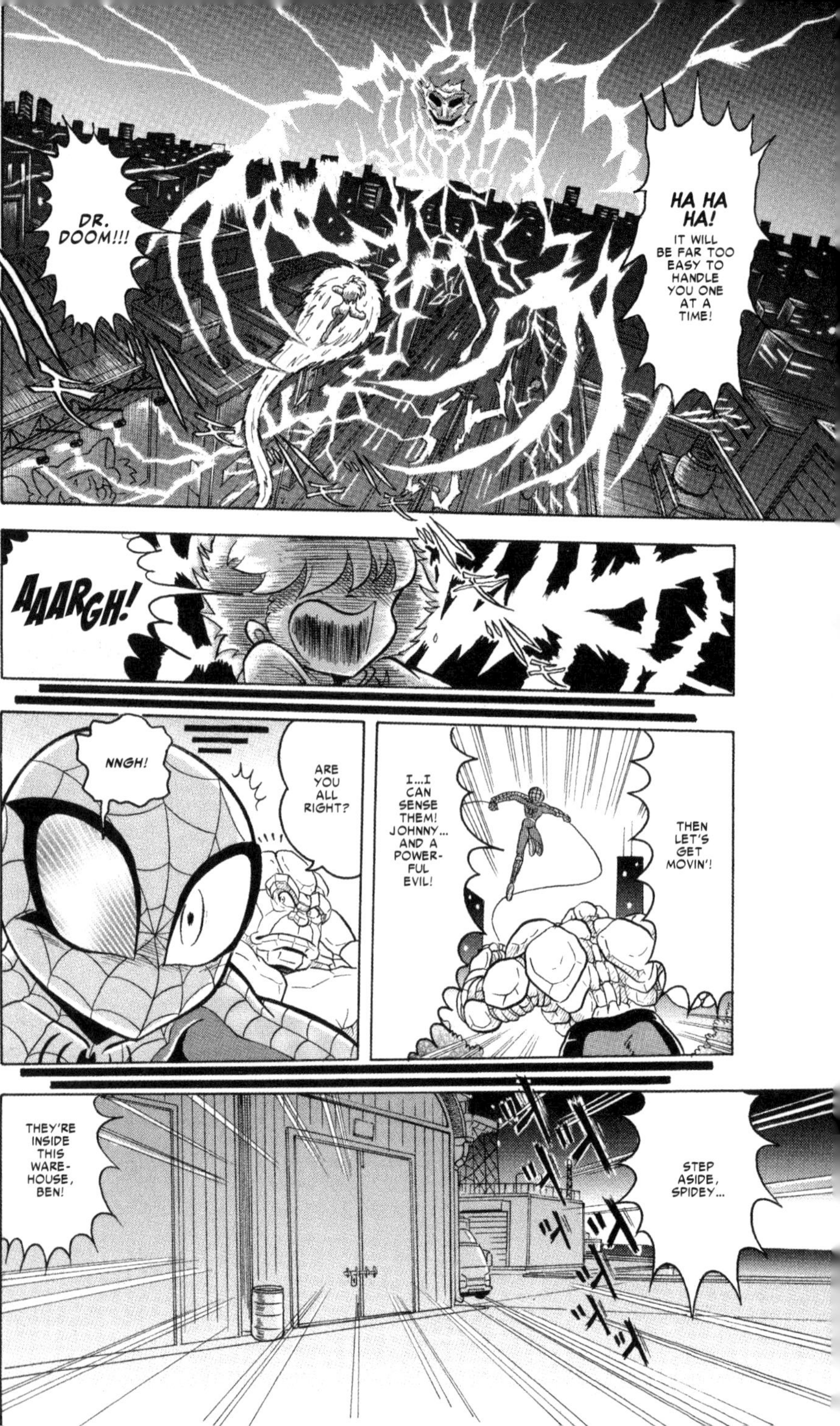
DR. DOOM!!!
HA HA HA! IT WILL BE FAR TOO EASY TO HANDLE YOU ONE AT A TIME!
AAARGH!
NNGH!
ARE YOU ALL RIGHT?
I...I CAN SENSE THEM! JOHNNY... AND A POWERFUL EVIL!
THEN LET'S GET MOVIN'!
THEY'RE INSIDE THIS WAREHOUSE, BEN!
STEP ASIDE, SPIDEY...

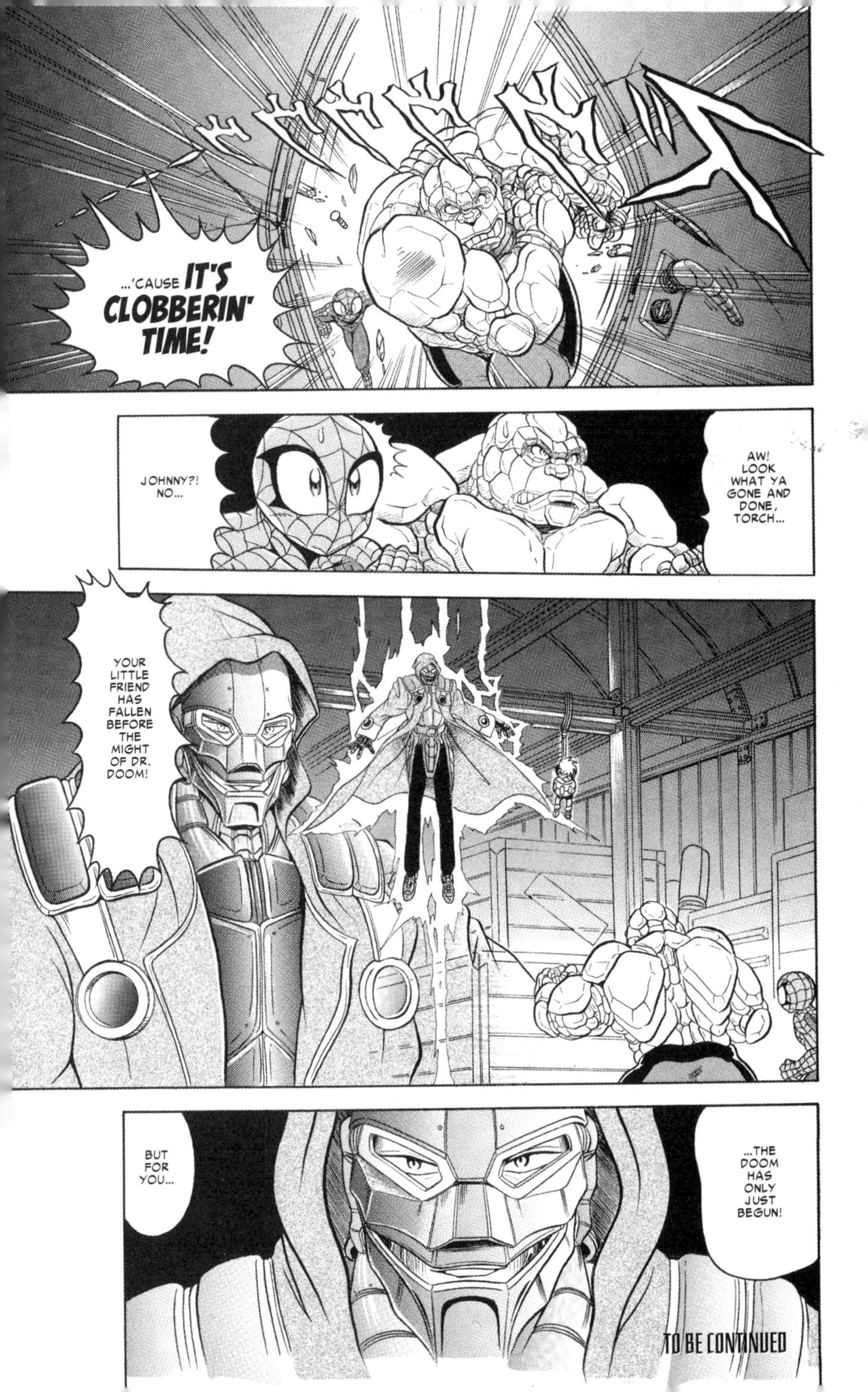
...'CAUSE IT'S CLOBBERIN' TIME!
JOHNNY?! NO...
AW! LOOK WHAT YA GONE AND DONE, TORCH...
YOUR LITTLE FRIEND HAS FALLEN BEFORE THE MIGHT OF DR. DOOM!
BUT FOR YOU...
...THE DOOM HAS ONLY JUST BEGUN!
TO BE CONTINUED

CHAPTER 4

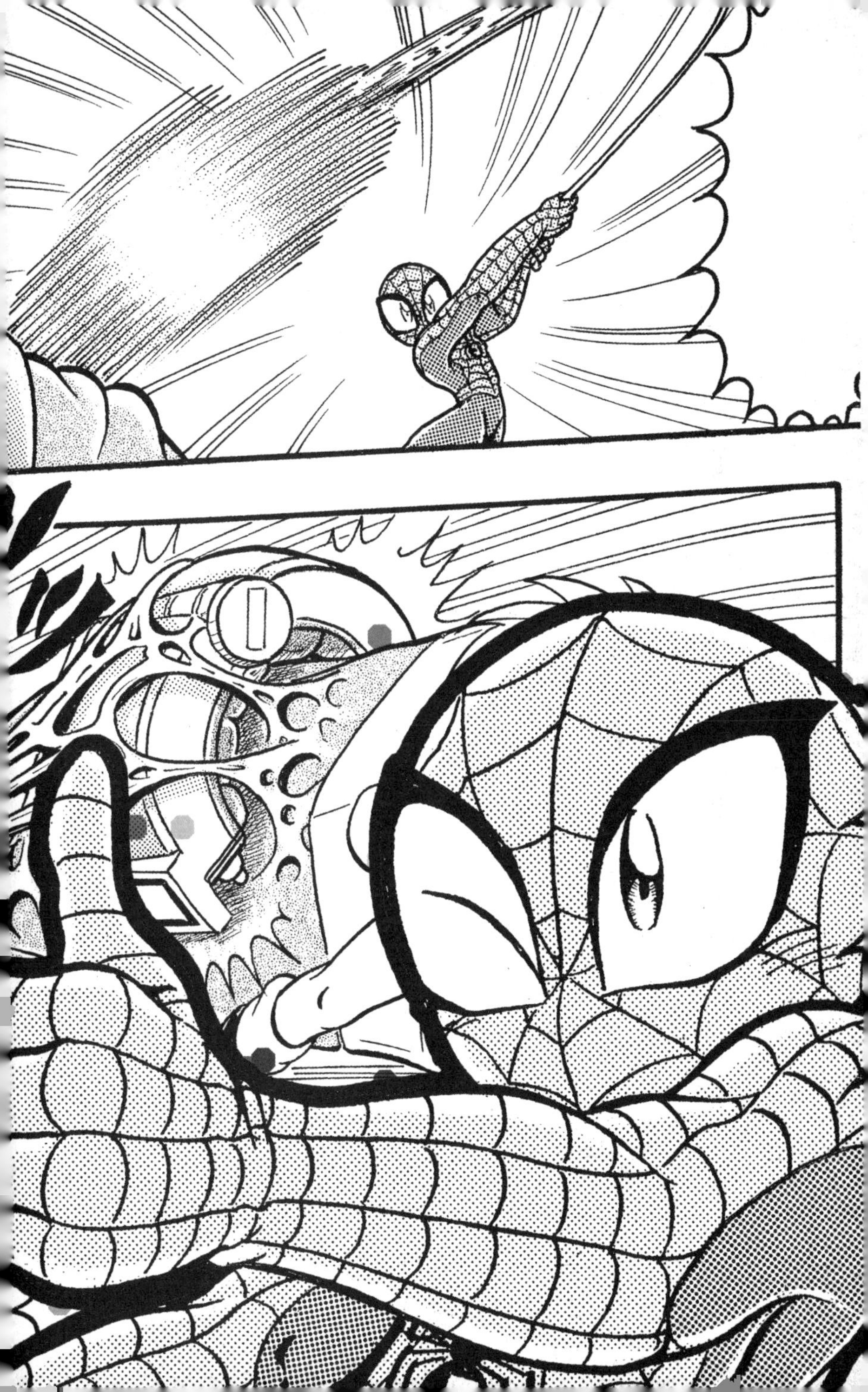

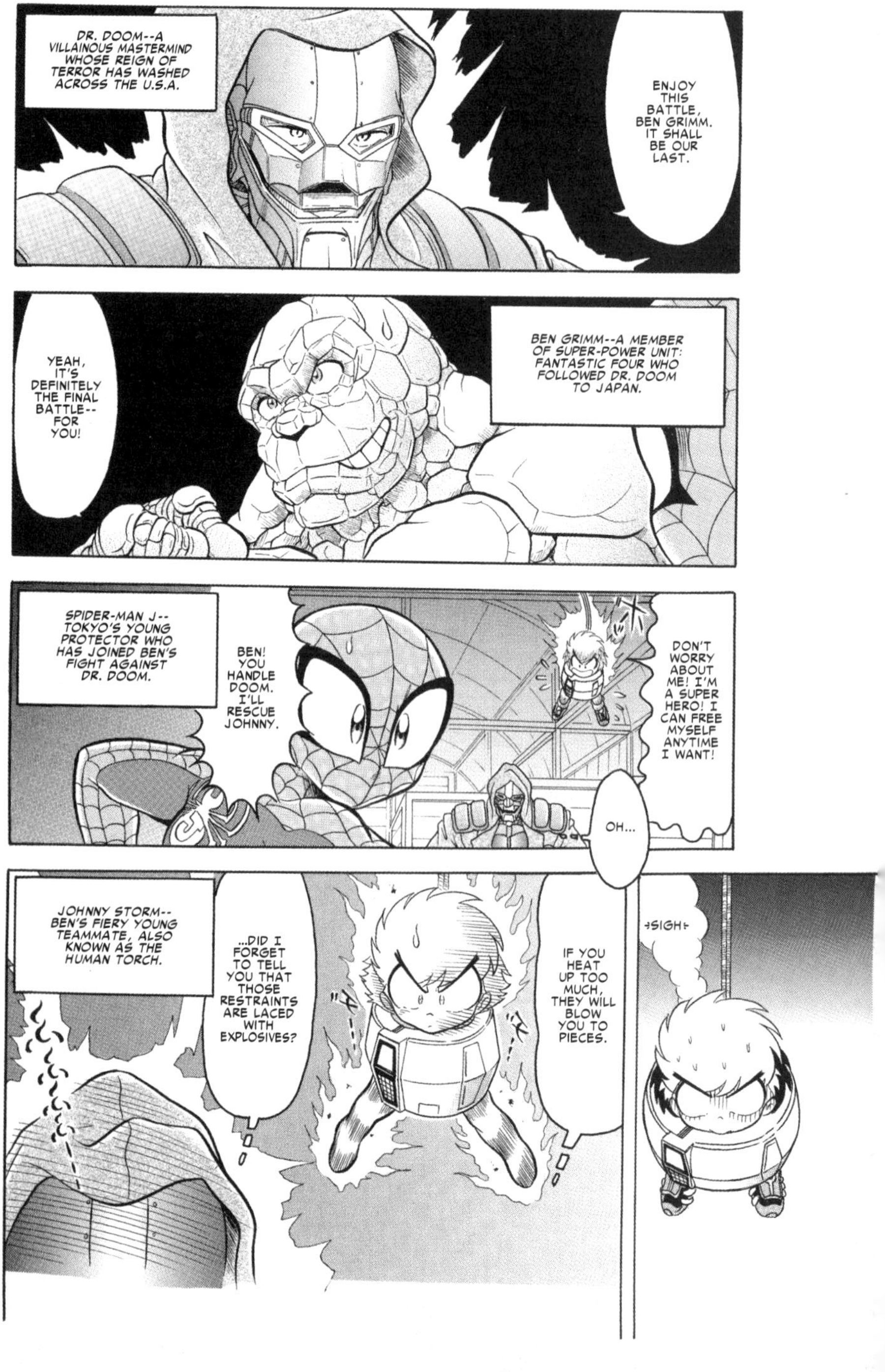
DR. DOOM--A VILLAINOUS MASTERMIND WHOSE REIGN OF TERROR HAS WASHED ACROSS THE U.S.A.
ENJOY THIS BATTLE, BEN GRIMM. IT SHALL BE OUR LAST.
BEN GRIMM--A MEMBER OF SUPER-POWER UNIT: FANTASTIC FOUR WHO FOLLOWED DR. DOOM TO JAPAN.
YEAH, IT'S DEFINITELY THE FINAL BATTLE--FOR YOU!
SPIDER-MAN J--TOKYO'S YOUNG PROTECTOR WHO HAS JOINED BEN'S FIGHT AGAINST DR. DOOM.
BEN! YOU HANDLE DOOM. I'LL RESCUE JOHNNY.
DON'T WORRY ABOUT ME! I'M A SUPER HERO! I CAN FREE MYSELF ANYTIME I WANT!
OH...
JOHNNY STORM--BEN'S FIERY YOUNG TEAMMATE, ALSO KNOWN AS THE HUMAN TORCH.
...DID I FORGET TO TELL YOU THAT THOSE RESTRAINTS ARE LACED WITH EXPLOSIVES?
IF YOU HEAT UP TOO MUCH, THEY WILL BLOW YOU TO PIECES.
+SIGH+

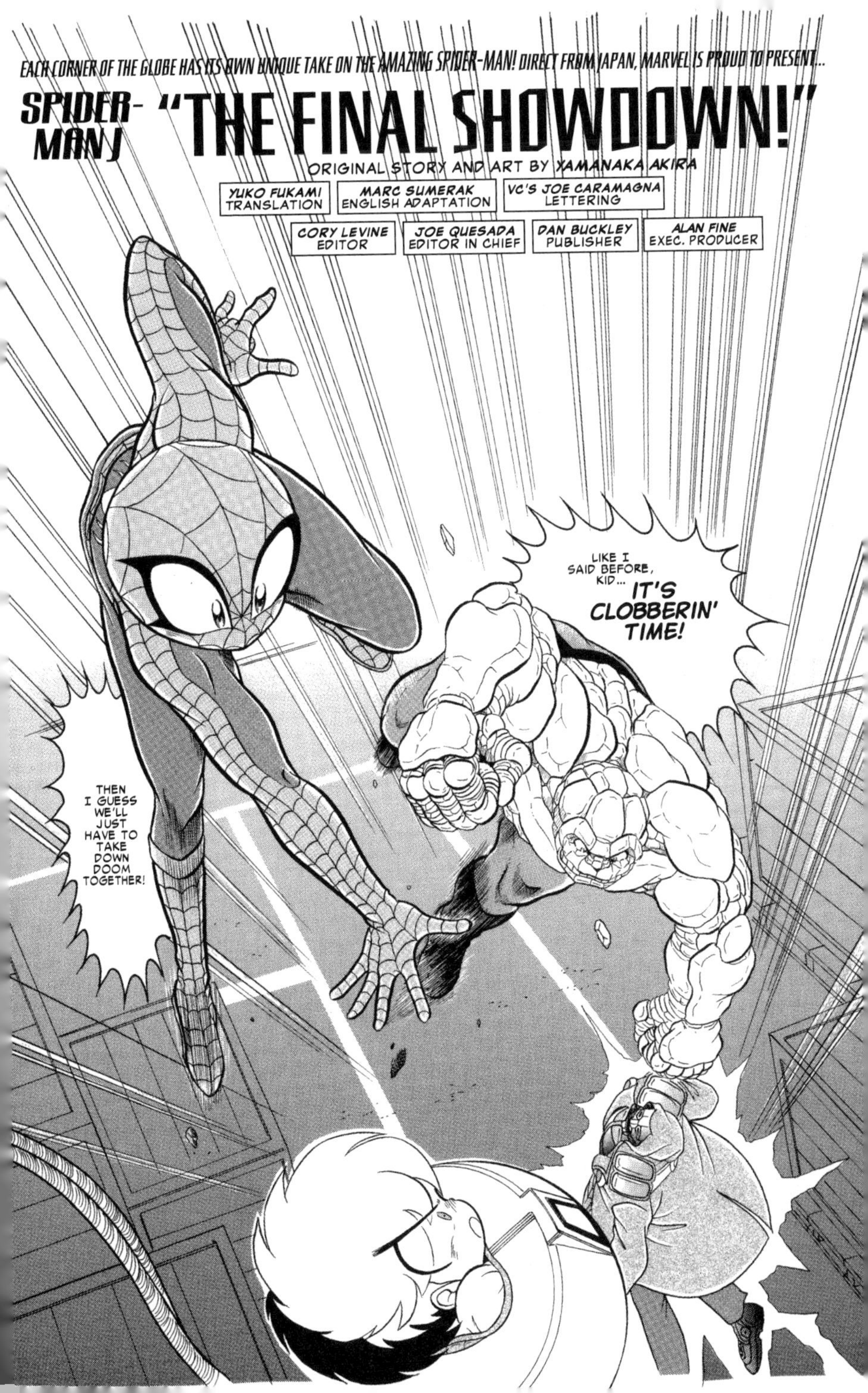
EACH CORNER OF THE GLOBE HAS ITS OWN UNIQUE TAKE ON THE AMAZING SPIDER-MAN! DIRECT FROM JAPAN, MARVEL IS PROUD TO PRESENT...
SPIDER-MAN J "THE FINAL SHOWDOWN!"
ORIGINAL STORY AND ART BY YAMANAKA AKIRA
YUKO FUKAMI TRANSLATION
MARC SUMERAK ENGLISH ADAPTATION
VC'S JOE CARAMAGNA LETTERING
CORY LEVINE EDITOR
JOE QUESADA EDITOR IN CHIEF
DAN BUCKLEY PUBLISHER
ALAN FINE EXEC. PRODUCER
LIKE I SAID BEFORE, KID... IT'S CLOBBERIN' TIME!
THEN I GUESS WE'LL JUST HAVE TO TAKE DOWN DOOM TOGETHER!

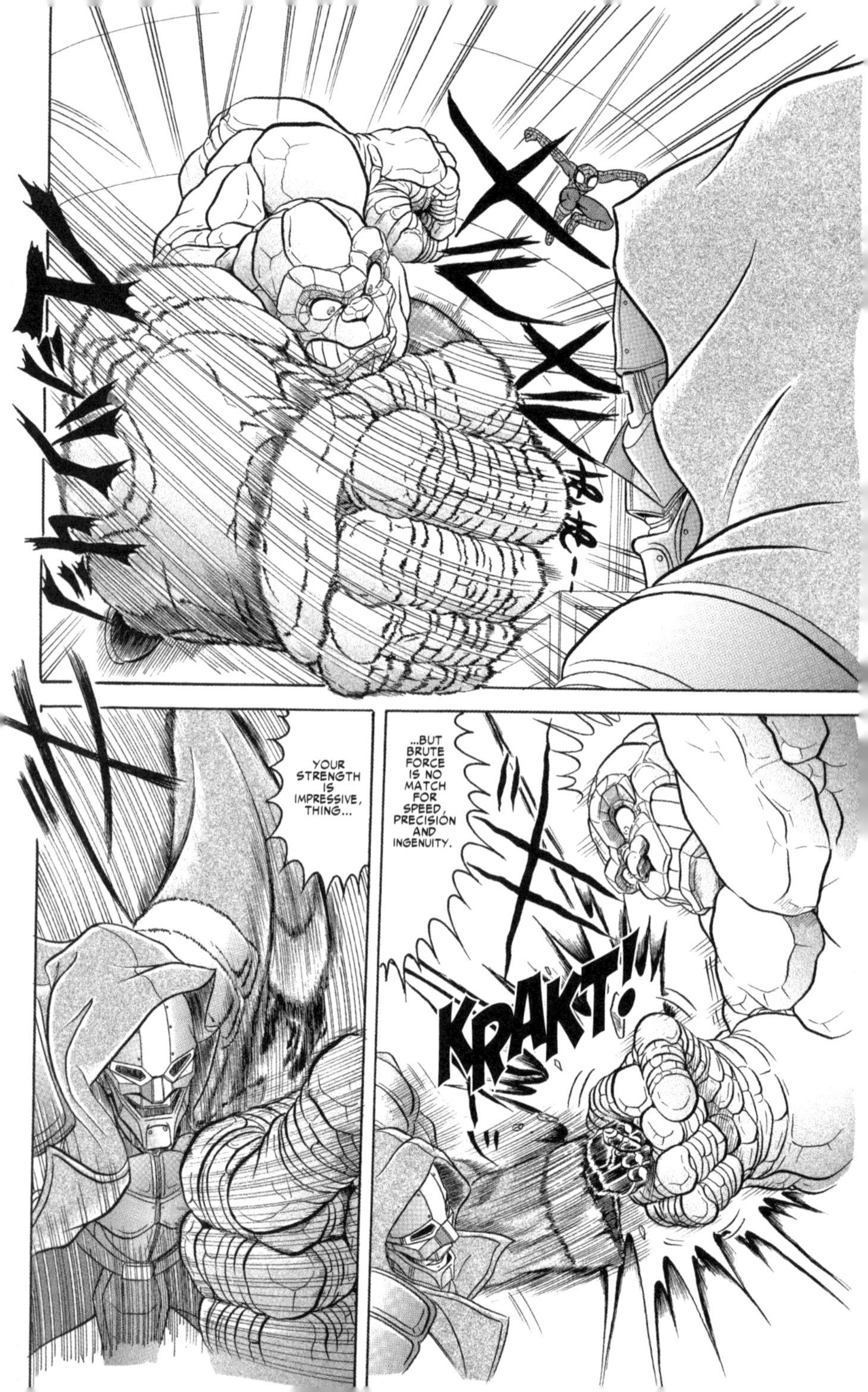
YOUR STRENGTH IS IMPRESSIVE, THING...
...BUT BRUTE FORCE IS NO MATCH FOR SPEED, PRECISION AND INGENUITY.
KRAKT!!

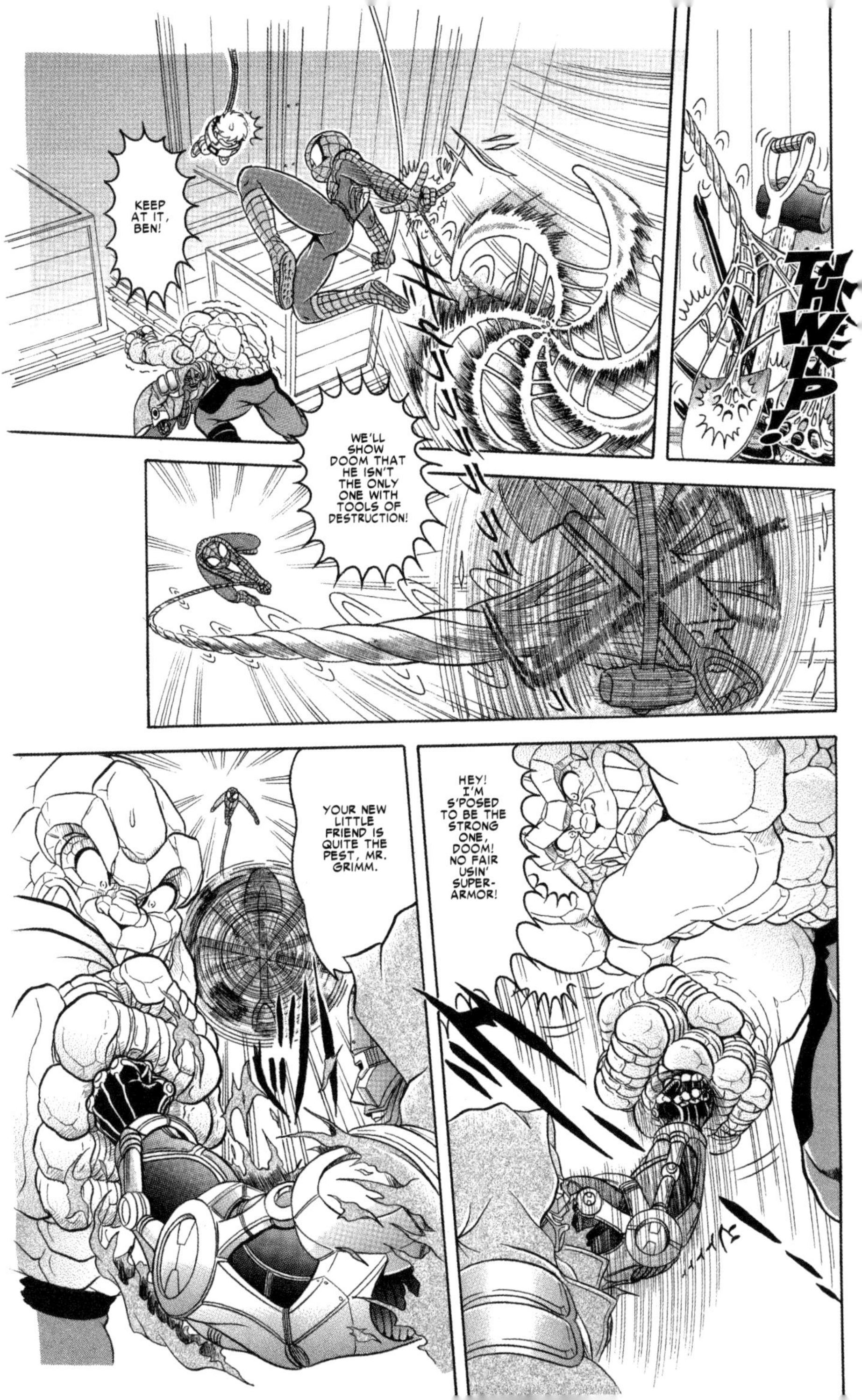
KEEP AT IT, BEN!
THWIP!
WE'LL SHOW DOOM THAT HE ISN'T THE ONLY ONE WITH TOOLS OF DESTRUCTION!
YOUR NEW LITTLE FRIEND IS QUITE THE PEST, MR. GRIMM.
HEY! I'M S'POSED TO BE THE STRONG ONE, DOOM! NO FAIR USIN' SUPER-ARMOR!

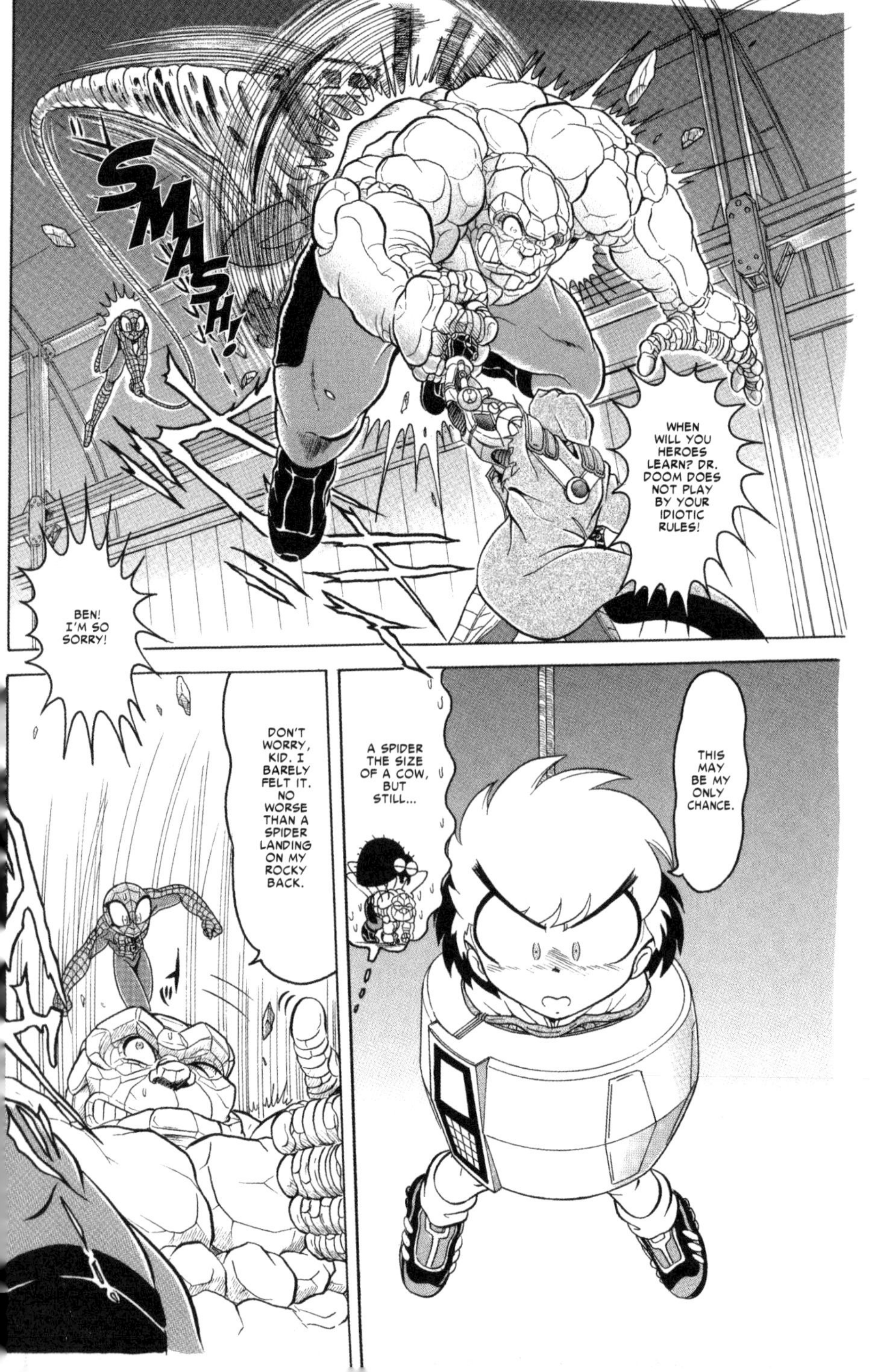

SMASH!
WHEN WILL YOU HEROES LEARN? DR. DOOM DOES NOT PLAY BY YOUR IDIOTIC RULES!
BEN! I'M SO SORRY!
DON'T WORRY, KID. I BARELY FELT IT. NO WORSE THAN A SPIDER LANDING ON MY ROCKY BACK.
A SPIDER THE SIZE OF A COW, BUT STILL...
THIS MAY BE MY ONLY CHANCE.

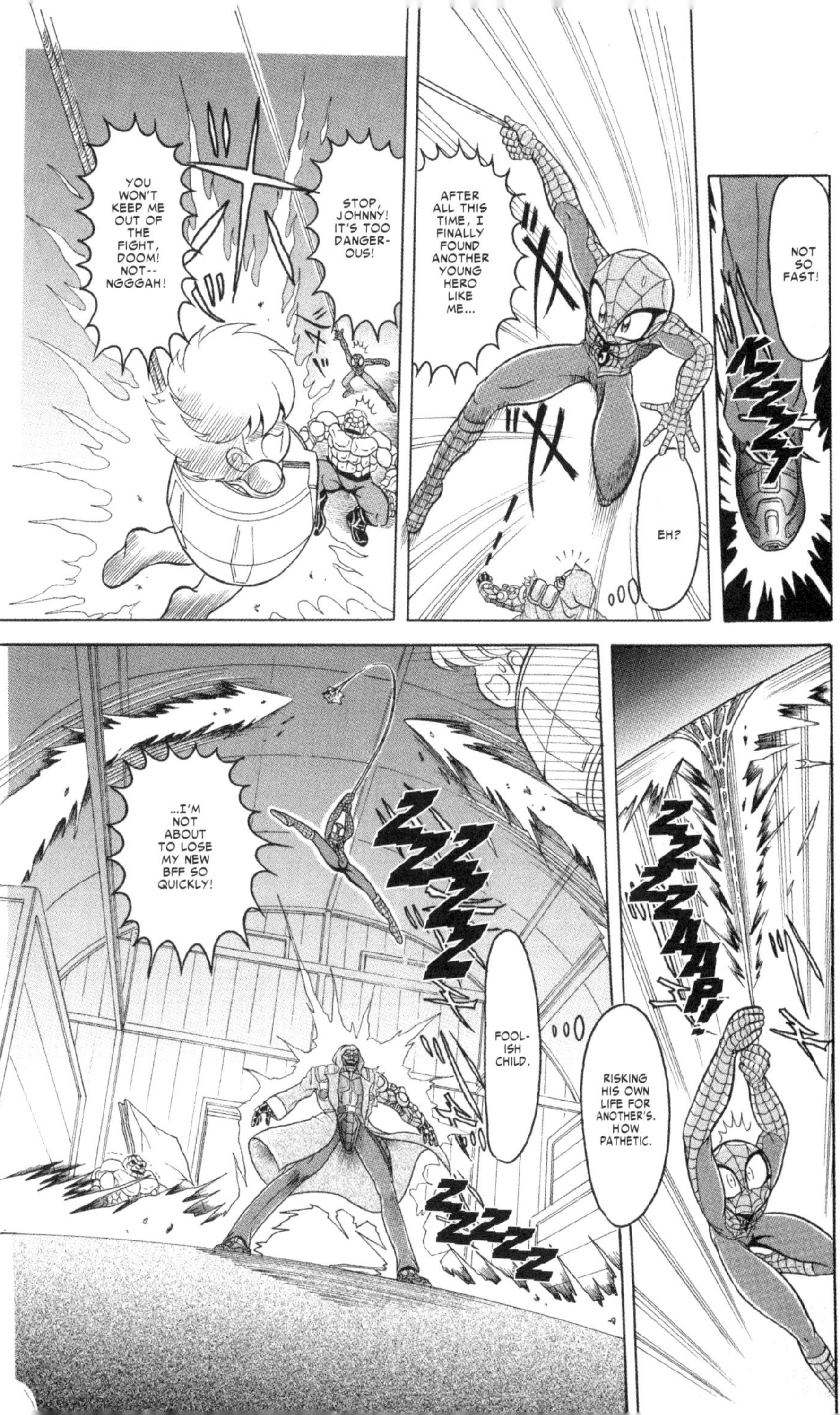
YOU WON'T KEEP ME OUT OF THE FIGHT, DOOM! NOT-- NGGGAH!
STOP, JOHNNY! IT'S TOO DANGER-OUS!
AFTER ALL THIS TIME, I FINALLY FOUND ANOTHER YOUNG HERO LIKE ME...
EH?
NOT SO FAST!
...I'M NOT ABOUT TO LOSE MY NEW BFF SO QUICKLY!
FOOL-ISH CHILD.
RISKING HIS OWN LIFE FOR ANOTHER'S. HOW PATHETIC.

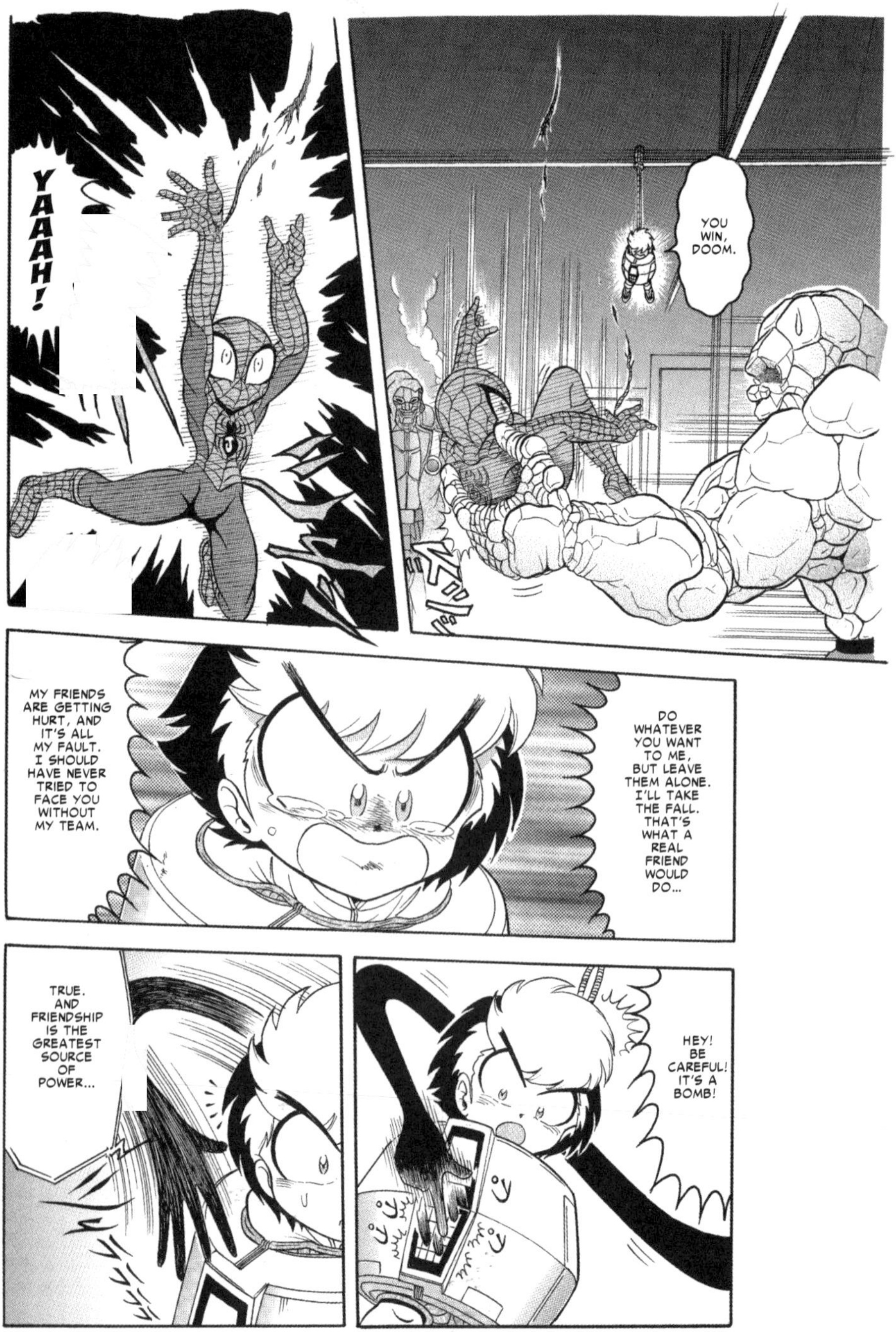
YAAAH!
YOU WIN, DOOM.
MY FRIENDS ARE GETTING HURT, AND IT'S ALL MY FAULT. I SHOULD HAVE NEVER TRIED TO FACE YOU WITHOUT MY TEAM.
DO WHATEVER YOU WANT TO ME, BUT LEAVE THEM ALONE. I'LL TAKE THE FALL. THAT'S WHAT A REAL FRIEND WOULD DO...
TRUE. AND FRIENDSHIP IS THE GREATEST SOURCE OF POWER...
HEY! BE CAREFUL! IT'S A BOMB!

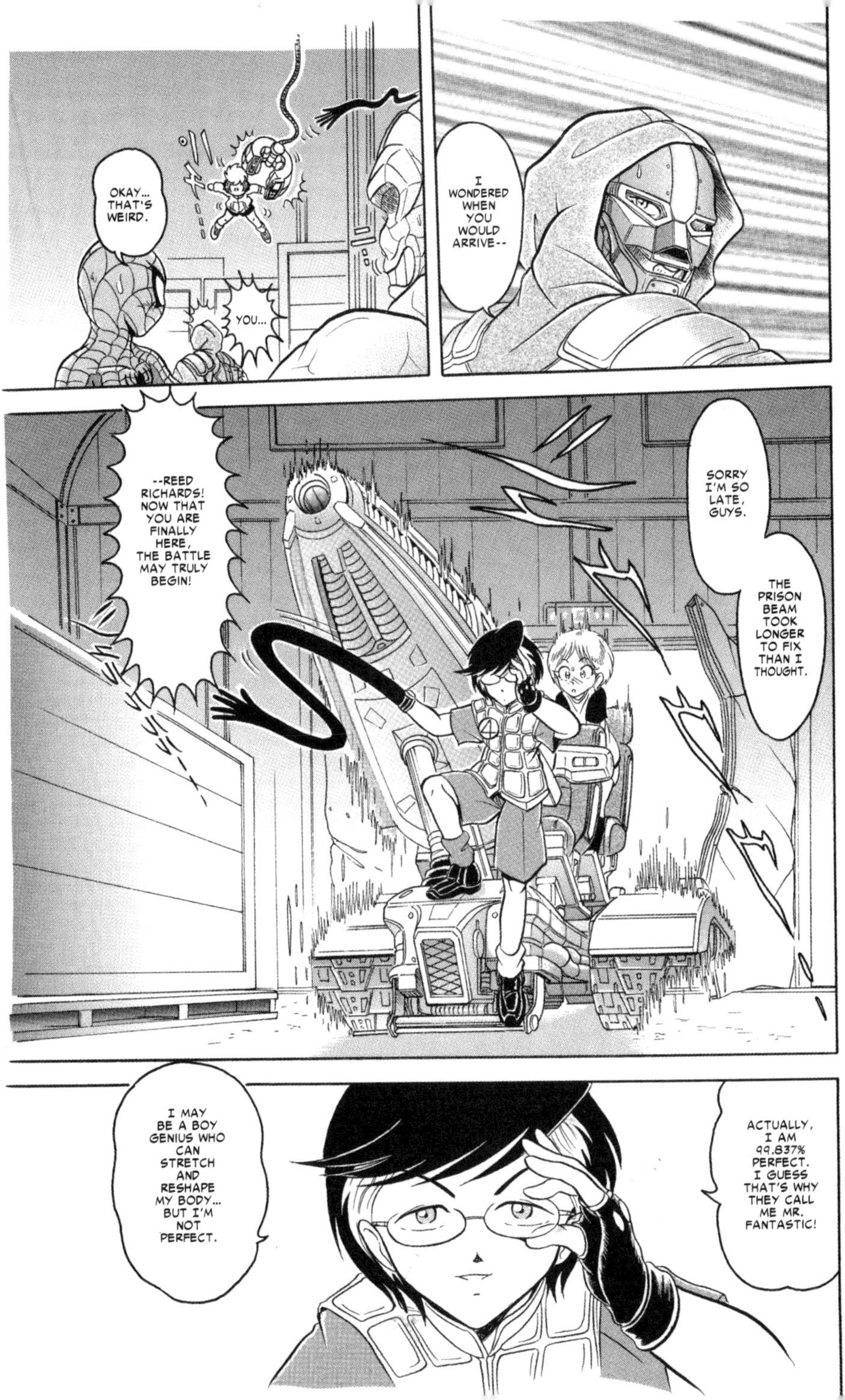
OKAY... THAT'S WEIRD.
YOU...
I WONDERED WHEN YOU WOULD ARRIVE--
--REED RICHARDS! NOW THAT YOU ARE FINALLY HERE, THE BATTLE MAY TRULY BEGIN!
SORRY I'M SO LATE, GUYS.
THE PRISON BEAM TOOK LONGER TO FIX THAN I THOUGHT.
I MAY BE A BOY GENIUS WHO CAN STRETCH AND RESHAPE MY BODY... BUT I'M NOT PERFECT.
ACTUALLY, I AM 99.837% PERFECT. I GUESS THAT'S WHY THEY CALL ME MR. FANTASTIC!

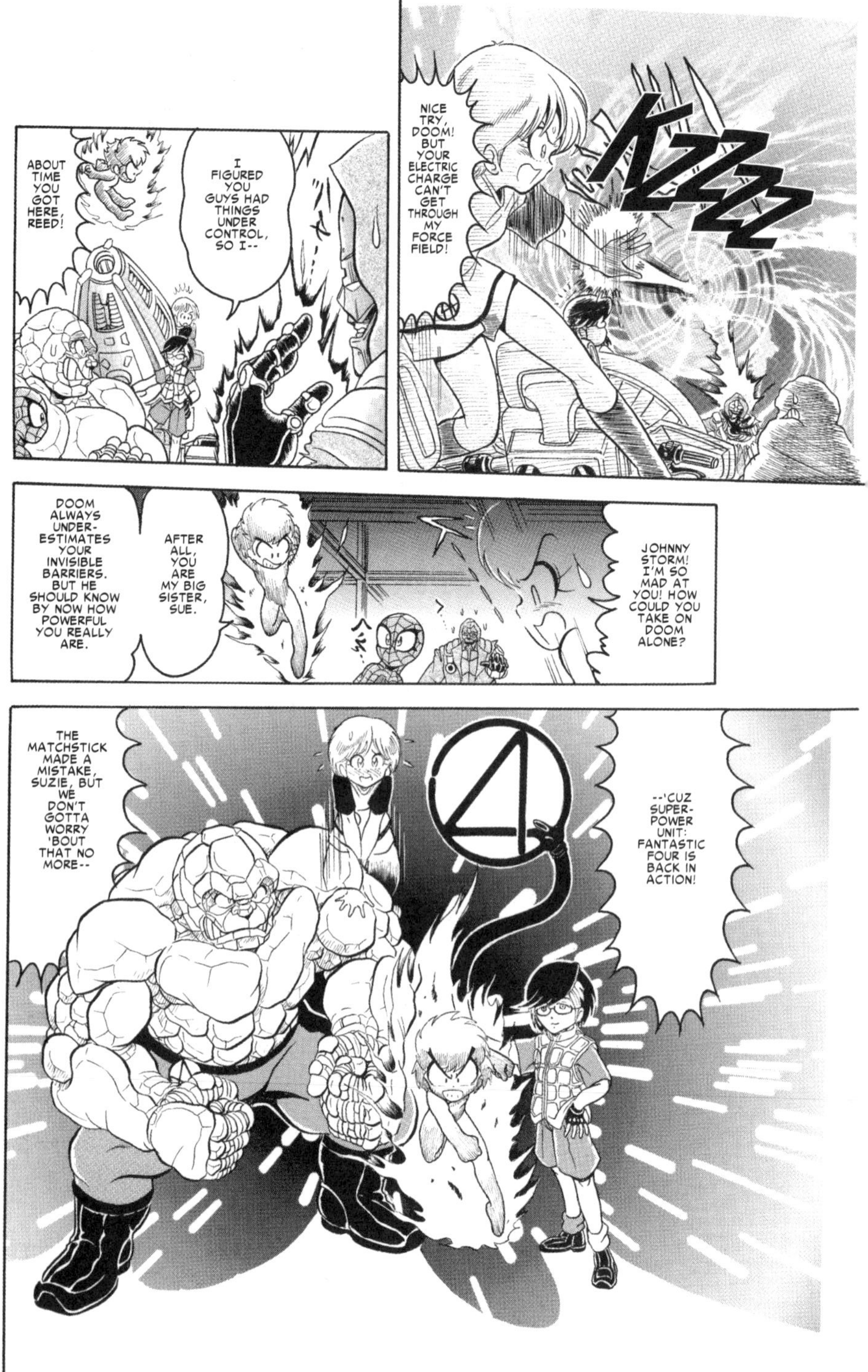

KZZZZ
NICE TRY, DOOM! BUT YOUR ELECTRIC CHARGE CAN'T GET THROUGH MY FORCE FIELD!
ABOUT TIME YOU GOT HERE, REED!
I FIGURED YOU GUYS HAD THINGS UNDER CONTROL, SO I--
JOHNNY STORM! I'M SO MAD AT YOU! HOW COULD YOU TAKE ON DOOM ALONE?
DOOM ALWAYS UNDER-ESTIMATES YOUR INVISIBLE BARRIERS. BUT HE SHOULD KNOW BY NOW HOW POWERFUL YOU REALLY ARE.
AFTER ALL, YOU ARE MY BIG SISTER, SUE.
THE MATCHSTICK MADE A MISTAKE, SUZIE, BUT WE DON'T GOTTA WORRY 'BOUT THAT NO MORE--
--'CUZ SUPER-POWER UNIT: FANTASTIC FOUR IS BACK IN ACTION!

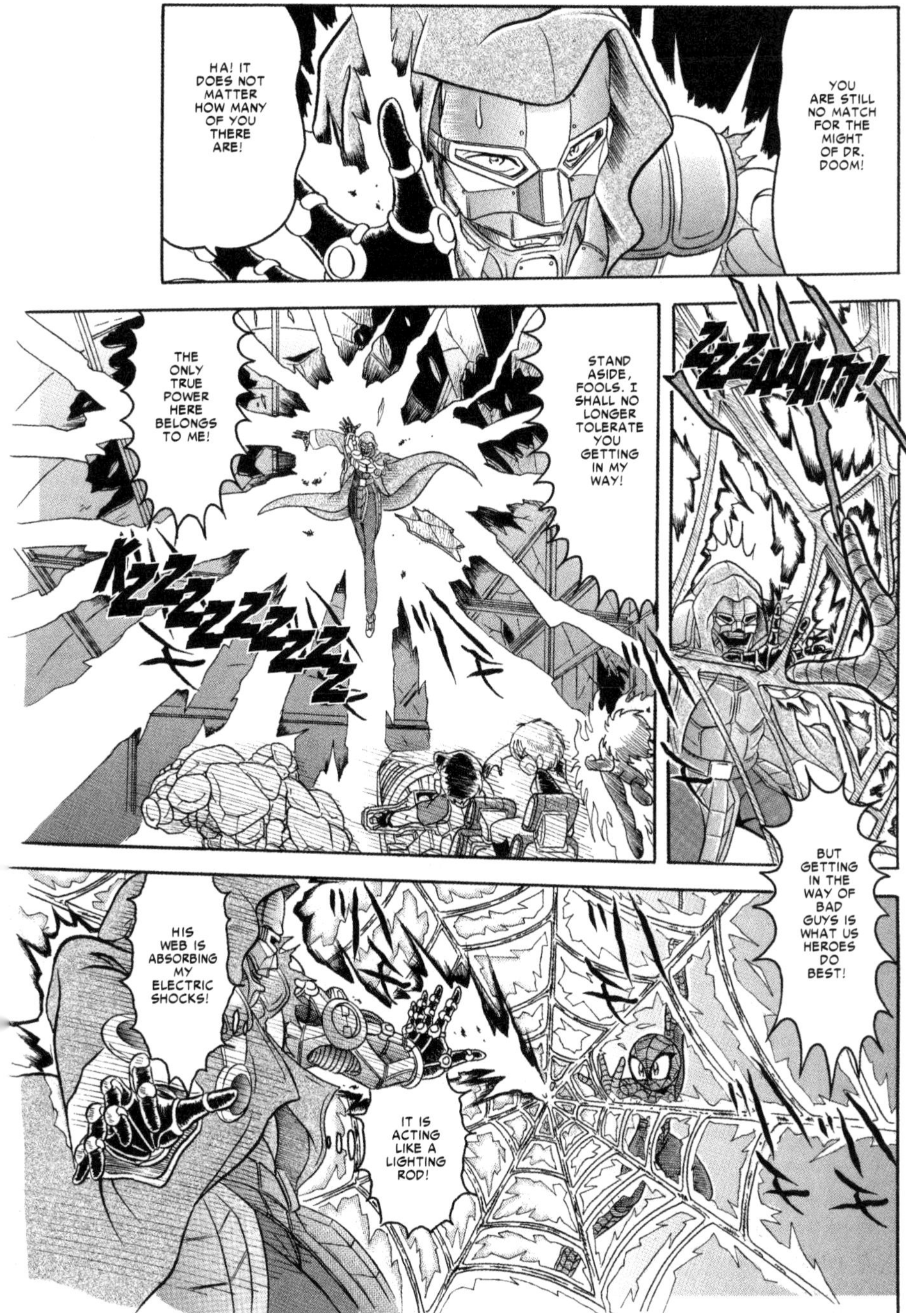
HA! IT DOES NOT MATTER HOW MANY OF YOU THERE ARE!
YOU ARE STILL NO MATCH FOR THE MIGHT OF DR. DOOM!
THE ONLY TRUE POWER HERE BELONGS TO ME!
STAND ASIDE, FOOLS. I SHALL NO LONGER TOLERATE YOU GETTING IN MY WAY!
KZZZZZZZZZZZZ
ZZZZAAATT!
BUT GETTING IN THE WAY OF BAD GUYS IS WHAT US HEROES DO BEST!
HIS WEB IS ABSORBING MY ELECTRIC SHOCKS!
IT IS ACTING LIKE A LIGHTING ROD!

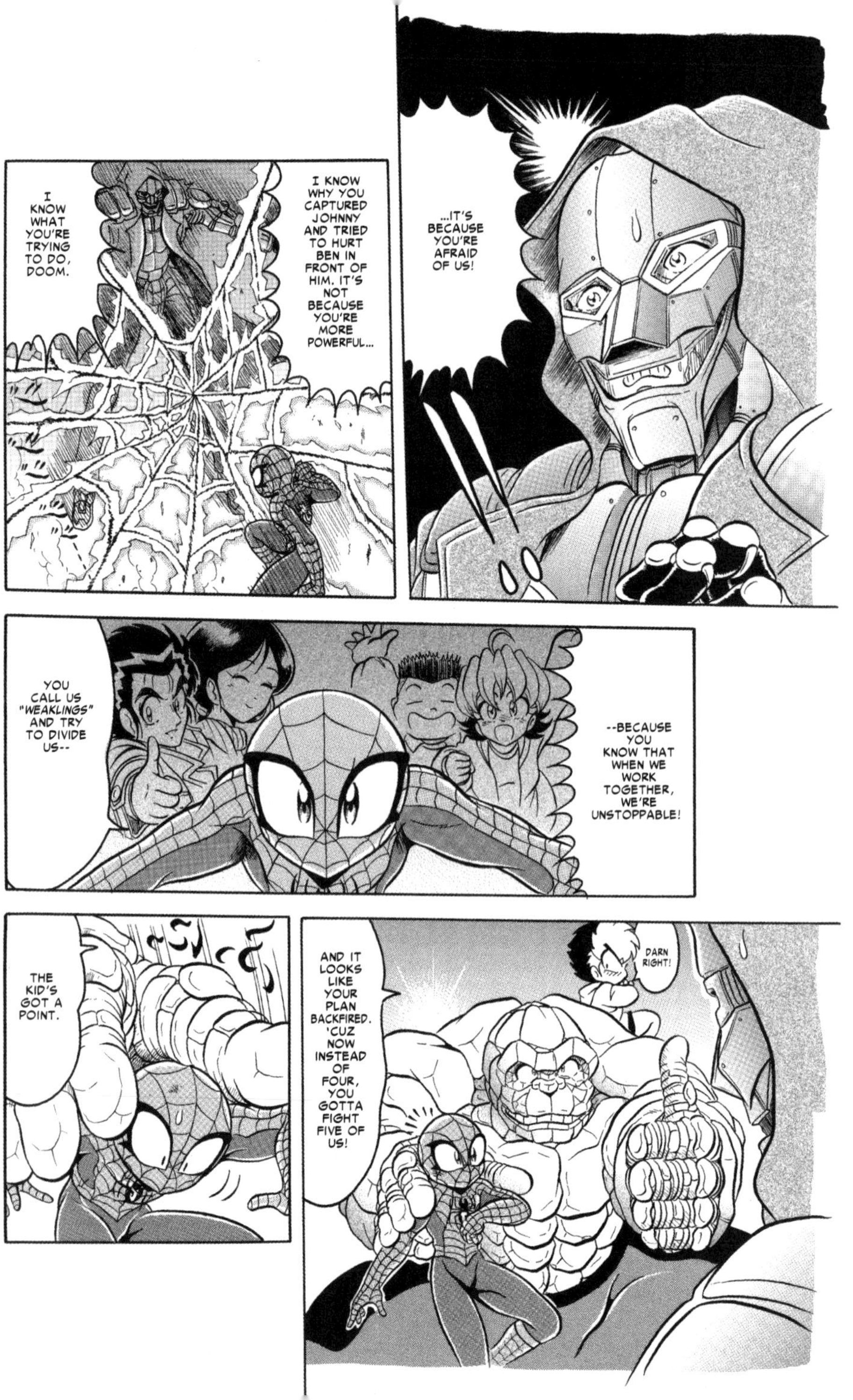
I KNOW WHAT YOU'RE TRYING TO DO, DOOM.
I KNOW WHY YOU CAPTURED JOHNNY AND TRIED TO HURT BEN IN FRONT OF HIM. IT'S NOT BECAUSE YOU'RE MORE POWERFUL...
...IT'S BECAUSE YOU'RE AFRAID OF US!
YOU CALL US "WEAKLINGS" AND TRY TO DIVIDE US--
--BECAUSE YOU KNOW THAT WHEN WE WORK TOGETHER, WE'RE UNSTOPPABLE!
THE KID'S GOT A POINT.
AND IT LOOKS LIKE YOUR PLAN BACKFIRED. 'CUZ NOW INSTEAD OF FOUR, YOU GOTTA FIGHT FIVE OF US!
DARN RIGHT!

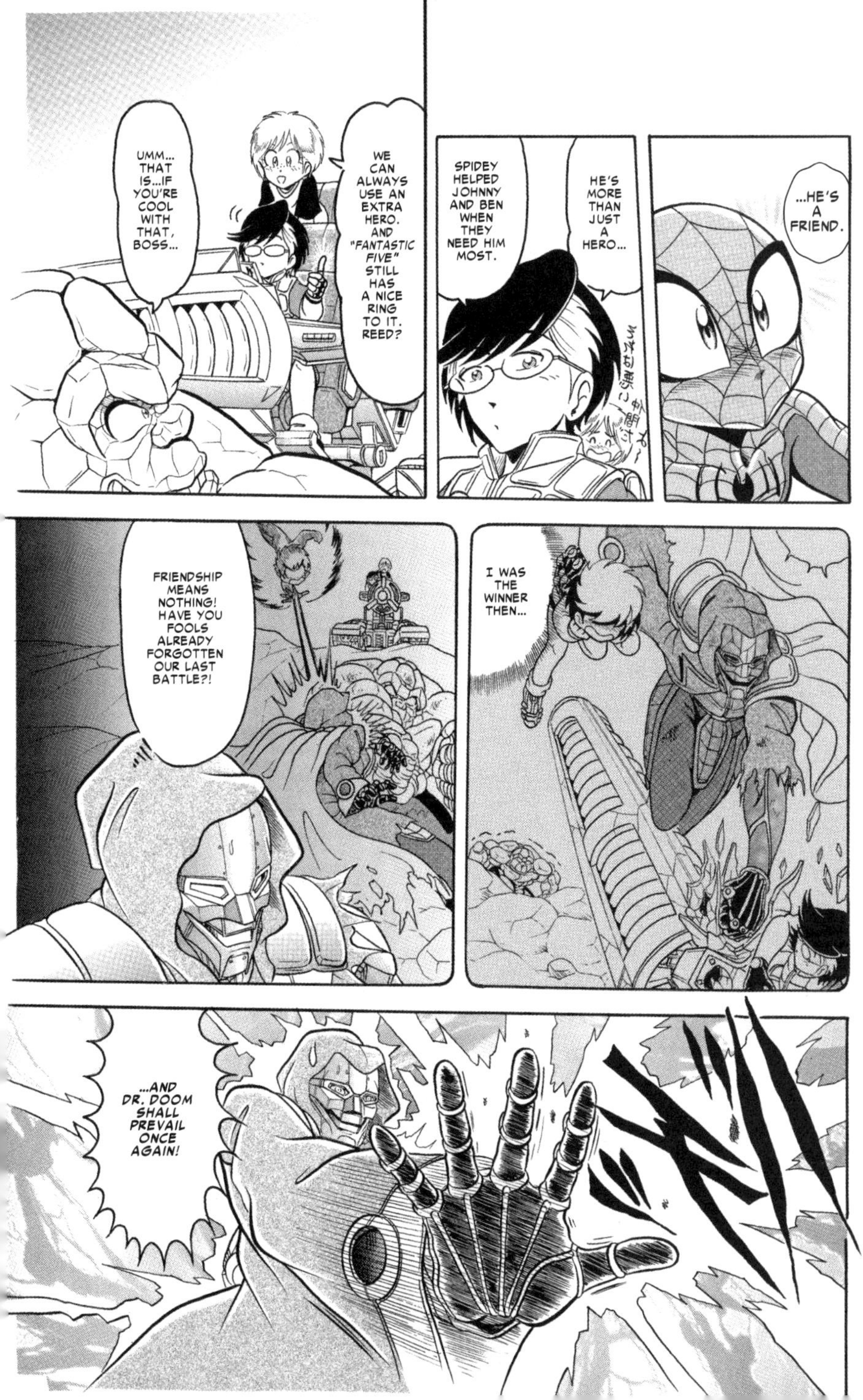
UMM... THAT IS...IF YOU'RE COOL WITH THAT, BOSS...
WE CAN ALWAYS USE AN EXTRA HERO. AND "FANTASTIC FIVE" STILL HAS A NICE RING TO IT. REED?
SPIDEY HELPED JOHNNY AND BEN WHEN THEY NEED HIM MOST.
HE'S MORE THAN JUST A HERO...
...HE'S A FRIEND.
FRIENDSHIP MEANS NOTHING! HAVE YOU FOOLS ALREADY FORGOTTEN OUR LAST BATTLE?!
I WAS THE WINNER THEN...
...AND DR. DOOM SHALL PREVAIL ONCE AGAIN!

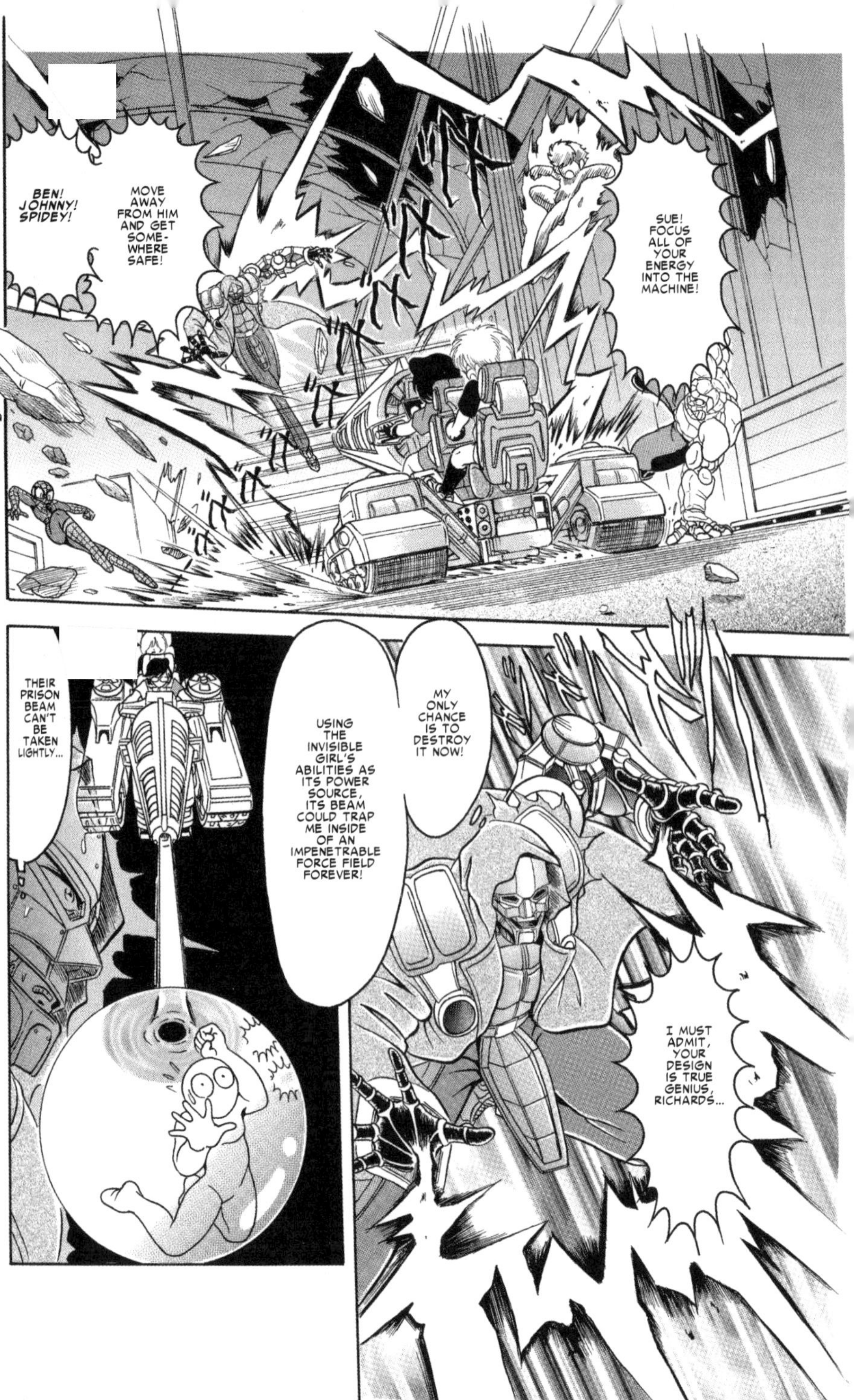
BEN! JOHNNY! SPIDEY!
MOVE AWAY FROM HIM AND GET SOME-WHERE SAFE!
SUE! FOCUS ALL OF YOUR ENERGY INTO THE MACHINE!
THEIR PRISON BEAM CAN'T BE TAKEN LIGHTLY...
USING THE INVISIBLE GIRL'S ABILITIES AS ITS POWER SOURCE, ITS BEAM COULD TRAP ME INSIDE OF AN IMPENETRABLE FORCE FIELD FOREVER!
MY ONLY CHANCE IS TO DESTROY IT NOW!
I MUST ADMIT, YOUR DESIGN IS TRUE GENIUS, RICHARDS...

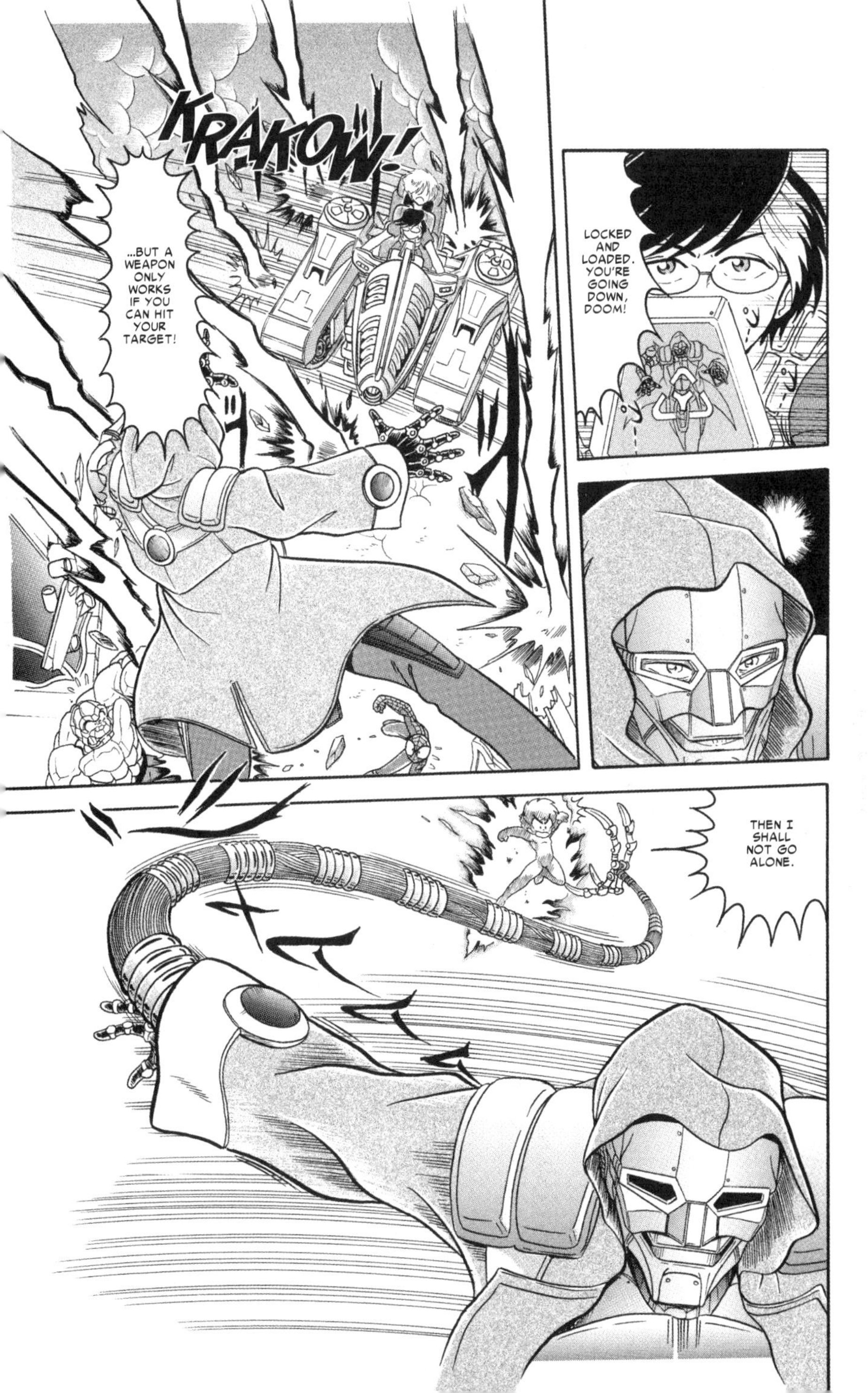
KRAKOW!
...BUT A WEAPON ONLY WORKS IF YOU CAN HIT YOUR TARGET!
LOCKED AND LOADED. YOU'RE GOING DOWN, DOOM!
THEN I SHALL NOT GO ALONE.

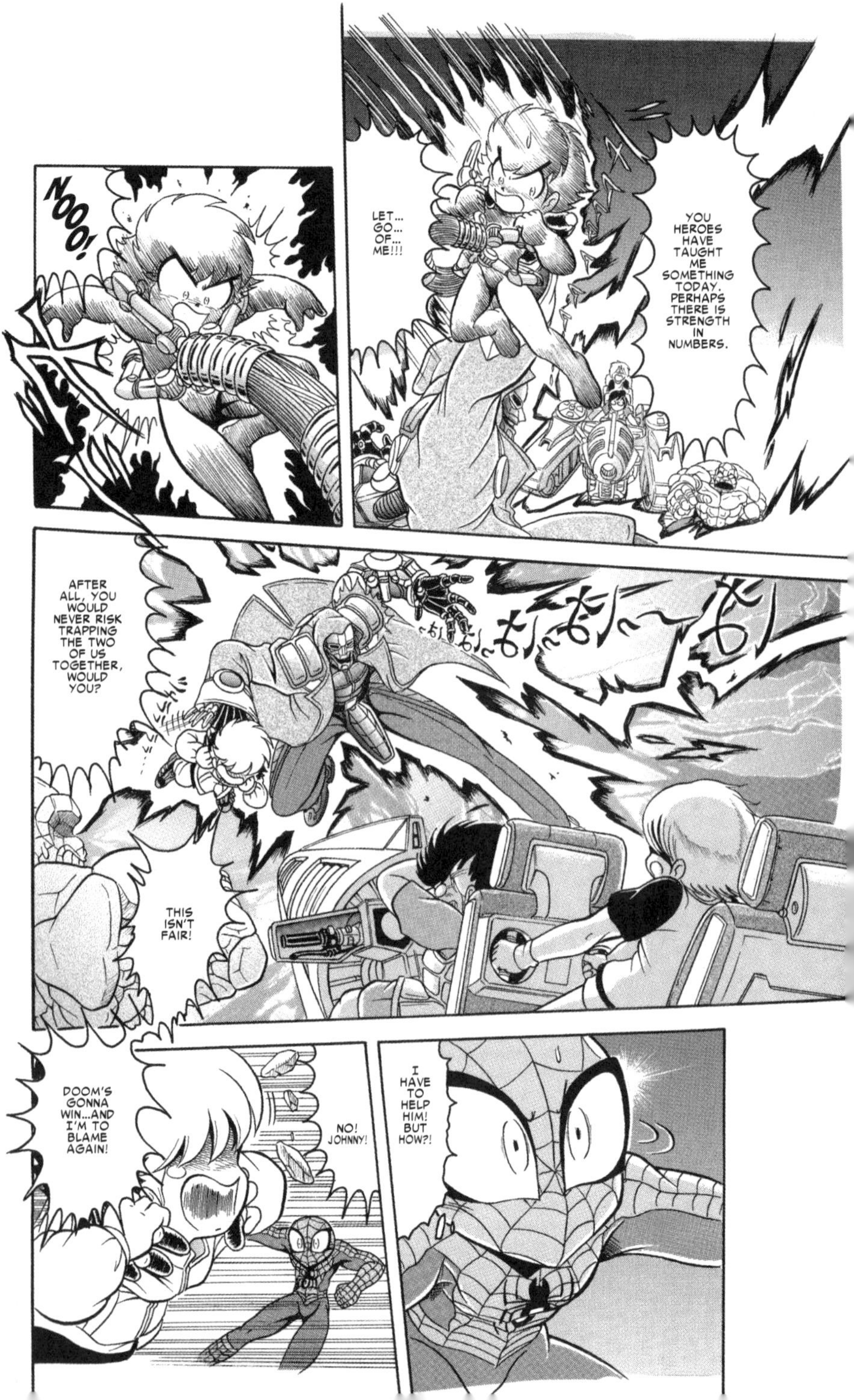
YOU HEROES HAVE TAUGHT ME SOMETHING TODAY. PERHAPS THERE IS STRENGTH IN NUMBERS.
LET... GO... OF... ME!!!
NOOO!
AFTER ALL, YOU WOULD NEVER RISK TRAPPING THE TWO OF US TOGETHER, WOULD YOU?
THIS ISN'T FAIR!
I HAVE TO HELP HIM! BUT HOW?!
NO! JOHNNY!
DOOM'S GONNA WIN...AND I'M TO BLAME AGAIN!

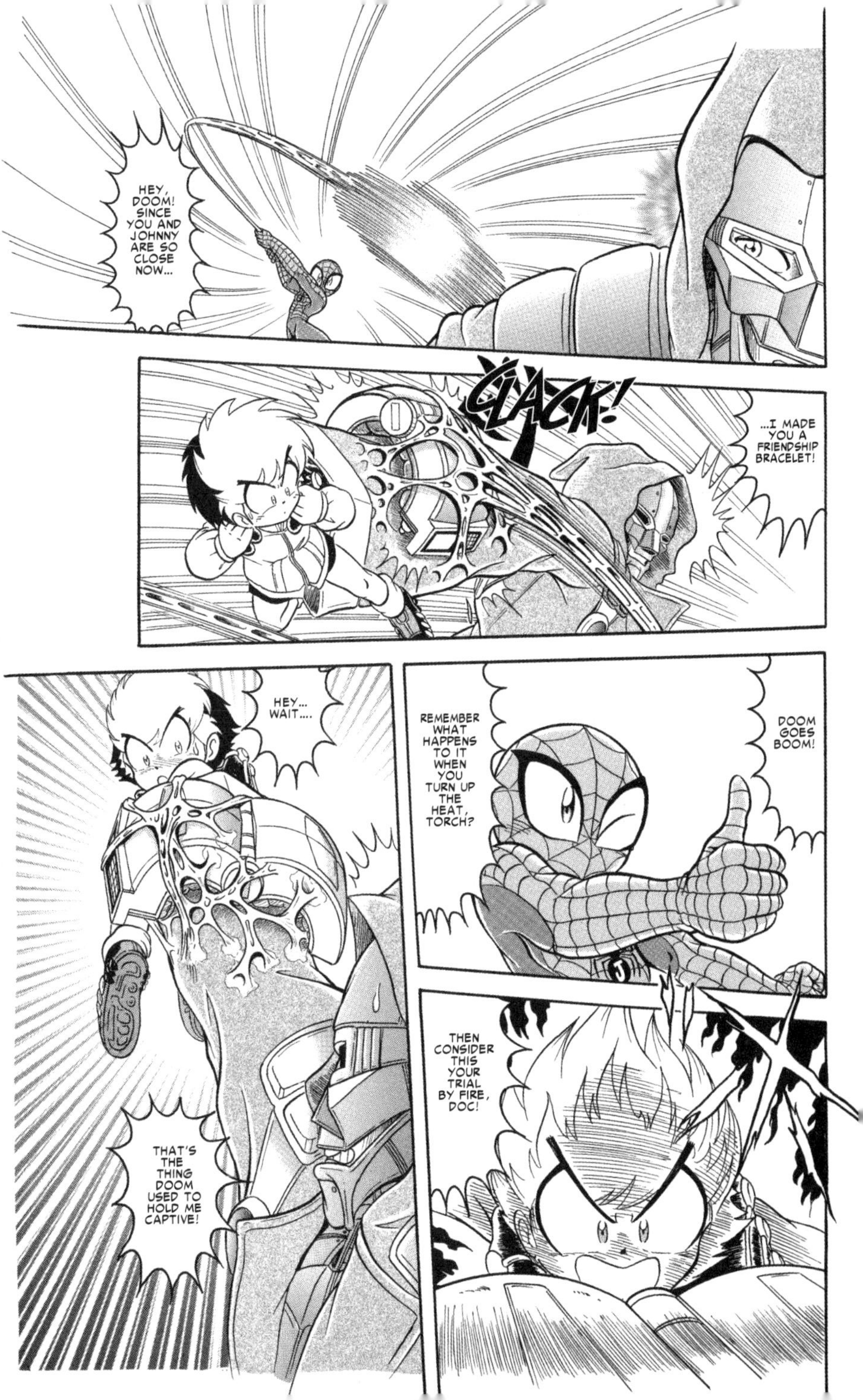
HEY, DOOM! SINCE YOU AND JOHNNY ARE SO CLOSE NOW...
CLACK!
...I MADE YOU A FRIENDSHIP BRACELET!
HEY... WAIT....
THAT'S THE THING DOOM USED TO HOLD ME CAPTIVE!
REMEMBER WHAT HAPPENS TO IT WHEN YOU TURN UP THE HEAT, TORCH?
DOOM GOES BOOM!
THEN CONSIDER THIS YOUR TRIAL BY FIRE, DOC!

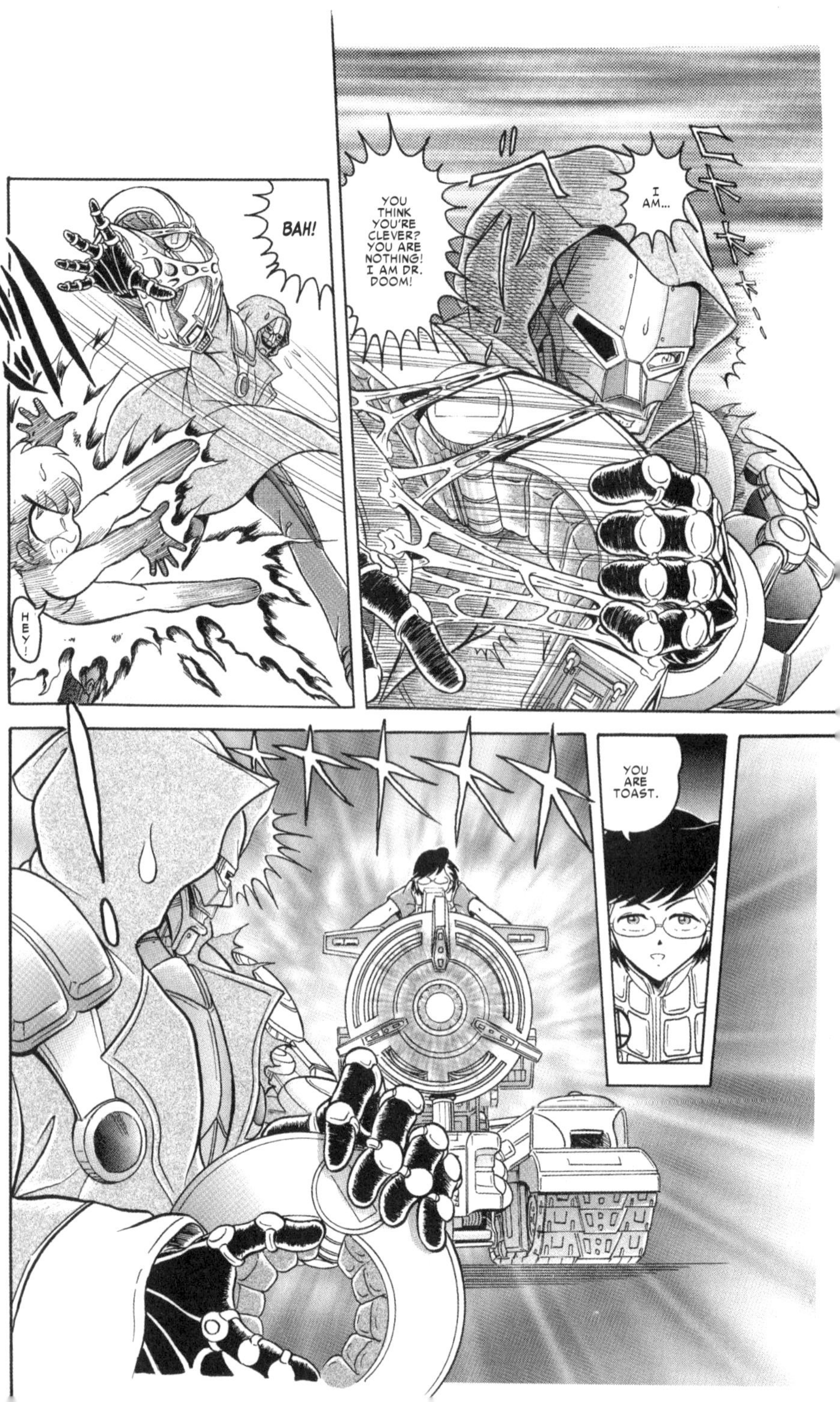
I AM...
YOU THINK YOU'RE CLEVER? YOU ARE NOTHING! I AM DR. DOOM!
BAH!
HEY!
YOU ARE TOAST.

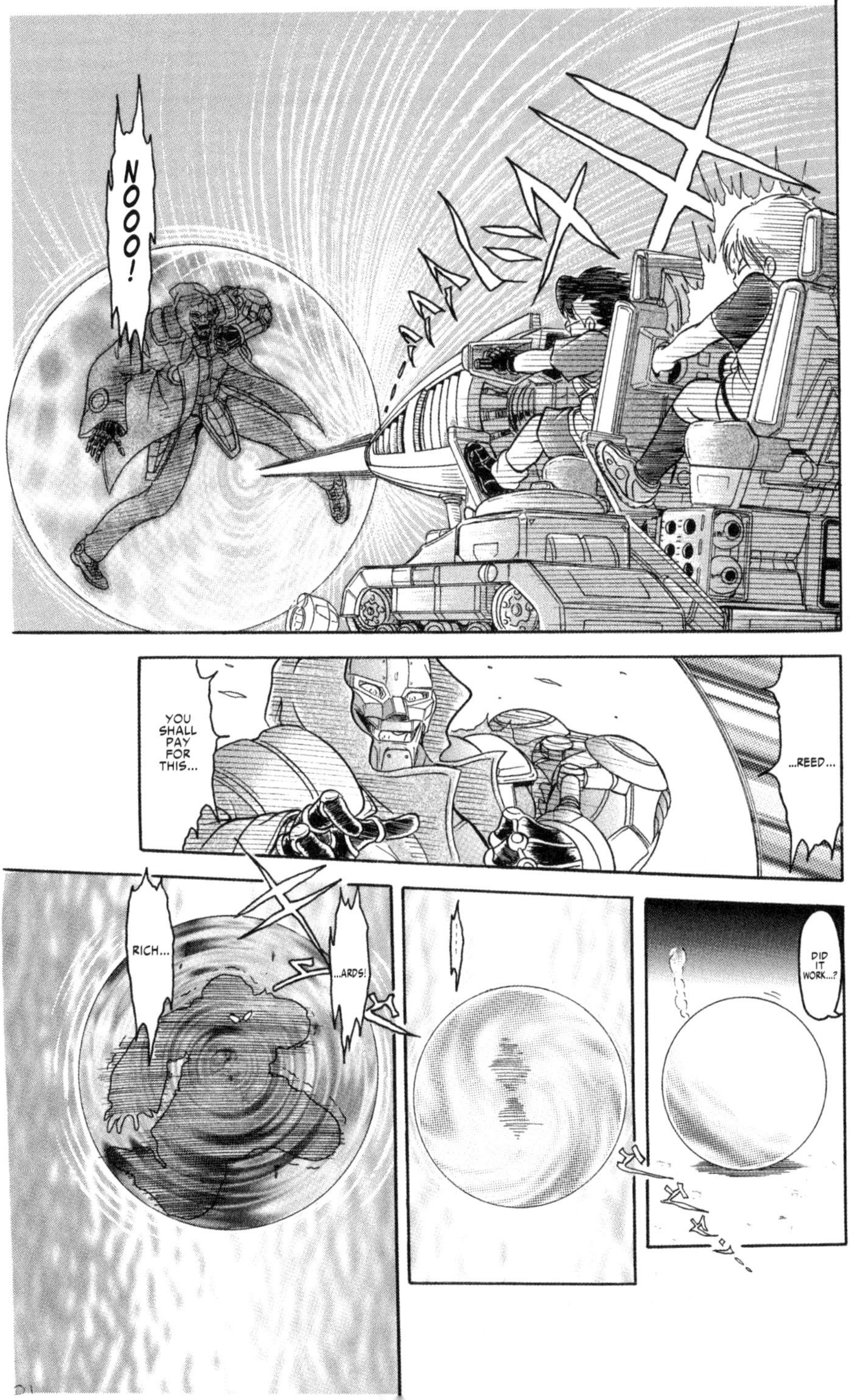
NOOOO!
YOU SHALL PAY FOR THIS...
...REED...
RICH...
...ARDS!
DID IT WORK...?

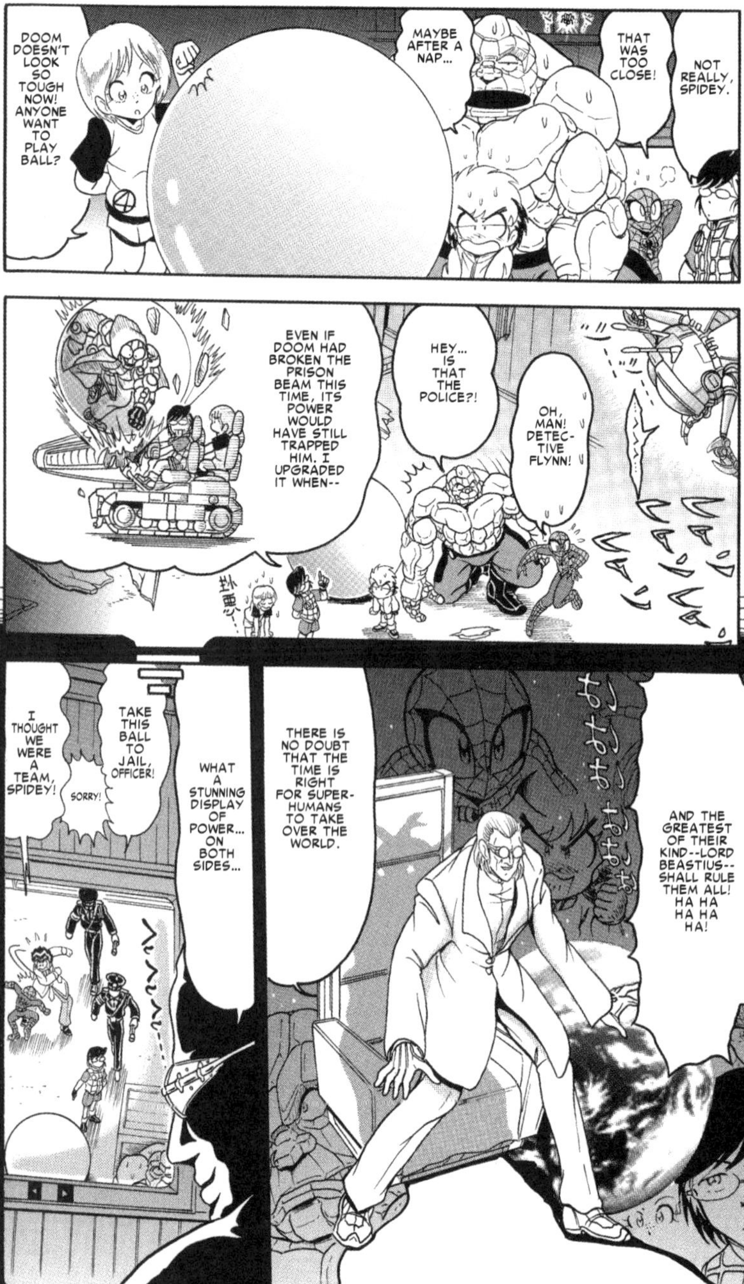

DOOM DOESN'T LOOK SO TOUGH NOW! ANYONE WANT TO PLAY BALL?
MAYBE AFTER A NAP...
THAT WAS TOO CLOSE!
NOT REALLY, SPIDEY.
EVEN IF DOOM HAD BROKEN THE PRISON BEAM THIS TIME, ITS POWER WOULD HAVE STILL TRAPPED HIM. I UPGRADED IT WHEN--
HEY... IS THAT THE POLICE?!
OH, MAN! DETECTIVE FLYNN!
I THOUGHT WE WERE A TEAM, SPIDEY!
SORRY!
TAKE THIS BALL TO JAIL, OFFICER!
WHAT A STUNNING DISPLAY OF POWER... ON BOTH SIDES...
THERE IS NO DOUBT THAT THE TIME IS RIGHT FOR SUPER-HUMANS TO TAKE OVER THE WORLD.
AND THE GREATEST OF THEIR KIND--LORD BEASTIUS--SHALL RULE THEM ALL! HA HA HA HA HA!

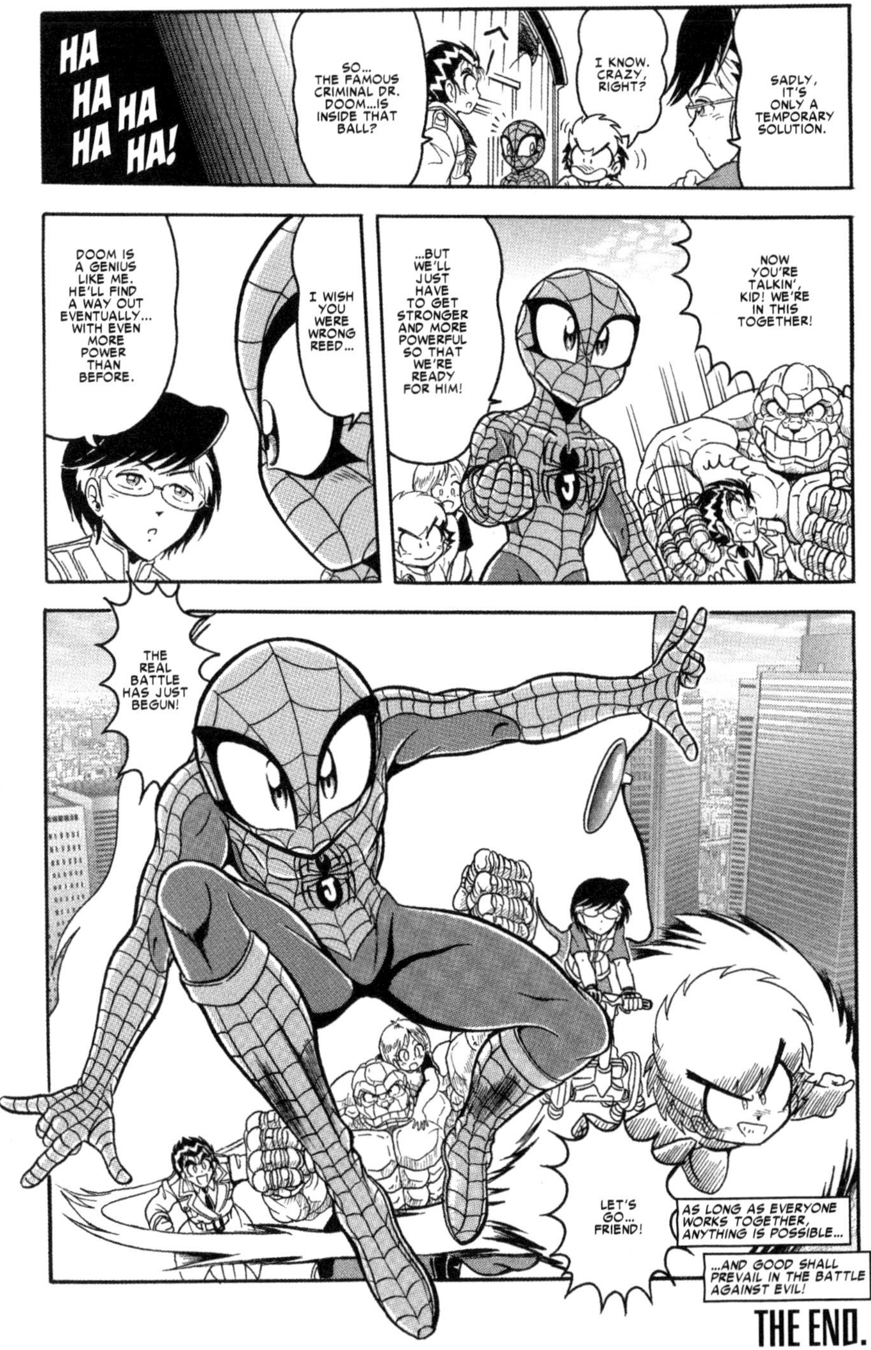
HA HA HA HA HA!
SO... THE FAMOUS CRIMINAL DR. DOOM...IS INSIDE THAT BALL?
I KNOW. CRAZY, RIGHT?
SADLY, IT'S ONLY A TEMPORARY SOLUTION.
DOOM IS A GENIUS LIKE ME. HE'LL FIND A WAY OUT EVENTUALLY... WITH EVEN MORE POWER THAN BEFORE.
I WISH YOU WERE WRONG REED...
...BUT WE'LL JUST HAVE TO GET STRONGER AND MORE POWERFUL SO THAT WE'RE READY FOR HIM!
NOW YOU'RE TALKIN', KID! WE'RE IN THIS TOGETHER!
THE REAL BATTLE HAS JUST BEGUN!
LET'S GO... FRIEND!
AS LONG AS EVERYONE WORKS TOGETHER, ANYTHING IS POSSIBLE...
...AND GOOD SHALL PREVAIL IN THE BATTLE AGAINST EVIL!
THE END.

CHAPTER 5

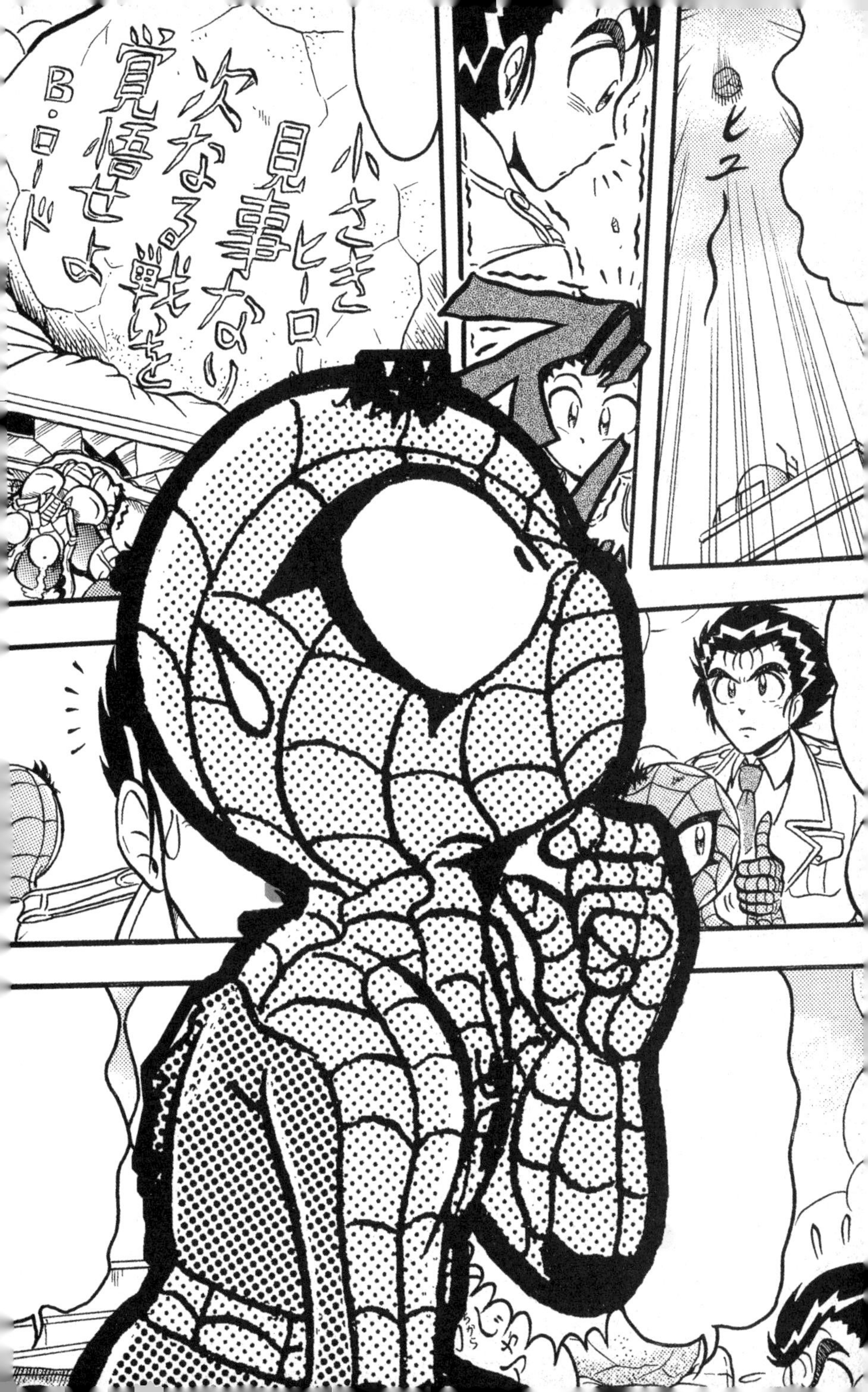
小さきヒーロー
見事なり
次なる戦いを
覚悟せよ
B・ロード
ヒュ

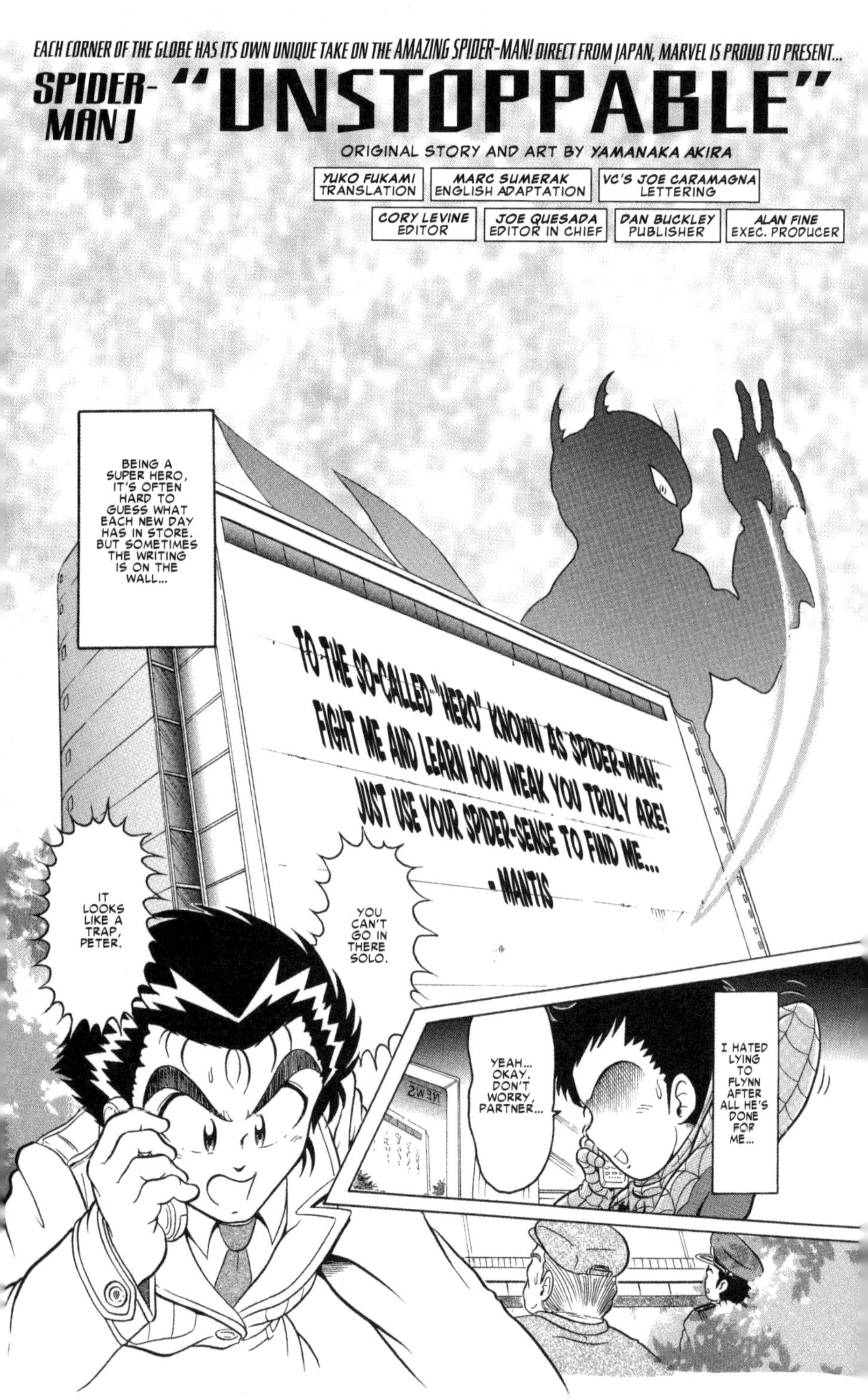
EACH CORNER OF THE GLOBE HAS ITS OWN UNIQUE TAKE ON THE AMAZING SPIDER-MAN! DIRECT FROM JAPAN, MARVEL IS PROUD TO PRESENT...
SPIDER-MAN J
"UNSTOPPABLE"
ORIGINAL STORY AND ART BY YAMANAKA AKIRA
YUKO FUKAMI TRANSLATION
MARC SUMERAK ENGLISH ADAPTATION
VC'S JOE CARAMAGNA LETTERING
CORY LEVINE EDITOR
JOE QUESADA EDITOR IN CHIEF
DAN BUCKLEY PUBLISHER
ALAN FINE EXEC. PRODUCER
BEING A SUPER HERO, IT'S OFTEN HARD TO GUESS WHAT EACH NEW DAY HAS IN STORE. BUT SOMETIMES THE WRITING IS ON THE WALL...
TO THE SO-CALLED "HERO" KNOWN AS SPIDER-MAN: FIGHT ME AND LEARN HOW WEAK YOU TRULY ARE! JUST USE YOUR SPIDER-SENSE TO FIND ME... - MANTIS
IT LOOKS LIKE A TRAP, PETER.
YOU CAN'T GO IN THERE SOLO.
YEAH... OKAY. DON'T WORRY, PARTNER...
I HATED LYING TO FLYNN AFTER ALL HE'S DONE FOR ME...

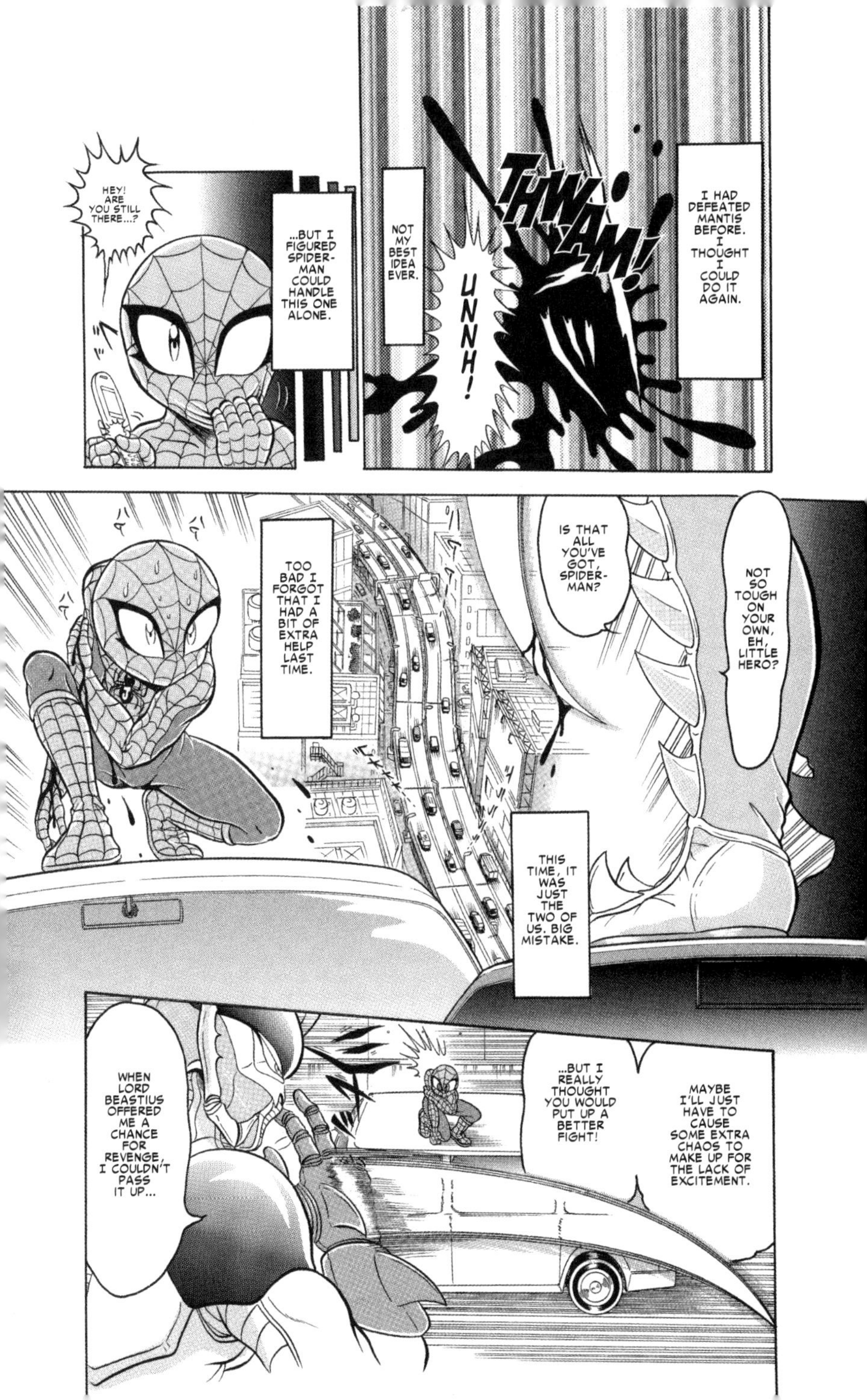
I HAD DEFEATED MANTIS BEFORE. I THOUGHT I COULD DO IT AGAIN.
THWAAM!
UNNH!
NOT MY BEST IDEA EVER.
...BUT I FIGURED SPIDER-MAN COULD HANDLE THIS ONE ALONE.
HEY! ARE YOU STILL THERE...?
NOT SO TOUGH ON YOUR OWN, EH, LITTLE HERO?
IS THAT ALL YOU'VE GOT, SPIDER-MAN?
TOO BAD I FORGOT THAT I HAD A BIT OF EXTRA HELP LAST TIME.
THIS TIME, IT WAS JUST THE TWO OF US. BIG MISTAKE.
MAYBE I'LL JUST HAVE TO CAUSE SOME EXTRA CHAOS TO MAKE UP FOR THE LACK OF EXCITEMENT.
...BUT I REALLY THOUGHT YOU WOULD PUT UP A BETTER FIGHT!
WHEN LORD BEASTIUS OFFERED ME A CHANCE FOR REVENGE, I COULDN'T PASS IT UP...

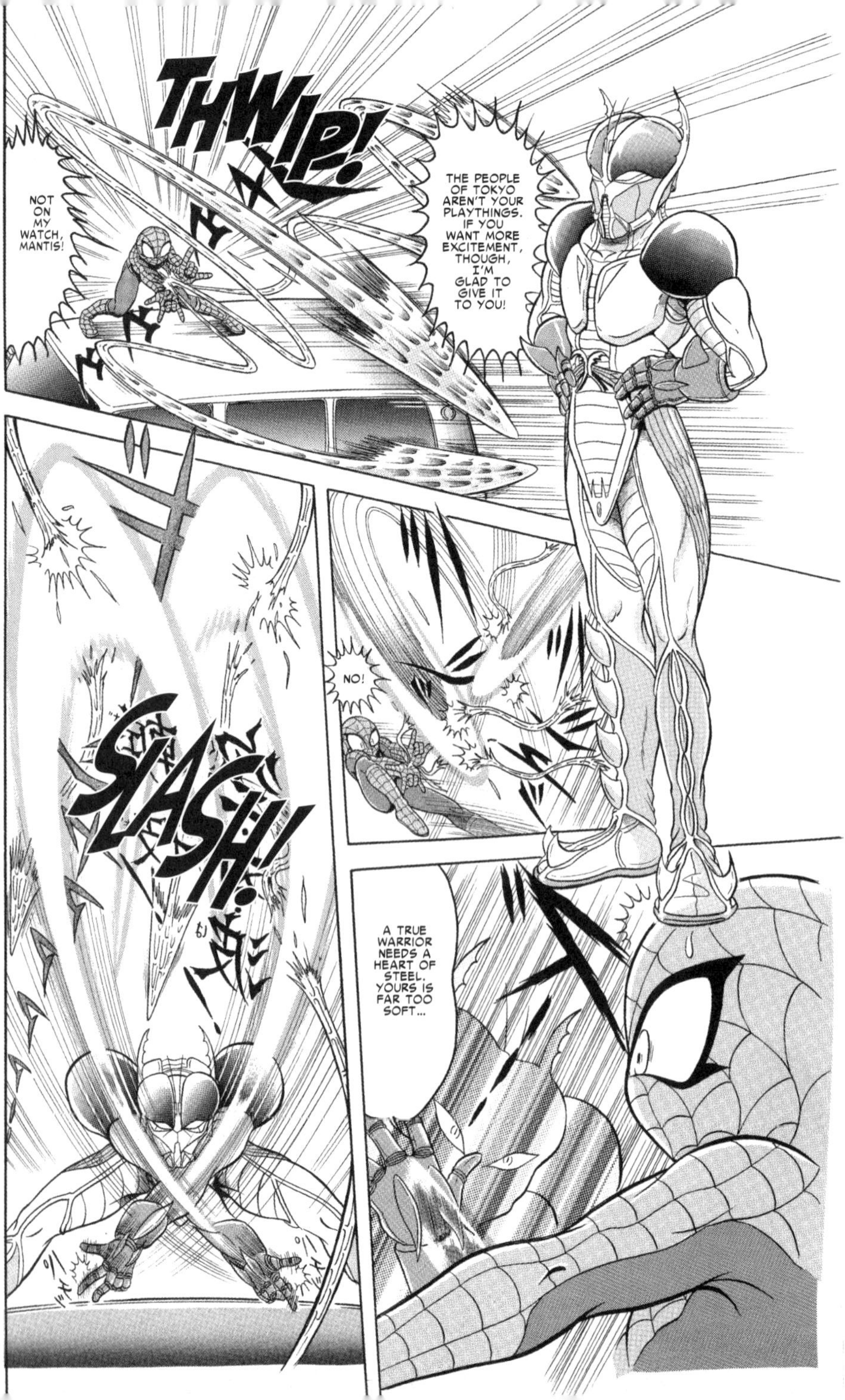
THWIP!
NOT ON MY WATCH, MANTIS!
THE PEOPLE OF TOKYO AREN'T YOUR PLAYTHINGS. IF YOU WANT MORE EXCITEMENT, THOUGH, I'M GLAD TO GIVE IT TO YOU!
SLASH!
NO!
A TRUE WARRIOR NEEDS A HEART OF STEEL. YOURS IS FAR TOO SOFT...

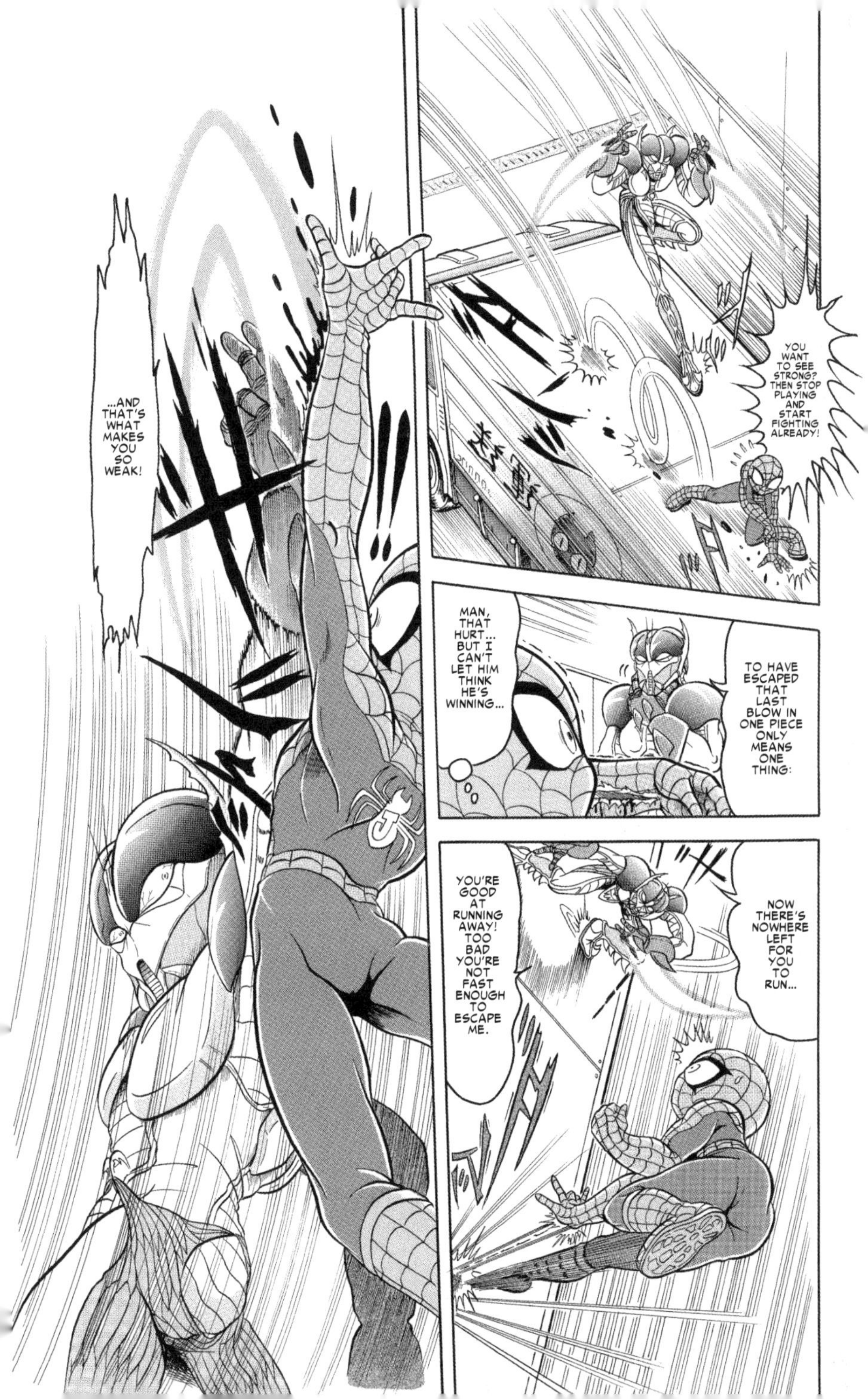

YOU WANT TO SEE STRONG? THEN STOP PLAYING AND START FIGHTING ALREADY!
TO HAVE ESCAPED THAT LAST BLOW IN ONE PIECE ONLY MEANS ONE THING:
MAN, THAT HURT... BUT I CAN'T LET HIM THINK HE'S WINNING...
NOW THERE'S NOWHERE LEFT FOR YOU TO RUN...
YOU'RE GOOD AT RUNNING AWAY! TOO BAD YOU'RE NOT FAST ENOUGH TO ESCAPE ME.
...AND THAT'S WHAT MAKES YOU SO WEAK!

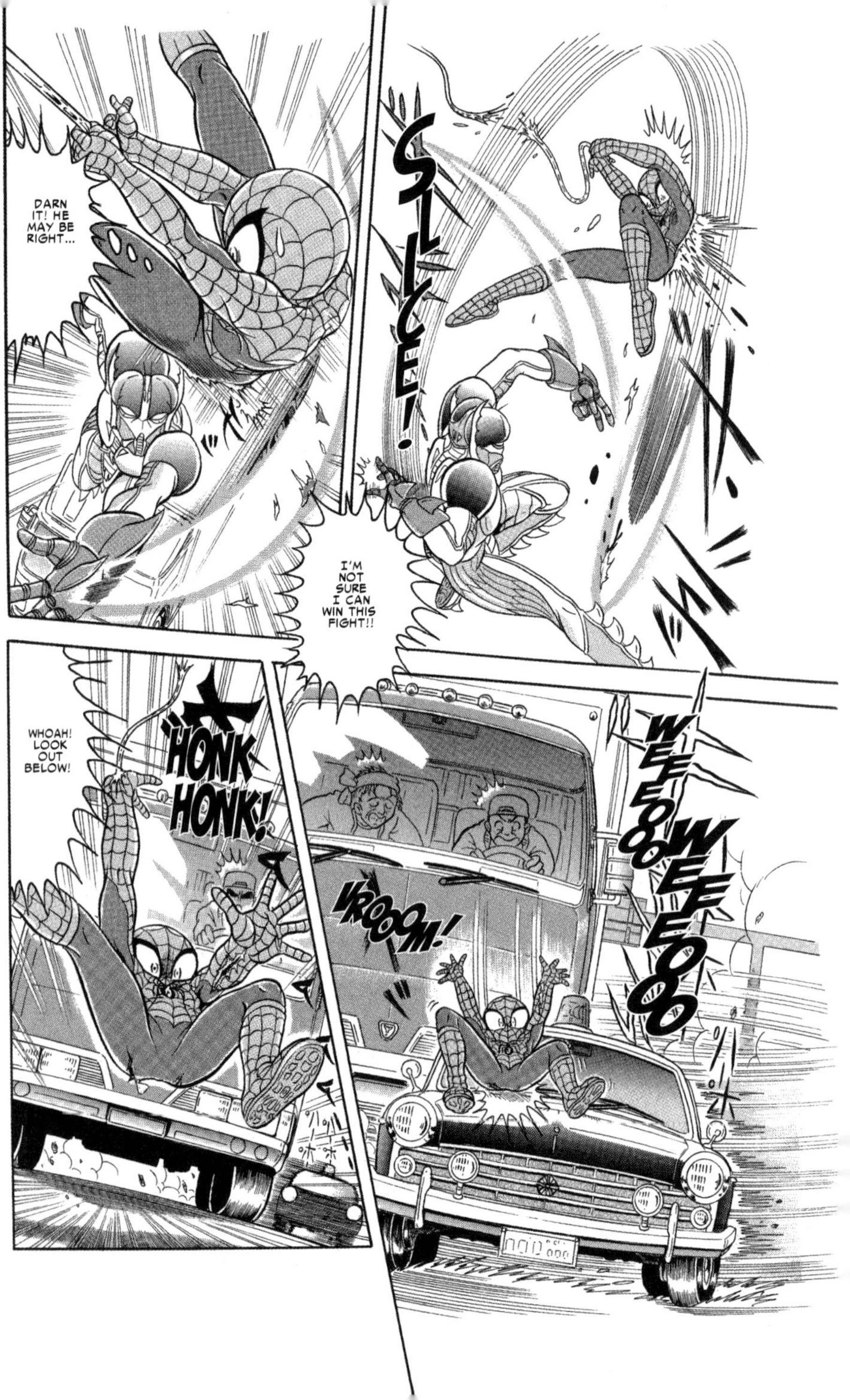
DARN IT! HE MAY BE RIGHT...
SLICE!
I'M NOT SURE I CAN WIN THIS FIGHT!!
WHOAH! LOOK OUT BELOW!
HONK HONK!
VROOOOM!
WEEEOOO
WEEEOOO

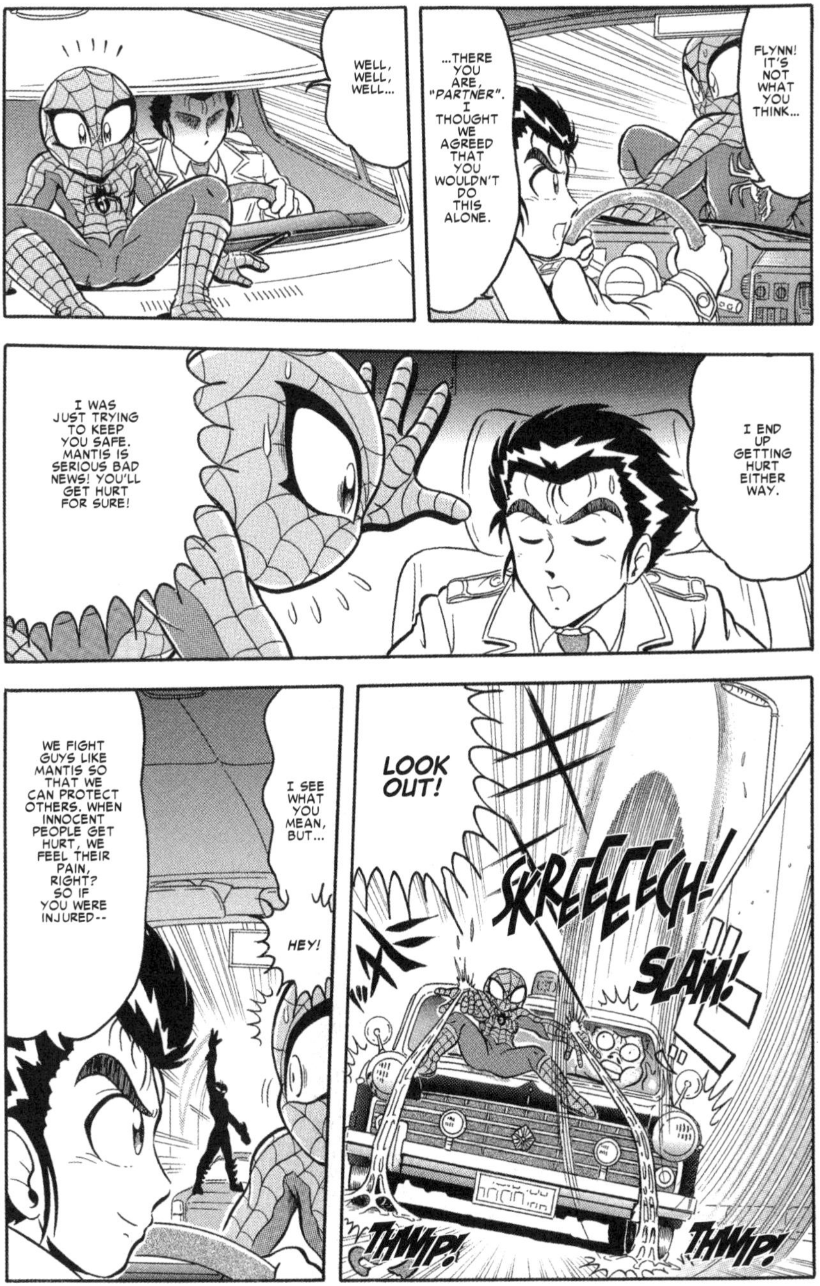

WELL, WELL, WELL...
...THERE YOU ARE, "PARTNER". I THOUGHT WE AGREED THAT YOU WOULDN'T DO THIS ALONE.
FLYNN! IT'S NOT WHAT YOU THINK...
I WAS JUST TRYING TO KEEP YOU SAFE. MANTIS IS SERIOUS BAD NEWS! YOU'LL GET HURT FOR SURE!
I END UP GETTING HURT EITHER WAY.
WE FIGHT GUYS LIKE MANTIS SO THAT WE CAN PROTECT OTHERS. WHEN INNOCENT PEOPLE GET HURT, WE FEEL THEIR PAIN, RIGHT? SO IF YOU WERE INJURED--
I SEE WHAT YOU MEAN, BUT...
HEY!
LOOK OUT!
SKREEEECH!
SLAM!
THWIP!
THWIP!

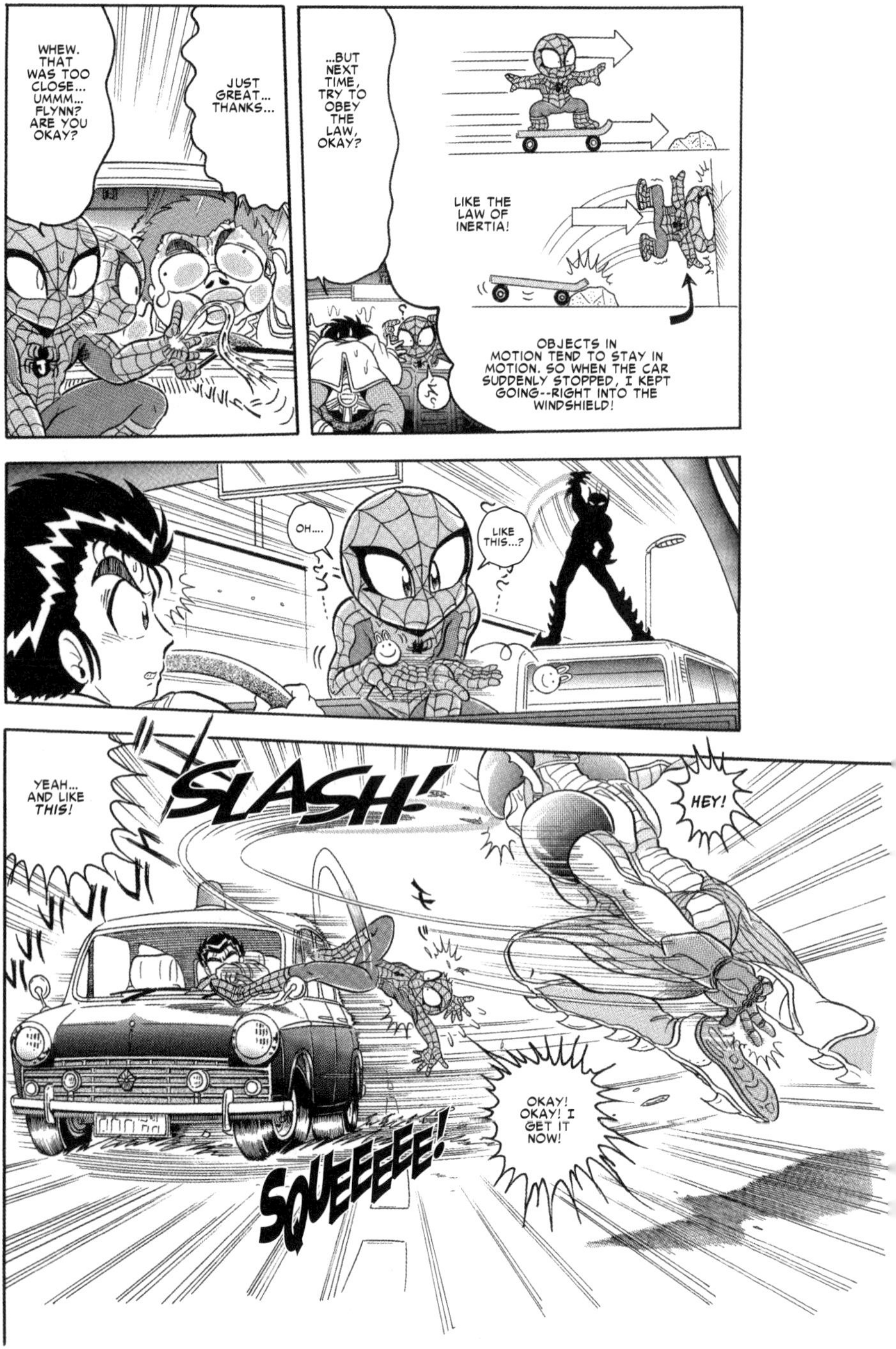
WHEW. THAT WAS TOO CLOSE... UMMM... FLYNN? ARE YOU OKAY?
JUST GREAT... THANKS...
...BUT NEXT TIME, TRY TO OBEY THE LAW, OKAY?
LIKE THE LAW OF INERTIA!
OBJECTS IN MOTION TEND TO STAY IN MOTION. SO WHEN THE CAR SUDDENLY STOPPED, I KEPT GOING--RIGHT INTO THE WINDSHIELD!
OH....
LIKE THIS...?
YEAH... AND LIKE THIS!
SLASH!
HEY!
OKAY! OKAY! I GET IT NOW!
SQUEEEEEE!

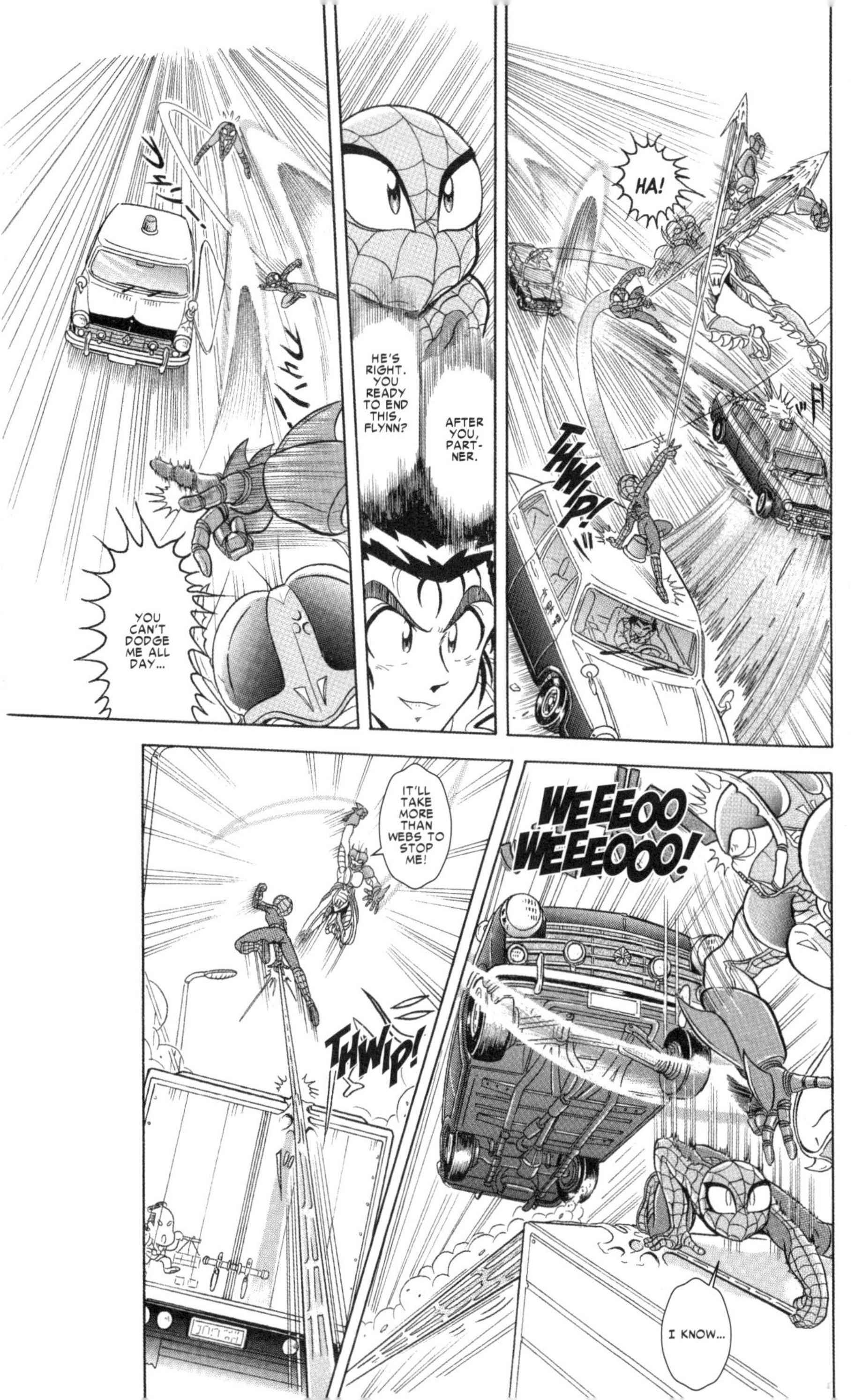

YOU CAN'T DODGE ME ALL DAY...
HE'S RIGHT. YOU READY TO END THIS, FLYNN?
AFTER YOU, PART-NER.
HA!
THWIP!
IT'LL TAKE MORE THAN WEBS TO STOP ME!
THWIP!
WEEEOO WEEEOOO!
I KNOW...

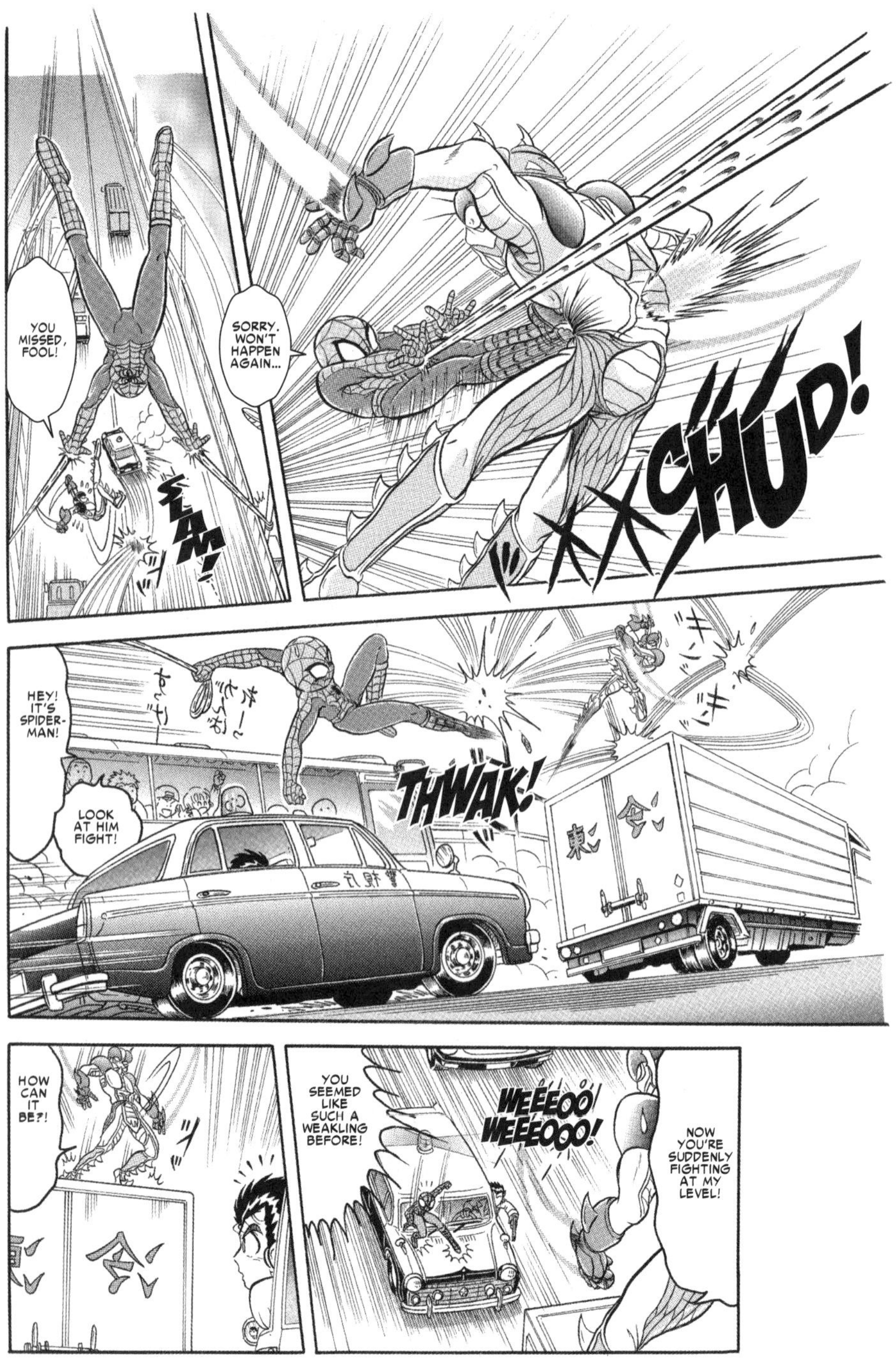
SORRY. WON'T HAPPEN AGAIN...
CHUD!
YOU MISSED, FOOL!
SLAM!
HEY! IT'S SPIDER-MAN!
LOOK AT HIM FIGHT!
THWAK!
HOW CAN IT BE?!
YOU SEEMED LIKE SUCH A WEAKLING BEFORE!
WEEEOO WEEEOOO!
NOW YOU'RE SUDDENLY FIGHTING AT MY LEVEL!

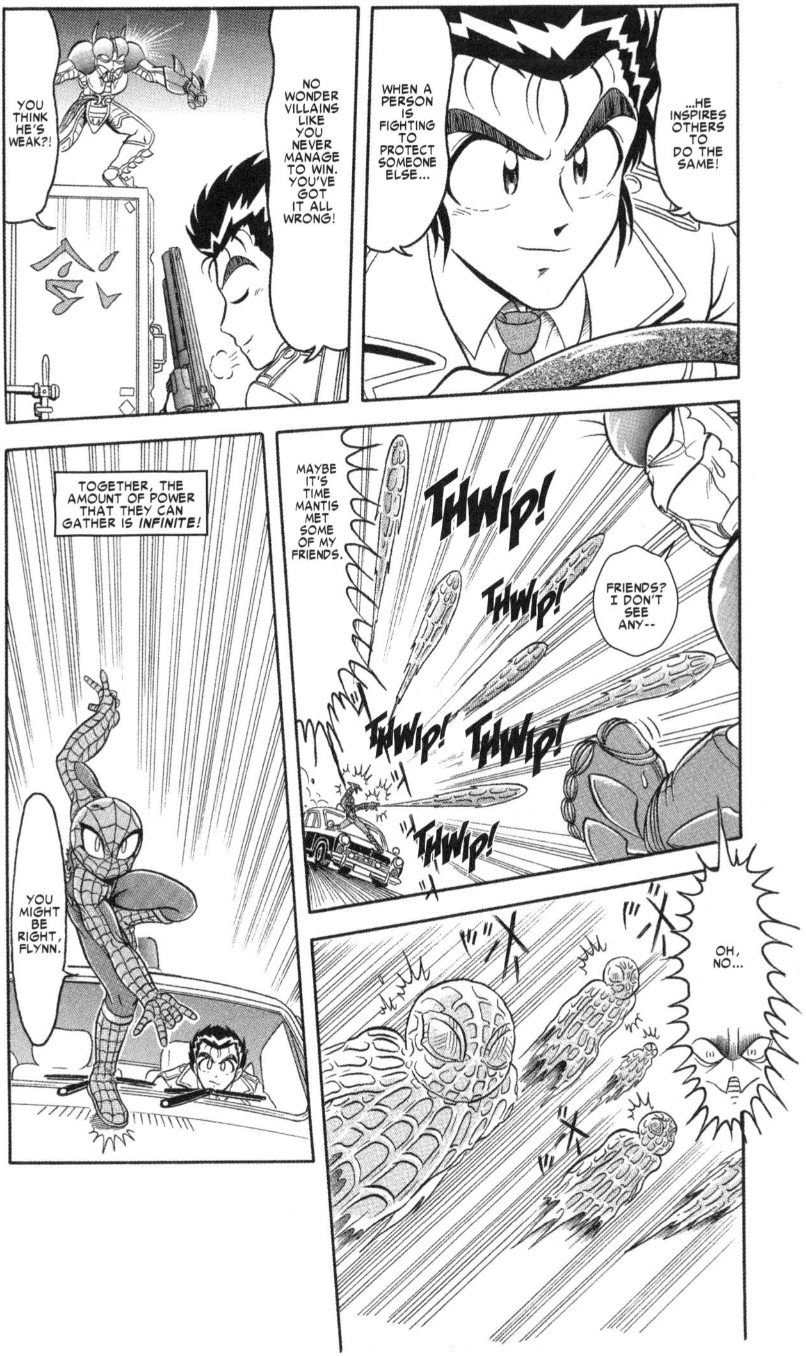
YOU THINK HE'S WEAK?!
NO WONDER VILLAINS LIKE YOU NEVER MANAGE TO WIN. YOU'VE GOT IT ALL WRONG!
WHEN A PERSON IS FIGHTING TO PROTECT SOMEONE ELSE...
...HE INSPIRES OTHERS TO DO THE SAME!
TOGETHER, THE AMOUNT OF POWER THAT THEY CAN GATHER IS *INFINITE!*
YOU MIGHT BE RIGHT, FLYNN.
MAYBE IT'S TIME MANTIS MET SOME OF MY FRIENDS.
THWIP!
THWIP!
FRIENDS? I DON'T SEE ANY--
THWIP!
THWIP!
THWIP!
OH, NO...

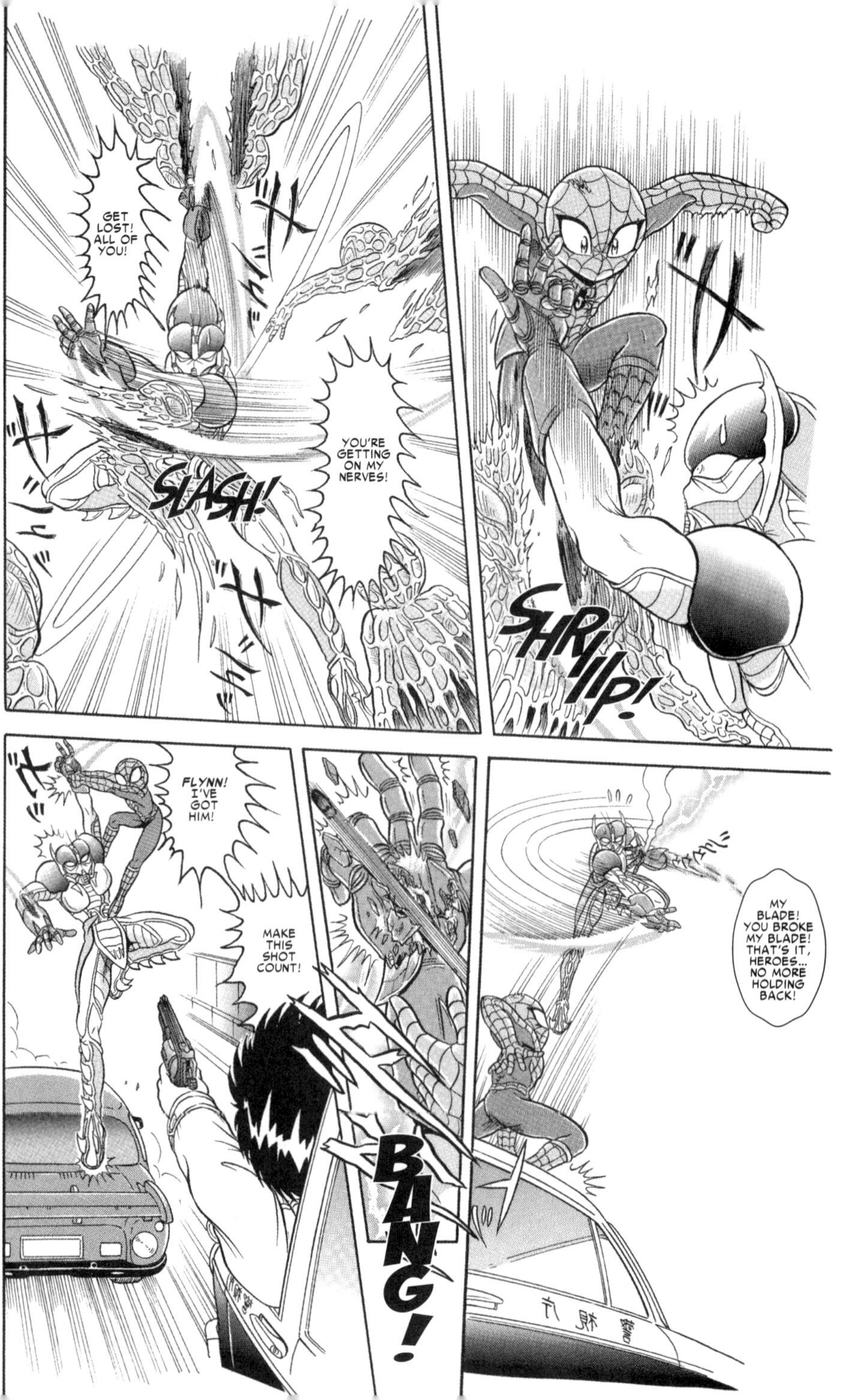
GET LOST! ALL OF YOU!
YOU'RE GETTING ON MY NERVES!
SLASH!
SHRIIIP!
FLYNN! I'VE GOT HIM!
MAKE THIS SHOT COUNT!
BANG!
MY BLADE! YOU BROKE MY BLADE! THAT'S IT, HEROES... NO MORE HOLDING BACK!

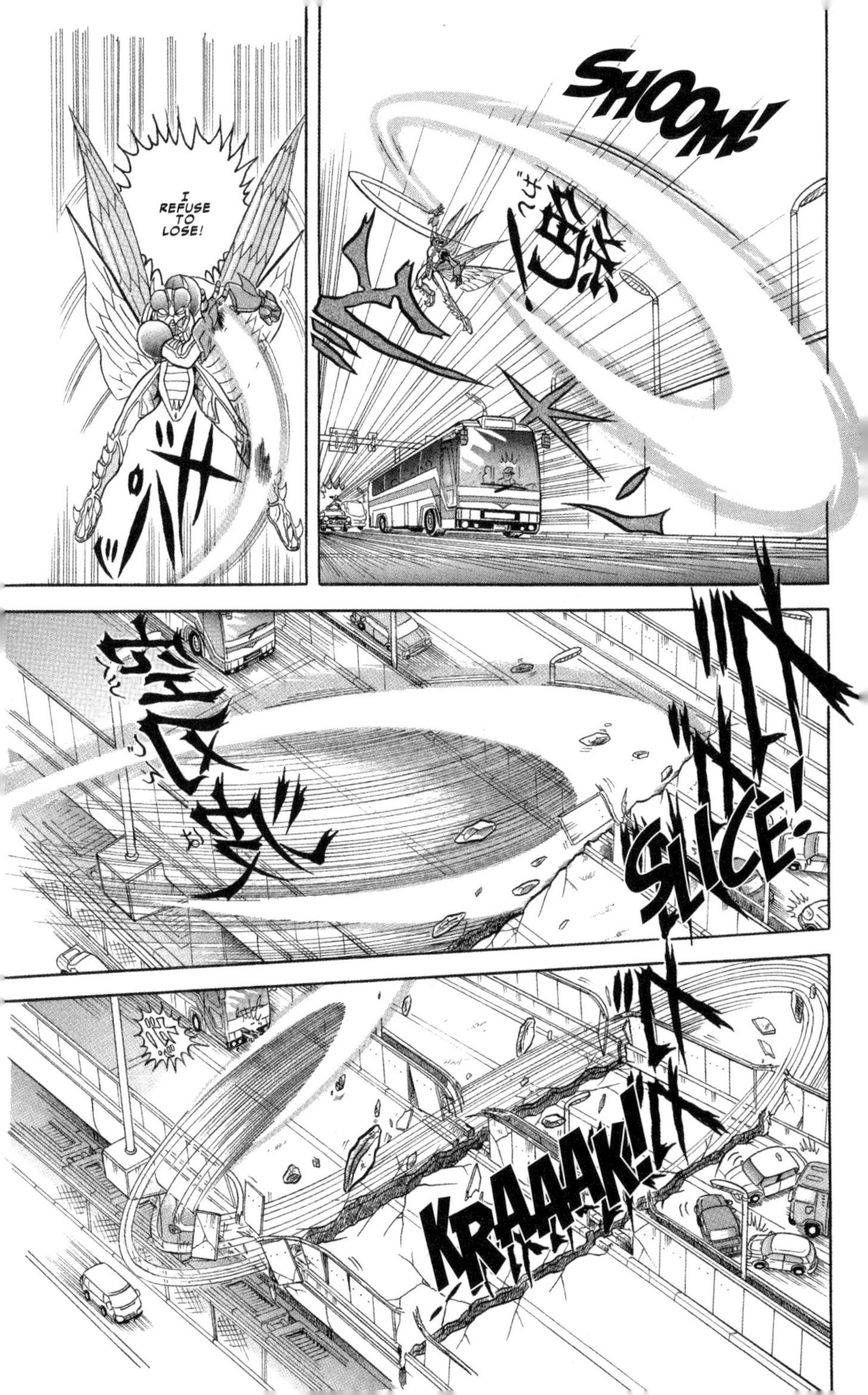
SHOOM!
I REFUSE TO LOSE!
SLICE!
KRAAAK!!

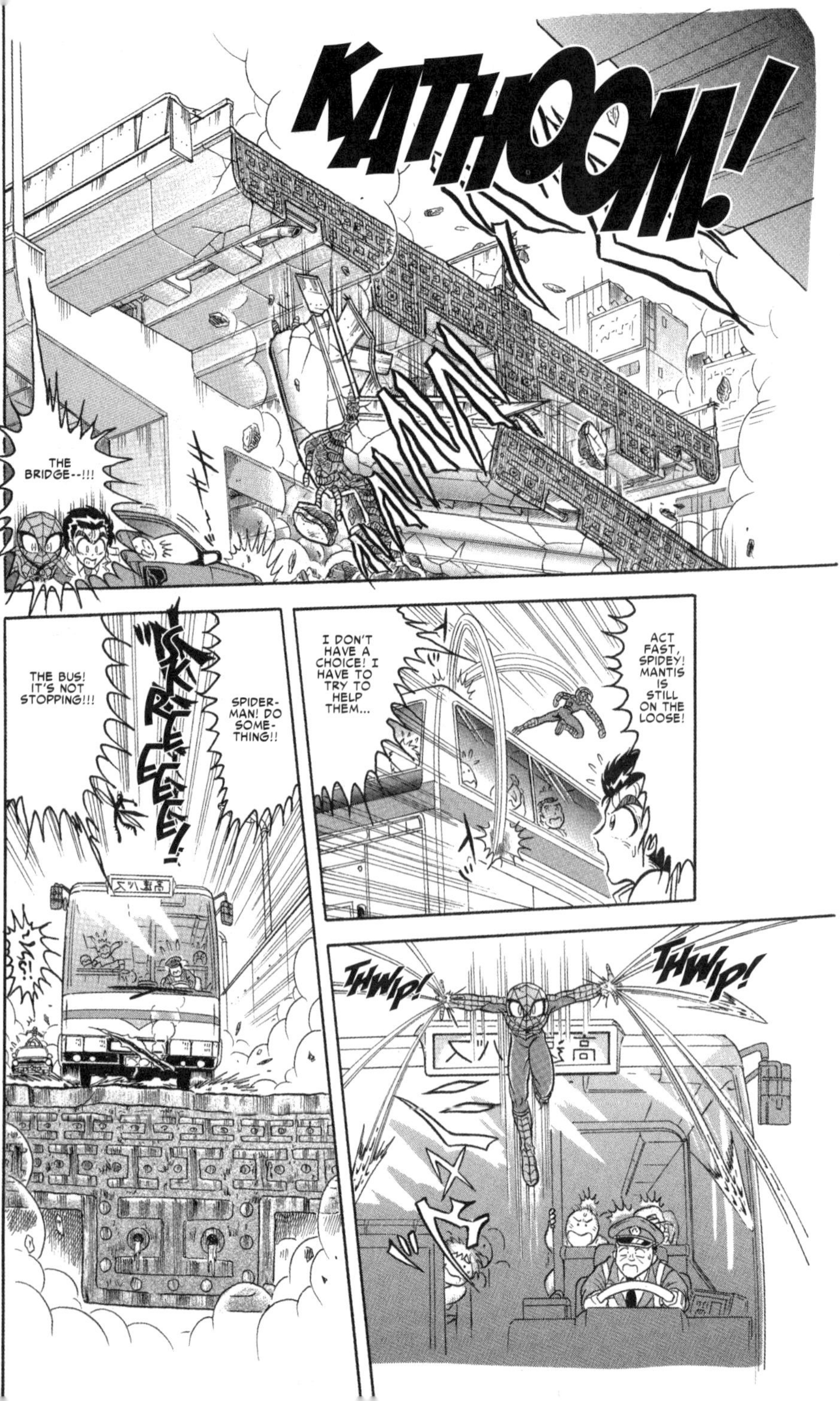
KATHOOM!
THE BRIDGE--!!!
THE BUS! IT'S NOT STOPPING!!!
SPIDER-MAN! DO SOME-THING!!
SKREEEE!!
I DON'T HAVE A CHOICE! I HAVE TO TRY TO HELP THEM...
ACT FAST, SPIDEY! MANTIS IS STILL ON THE LOOSE!
THWIP!
THWIP!

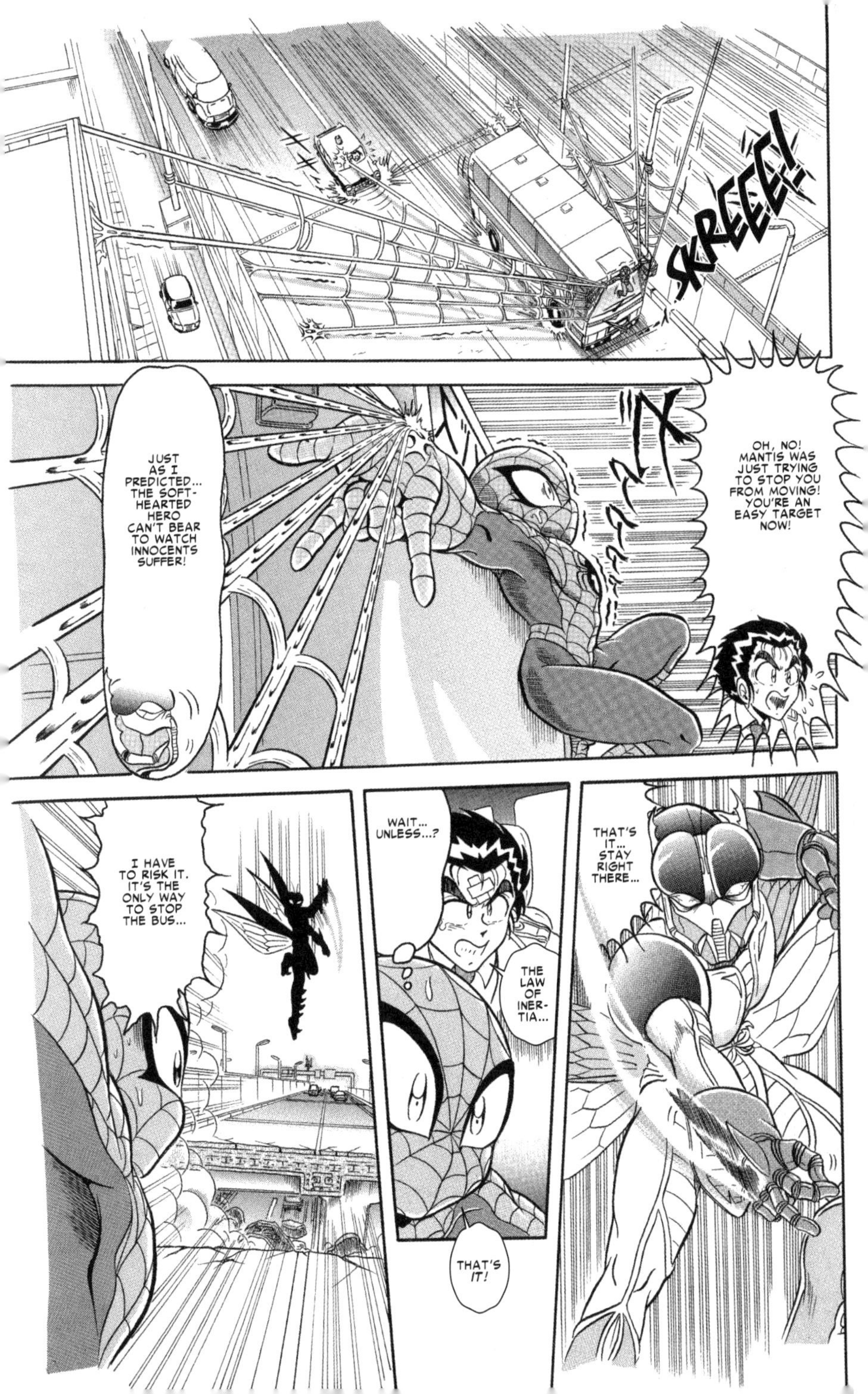
SKREEE!!
JUST AS I PREDICTED... THE SOFT-HEARTED HERO CAN'T BEAR TO WATCH INNOCENTS SUFFER!
OH, NO! MANTIS WAS JUST TRYING TO STOP YOU FROM MOVING! YOU'RE AN EASY TARGET NOW!
I HAVE TO RISK IT. IT'S THE ONLY WAY TO STOP THE BUS...
WAIT... UNLESS...?
THE LAW OF INER-TIA...
THAT'S IT!
THAT'S IT... STAY RIGHT THERE...

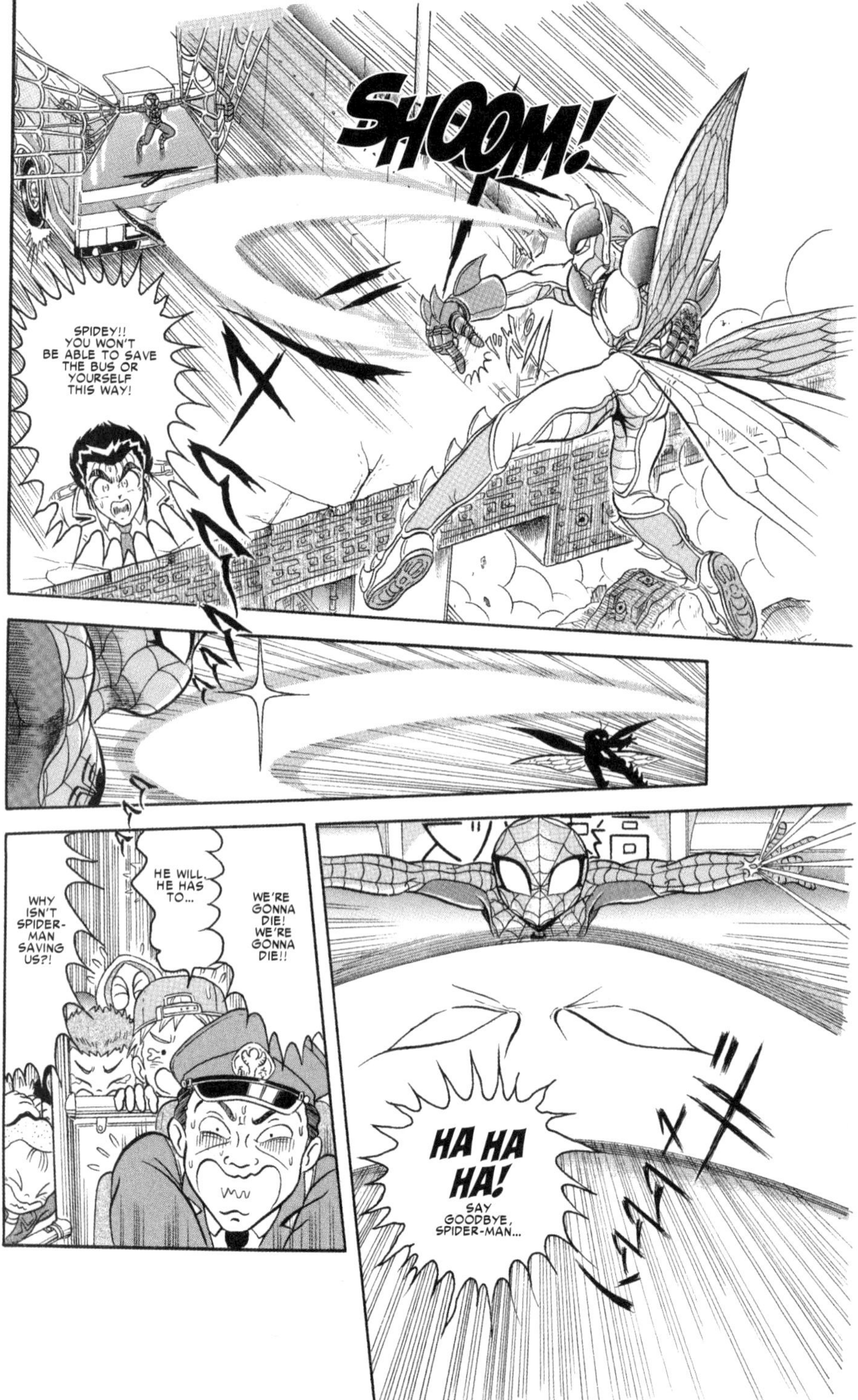
SHOOM!
SPIDEY!! YOU WON'T BE ABLE TO SAVE THE BUS OR YOURSELF THIS WAY!
WHY ISN'T SPIDER-MAN SAVING US?!
HE WILL. HE HAS TO...
WE'RE GONNA DIE! WE'RE GONNA DIE!!
HA HA HA!
SAY GOODBYE, SPIDER-MAN...

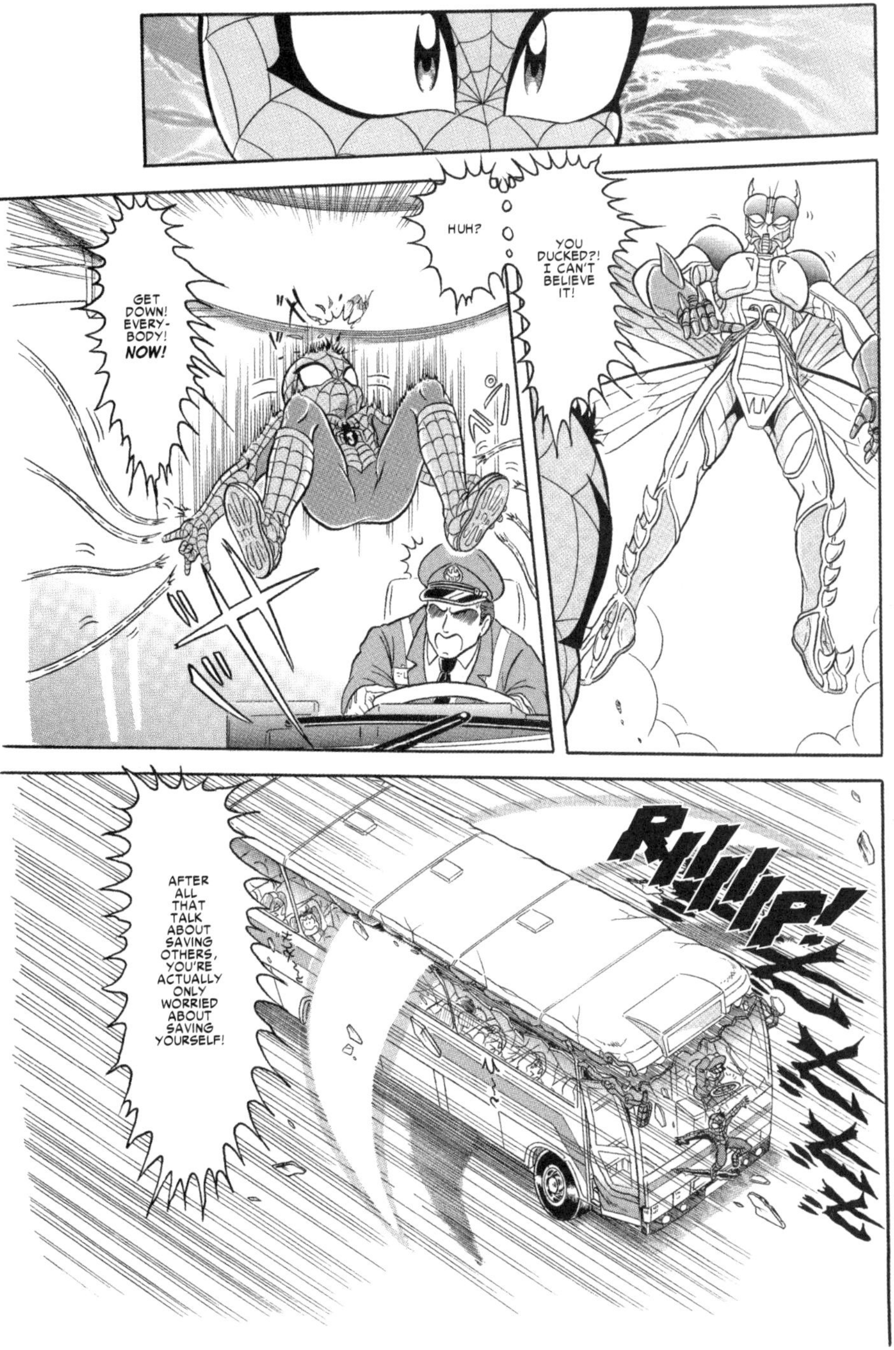

YOU DUCKED?! I CAN'T BELIEVE IT!
HUH?
GET DOWN! EVERYBODY! **NOW!**
AFTER ALL THAT TALK ABOUT SAVING OTHERS, YOU'RE ACTUALLY ONLY WORRIED ABOUT SAVING YOURSELF!
RIIIIP!

YOU JUST PUT EVERY-ONE ON THAT BUS IN DANGER TO PROTECT YOUR OWN LIFE!

RIIIIP!

MAYBE YOU'RE STRONGER THAN I THOUGHT, KID...

I AM STRONG. I'M A HERO!

I'LL SAVE MY-SELF...

THWIP!

...AND SAVE THE OTHERS!

THWIP!

BUT FIRST, IT'S TIME FOR THIS BUS TO MAKE ONE FINAL-- AND VERY SUDDEN-- STOP!

SKREEEE!

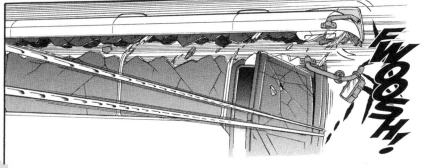

FWOOSH!

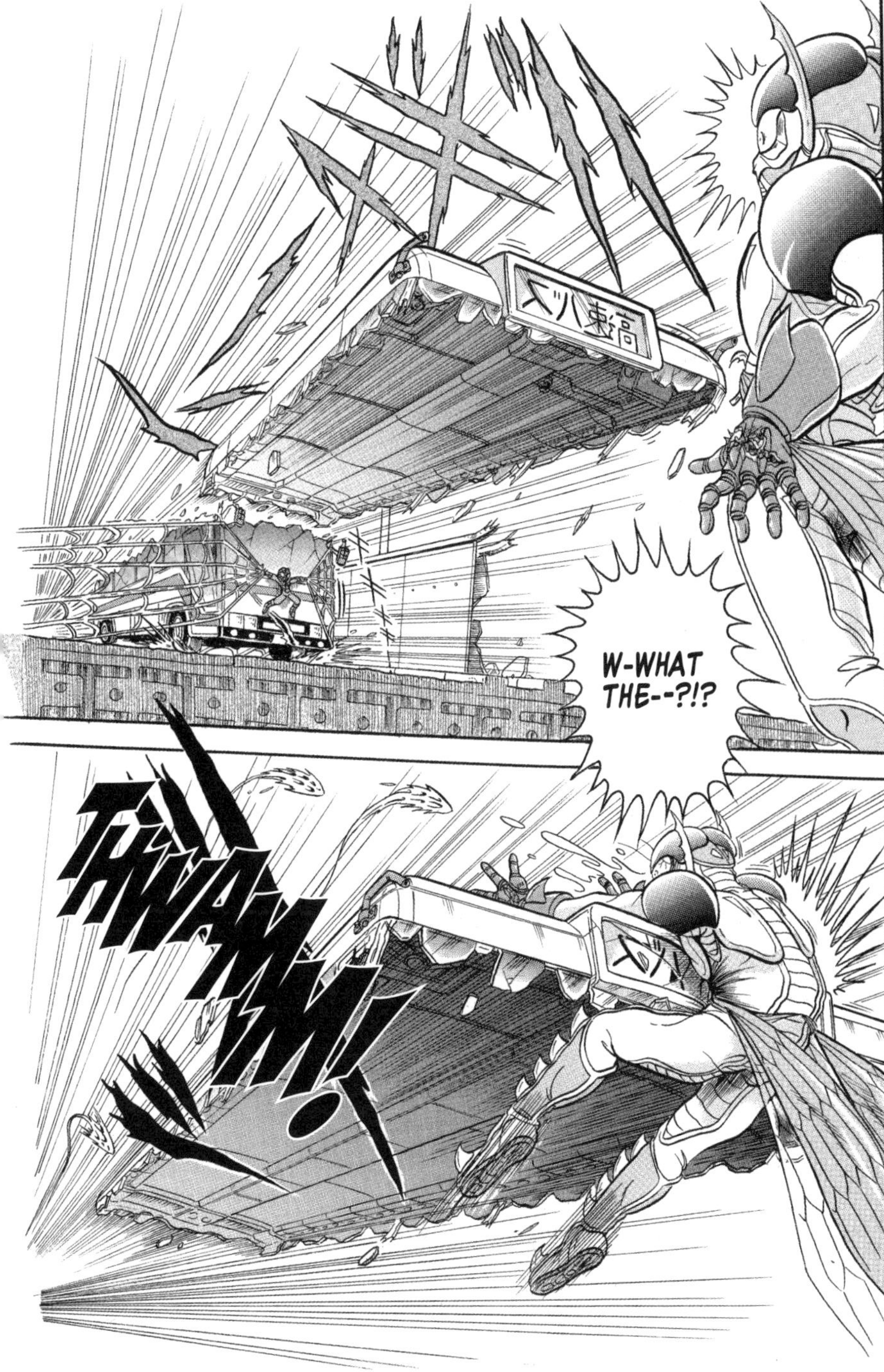
W-WHAT THE--?!?
THWAMM!

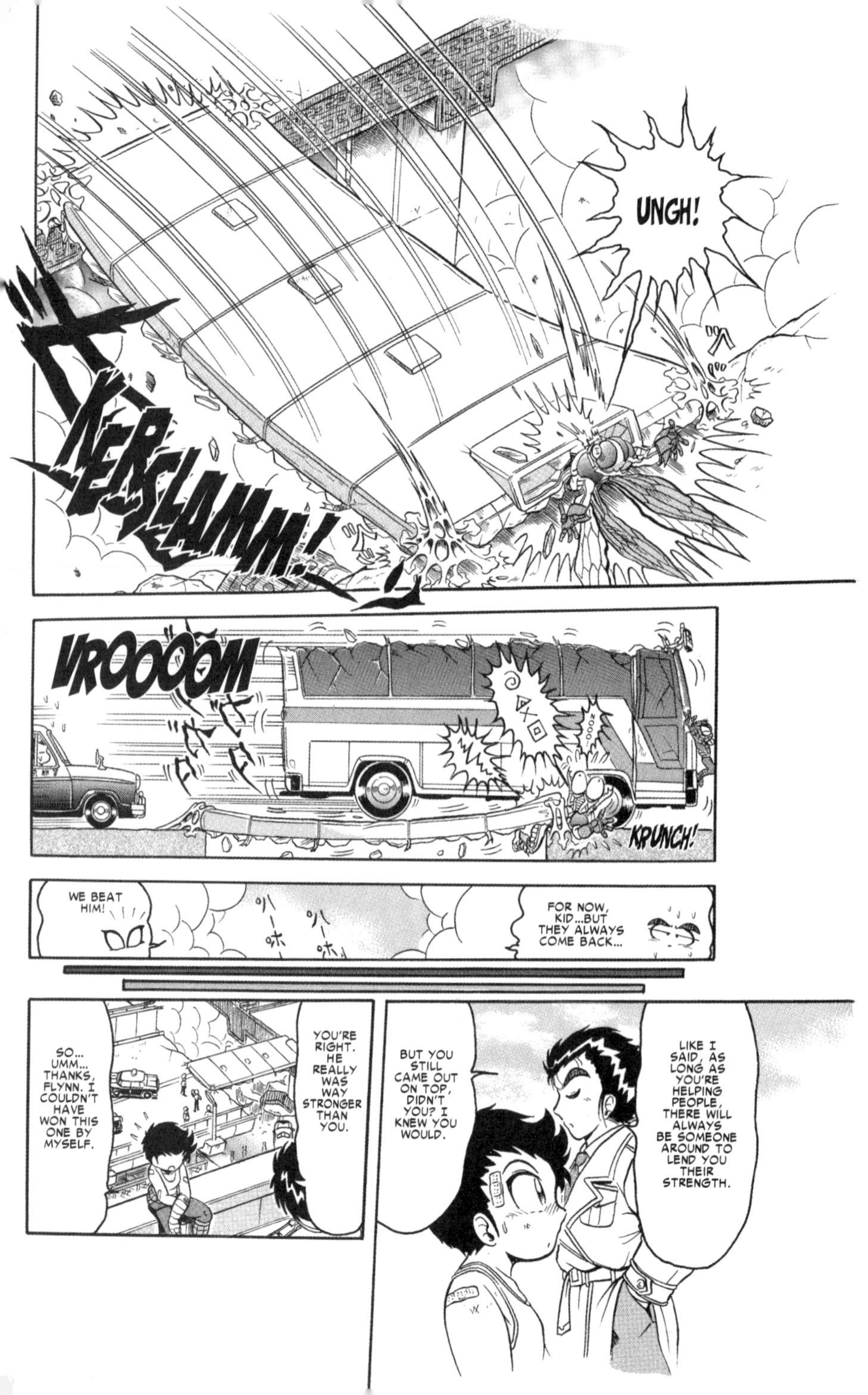
KERSLAMMM!
UNGH!
VROOOOM
KRUNCH!
WE BEAT HIM!
FOR NOW, KID...BUT THEY ALWAYS COME BACK...
SO... UMM... THANKS, FLYNN. I COULDN'T HAVE WON THIS ONE BY MYSELF.
YOU'RE RIGHT. HE REALLY WAS WAY STRONGER THAN YOU.
BUT YOU STILL CAME OUT ON TOP, DIDN'T YOU? I KNEW YOU WOULD.
LIKE I SAID, AS LONG AS YOU'RE HELPING PEOPLE, THERE WILL ALWAYS BE SOMEONE AROUND TO LEND YOU THEIR STRENGTH.

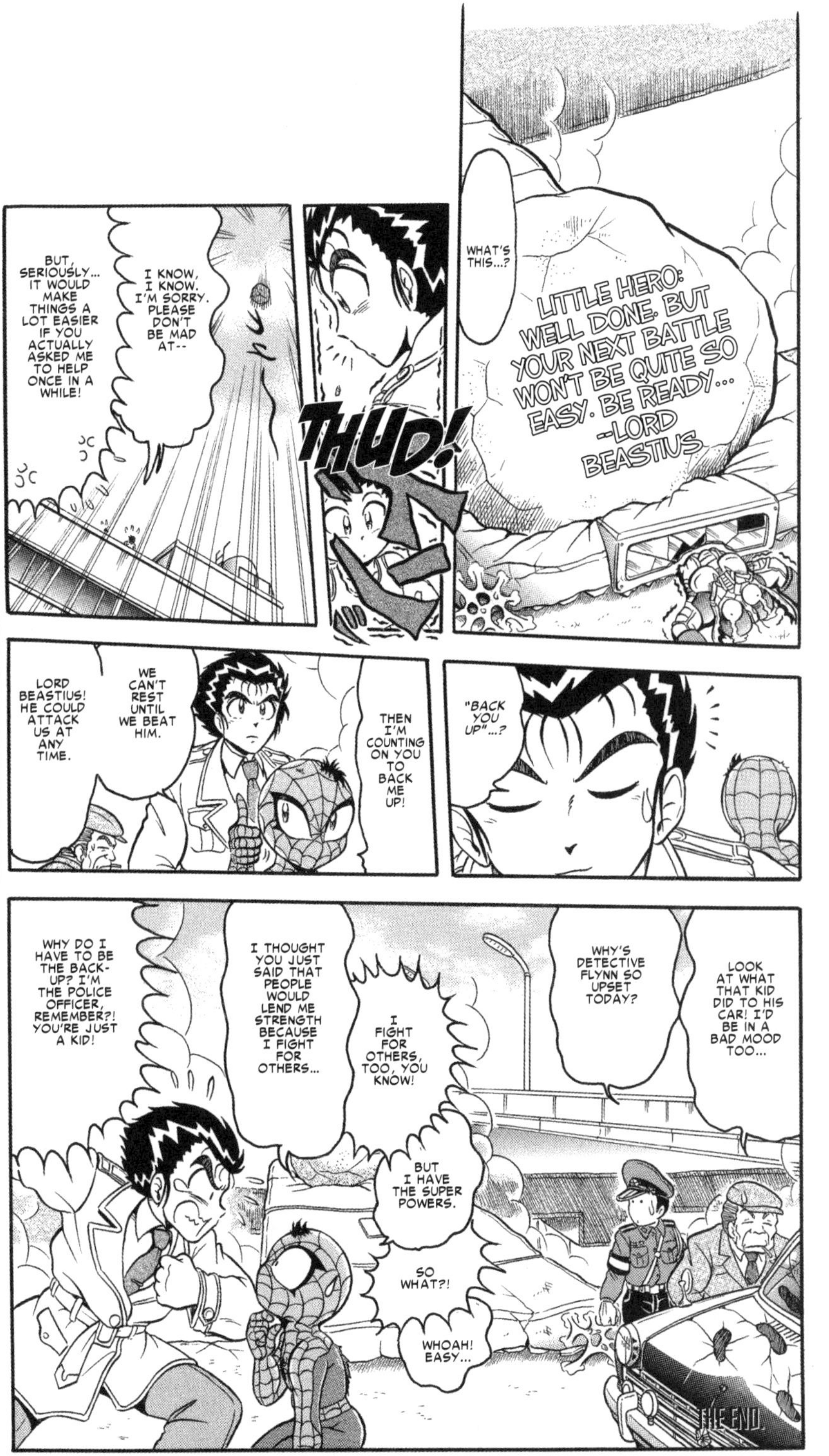
BUT, SERIOUSLY... IT WOULD MAKE THINGS A LOT EASIER IF YOU ACTUALLY ASKED ME TO HELP ONCE IN A WHILE!
I KNOW, I KNOW. I'M SORRY. PLEASE DON'T BE MAD AT--
THUD!
WHAT'S THIS...?
LITTLE HERO: WELL DONE. BUT YOUR NEXT BATTLE WON'T BE QUITE SO EASY. BE READY... --LORD BEASTIUS
LORD BEASTIUS! HE COULD ATTACK US AT ANY TIME.
WE CAN'T REST UNTIL WE BEAT HIM.
THEN I'M COUNTING ON YOU TO BACK ME UP!
"BACK YOU UP"...?
WHY DO I HAVE TO BE THE BACK-UP? I'M THE POLICE OFFICER, REMEMBER?! YOU'RE JUST A KID!
I THOUGHT YOU JUST SAID THAT PEOPLE WOULD LEND ME STRENGTH BECAUSE I FIGHT FOR OTHERS...
I FIGHT FOR OTHERS, TOO, YOU KNOW!
BUT I HAVE THE SUPER POWERS.
SO WHAT?!
WHOAH! EASY...
WHY'S DETECTIVE FLYNN SO UPSET TODAY?
LOOK AT WHAT THAT KID DID TO HIS CAR! I'D BE IN A BAD MOOD TOO...
THE END.

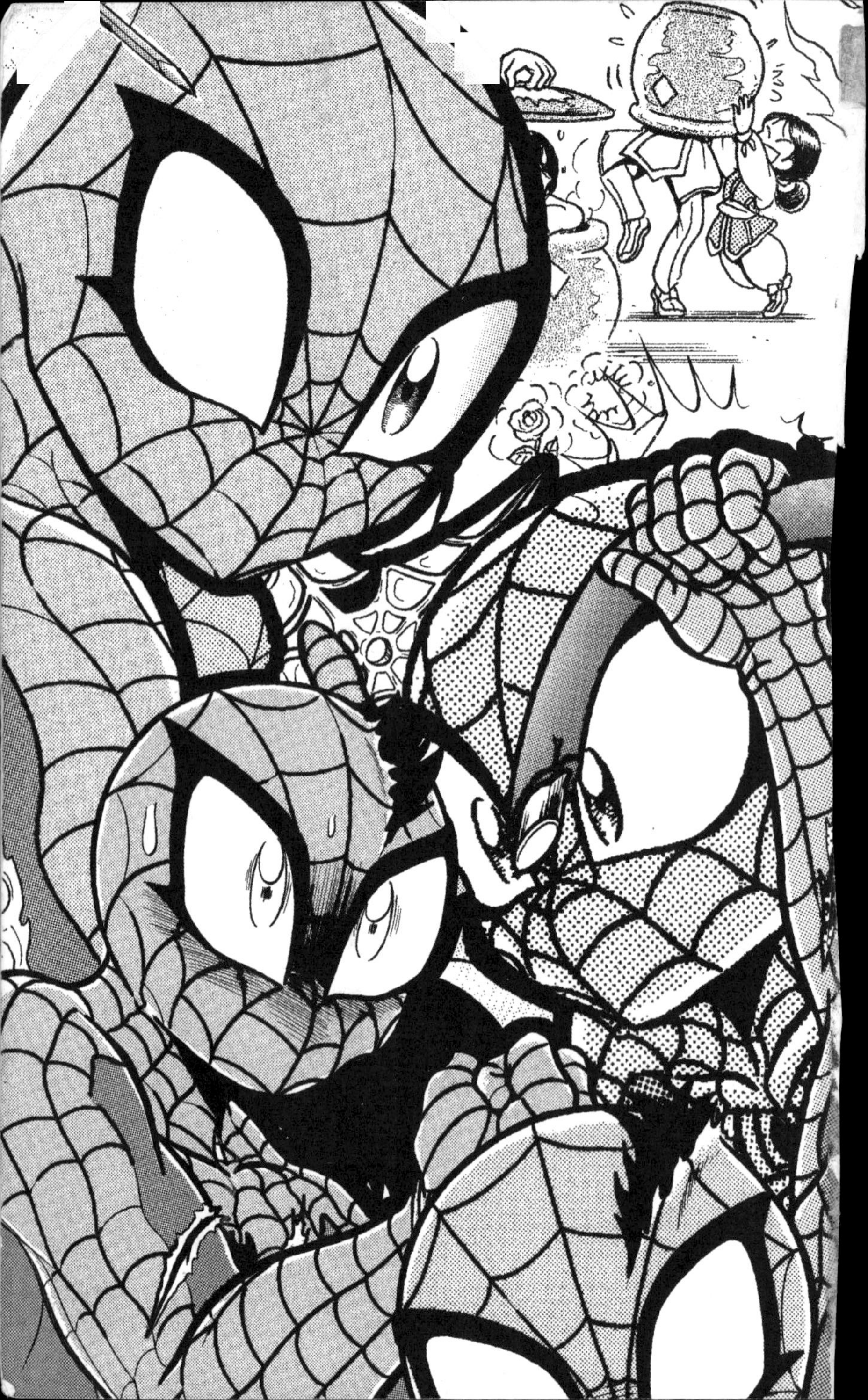